10660615

Joseph Pope

Confederation

Being a series of hithero unpublished documents bearing on the British North

America act

Joseph Pope

Confederation
Being a series of hithero unpublished documents bearing on the British North America act

ISBN/EAN: 9783337180584

Printed in Europe, USA, Canada, Australia, Japan

Cover: Foto ©Andreas Hilbeck / pixelio.de

More available books at **www.hansebooks.com**

CONFEDERATION:

BEING

A SERIES OF HITHERTO UNPUBLISHED DOCUMENTS
BEARING ON THE

BRITISH NORTH AMERICA ACT

EDITED BY

JOSEPH POPE,

Editor of "Memoirs of Sir John A. Macdonald, G.C.B."

TORONTO:
THE CARSWELL Co. Ltd. LAW PUBLISHERS, Etc.
1895.

PREFACE.

—

ONE of the chief disadvantages against which biographers of our public men have to contend arises from the dearth of new material at their command. Forced in many instances to make bricks without straw, they have been driven to supplement their scanty store by liberal draughts on the published reports of Parliament and other official documents, already common property. The result is that what purports to be a disclosure of the heretofore unrevealed side of a statesman's career, presents more often than otherwise the appearance of an abridged Hansard, convenient no doubt, and even interesting in a sense, but containing little or nothing not previously known.

It was my fortune as Sir John Macdonald's biographer to experience a difficulty precisely the reverse of this. When, on accepting the charge devolving upon me as literary executor of that great man, I approached the task which he had willed I should undertake, I was appalled at the mass of documents awaiting examination. Among them was a large collection of papers relating to the Confederation negotiations of 1864-1867. These documents gave promise of material from which could be prepared a history of Confederation as distinguished from accounts—chiefly reminiscent in their character—of concomitant social functions and after-dinner speeches Here were drafts of the Minutes of the Quebec Conference, reports of the discussions taken by Lt.-Colonel Bernard, the Secretary of the Conference, motions and amendments by the score in the handwriting of the movers, together with copious memoranda by the Fathers of Confederation. There were also sundry drafts of the British North America Bill in various stages of evolution, from the first rough trial to the Act itself. Not a line of these papers (other than the results arrived at) had ever been published.

The first thing to be done was to bring order out of chaos, to separate the wheat from the chaff, and thus to reduce the mass of valuable material to the smallest possible compass. But even when this had been accomplished it seemed hopeless to think of incorporating the contents of a volume relating exclusively to one subject, in a book of Memoirs dealing with the events of an exceptionally active political career extending over half a century. In this dilemma I had recourse to Sir John Thompson. "I would publish them all," said he, with special reference to the drafts of the British North America Bill. "As an appendix to the Memoirs?" I asked. "By all means," replied Sir John. "They will be useful to students of our Constitution, and add to the interest and importance of your work."

This advice I found impracticable to follow at the time. The injunction, however, of so distinguished a lawyer and statesman as Sir John Thompson is not lightly to be disregarded, and has impelled me to complete a labour the fulfilment of which I might otherwise have indefinitely postponed.

While the documents I publish are to a large extent self-explanatory, a very few words of mine may possibly lead to a more ready understanding of them. As regards the proceedings of the Quebec Conference, the key to the whole is to be found in the report made to His Excellency the Governor-General by the Provincial Secretary of Canada, dated 4th May, 1865, wherein Mr. McDougall makes the following observation :—

"As your Excellency is aware, the proceedings of the Conference towards the close of its deliberations were very much hurried."—(*Appendix to Pope's Memoirs of Sir John Macdonald, Vol. I., p. 356.*)

This is abundantly evident from the papers themselves. Apparently it was the intention at the outset to preserve a complete record of the proceedings of the Conference, for draft minutes of each day's proceedings up till the 20th October were printed. These drafts, however, are meagre, giving only the text of the motions as actually carried, omitting the proposed amendments, and in every case the names of the movers and seconders. On the other hand every scrap of writing has been preserved. The various draft motions, with scarcely an exception, are in the handwriting of the movers; and certain skeleton forms, indicating the order of each day's proceedings, have rendered the work of compiling the minutes a possible task. These minutes, with the exception of the three last sittings, are complete, and, with one or two qualifications which I have indicated in foot notes, may be accepted as constituting an accurate report of the Conference.

The record of the discussions, unfortunately, is obviously deficient, and, in places, fragmentary. I have contented myself with reproducing Colonel Bernard's notes, taken in longhand, supplying here and there such small words as are clearly necessary to bring out the sense, and leaving the elucidation of doubtful passages to those better qualified than myself to interpret them.

The minutes of the London Conference are printed as prepared by Colonel Bernard. They are merely in outline. No detailed record seems to have been kept at London as at Quebec, but from the loose notes and memoranda of Colonel Bernard I have been able to put together an interesting and, as far as it goes, an accurate account of the proceedings which transformed the Quebec Resolutions into those of the London Conference.

The various drafts of the Bill are absolutely to be relied upon, the originals being in every case printed and annotated, as well as distinguished by numbers and dates.

This little volume makes no pretension to be other than a compilation pure and simple. That it is not more full is

to be regretted. At the same time it should be borne in
mind (1) that it contains all the hitherto unpublished
information available upon the subject, and (2) that it is
exceedingly improbable there will ever be anything more
brought to light.

For these reasons, therefore, I feel that, viewed as sup-
plementary to the thirteenth and fourteenth chapters of
my 'Memoirs of Sir John Macdonald,' it may form a not
wholly unimportant contribution to the constitutional lit-
erature of Canada.

JOSEPH POPE.

OTTAWA, JULY 1ST, 1895.

CONTENTS.

LIST OF APPENDICES.

ERRATA.

Page 11, third line from bottom, for " noon " read " midnight."

Page 66, tenth line from bottom, for " pp. 13, 14 " read " page 19."

Page 70, sixth line from bottom, for " understand " read " understood."

Page 79, tenth line from top, for " pp. 22, 24, 43" read, " pp. 22, 23,"

MINUTES

OF THE

PROCEEDINGS IN CONFERENCE

OF THE

DELEGATES FROM THE PROVINCES

OF

BRITISH NORTH AMERICA.

OCTOBER, 1864.

CONFERENCE CHAMBER,
PARLIAMENT HOUSE,

Quebec, 10th October, 1864.

The following gentlemen assembled at the Conference Chamber in the Parliament House, Quebec, on Monday, the tenth day of October, 1864, at the hour of eleven o'clock in the forenoon :—

The Honourable Sir E. P. TACHÉ, M.L.C., Receiver-General and Minister of Militia of Canada.

The Honourable JOHN ALEXANDER MACDONALD, M.P.P., Attorney-General of Upper Canada.

The Honourable GEORGE ETIENNE CARTIER, M.P.P., Attorney-General of Lower Canada.

The Honourable GEORGE BROWN, M.P.P., President of the Executive Council of Canada.

The Honourable OLIVER MOWAT, M.P.P., Postmaster-General of Canada.

The Honourable ALEXANDER T. GALT, M.P.P., Minister of Finance of Canada.

The Honourable WILLIAM McDOUGALL, M.P.P., Provincial Secretary of Canada.

The Honourable T. D'ARCY McGEE, M.P.P., Minister of Agriculture of Canada.

The Honourable ALEXANDER CAMPBELL, M.L.C., Commissioner of Crown Lands.

The Honourable J. C. CHAPAIS, M.P.P., Commissioner of Public Works.

The Honourable H. L. LANGEVIN, M.P.P., Solicitor-General of Lower Canada.

The Honourable JAMES COCKBURN, M.P.P., Solicitor-General of Upper Canada.

Sir Etienne Taché stated that the several gentlemen representing the Province of Canada were Members of the Executive Council of Canada.

Sir Etienne Taché laid before the Conference a despatch dated 3rd October, 1864,* from His Excellency Sir Richard Graves MacDonnell, K.C.B., Lieutenant-Governor of Nova Scotia, to His Excellency The Governor-General of Canada, stating that he had appointed the following gentlemen to form a deputation to meet the delegates in Conference in Quebec, viz.:—

The Honourable CHARLES TUPPER, M.P.P., Provincial Secretary of Nova Scotia.

The Honourable WILLIAM A. HENRY, M.P.P., Attorney-General of Nova Scotia.

The Honourable R. B. DICKEY, M.L.C.

The Honourable JONATHAN McCULLY, M.L.C., and

ADAMS G. ARCHIBALD, Esquire, M.P.P.

The Honourable Charles Tupper then laid before the Conference an instrument* under the hand and seal at arms of His Excellency Sir R. G. MacDonnell, Lieutenant-Governor of Nova Scotia, appointing Charles Tupper, William A. Henry, Jonathan McCully, Robert B. Dickey and Adams G. Archibald, to be such delegates.

* See Appendix I.

The Honourable Samuel L. Tilley, Provincial Secretary of
New Brunswick, stated that in consequence of the late date at
which the despatch of His Excellency the Governor-General
of Canada to His Excellency the Honourable Arthur H. Gordon,
Lieutenant-Governor of New Brunswick, requesting the appointment of Members of the Conference, had been received, it had
been found impossible to forward a formal instrument of delegation or despatch to that effect, but that he was empowered to
present the following as delegates from the Province of New
Brunswick to the Conference, viz. :—

The Honourable SAMUEL L. TILLEY, M.P.P., Provincial Secretary of New Brunswick.

The Honourable WILLIAM H. STEEVES, M.L.C. and a Member
of the Executive Council.

The Honourable J. M. JOHNSON, M.P.P., Attorney-General of
New Brunswick.

The Honourable P. MITCHELL, M.L.C. and a Member of the
Executive Council.

The Honourable E. B. CHANDLER, M.L.C.

Lieut.-Colonel the Honourable JOHN HAMILTON GRAY, M.P.P.

The Honourable CHARLES FISHER, M.P.P.

Sir Etienne Taché also laid before the Conference a despatch,
dated 6th October, 1864,* from His Excellency George Dundas,
Esquire, Lieutenant-Governor of Prince Edward Island, to His
Excellency the Governor-General of Canada, stating that he had
named the following gentlemen to proceed to Quebec, to be present
at the Conference on the 10th October instant, viz.:—

Colonel the Honourable JOHN HAMILTON GRAY, M.P.P., President of the Executive Council of Prince Edward Island.

The Honourable EDWARD PALMER, M.L.C., Attorney-General
of Prince Edward Island.

The Honourable WILLIAM H. POPE, M.P.P., Colonial Secretary
of Prince Edward Island.

* See Appendix II.

The Honourable A. A. MACDONALD, M.L.C.

The Honourable GEORGE COLES, M.P.P.

The Honourable T. HEATH HAVILAND, M.P.P.

The Honourable EDWARD WHELAN, M.P.P.

The Conference then stood composed of the following gentlemen :—

CANADA.—The Honourable Sir E. P. TACHÉ, The Honourable JOHN A. MACDONALD, The Honourable G. E. CARTIER, The Honourable GEORGE BROWN, The Honourable OLIVER MOWAT, The Honourable ALEXANDER T. GALT, The Honourable W. MCDOUGALL, The Honourable T. D'ARCY MCGEE, The Honourable ALEX. CAMPBELL, The Honourable J. C. CHAPAIS, The Honourable H. L. LANGEVIN, and the Honourable J. COCKBURN.

NOVA SCOTIA.—The Honourable CHARLES TUPPER, The Honourable WILLIAM A. HENRY, The Honourable JONATHAN MCCULLY, The Honourable ROBERT B. DICKEY, and ADAMS G. ARCHIBALD, Esquire.

NEW BRUNSWICK.—The Honourable SAMUEL L. TILLEY, The Honourable W. H. STEEVES, The Honourable J. M. JOHNSON, The Honourable P. MITCHELL, The Honourable E. B. CHANDLER, Lieut.-Col. The Honourable JOHN H. GRAY, The Honourable CHARLES FISHER.

NEWFOUNDLAND.—The Honourable F. B. T. CARTER, The Honourable AMBROSE SHEA.

PRINCE EDWARD ISLAND.—Col. The Honourable J. H. GRAY, The Honourable E. PALMER, The Honourable W. H. POPE, The Honourable A. A. MACDONALD, The Honourable G. COLES, The Honourable T. H. HAVILAND, The Honourable E. WHELAN.

And the Conference stood accordingly convened.

It was moved by Colonel the Honourable John Hamilton Gray (of Prince Edward Island), seconded by the Honourable Mr. Tilley, that the Honourable Sir E. P. Taché be Chairman of the Conference.

And the question of concurrence being put thereon, the same was resolved in the affirmative.

It was moved by the Honourable Mr. Campbell, seconded by the Honourable Mr. McGee :—

That the Provincial Secretaries of each of the Provinces represented at the Conference, and the Honourable Mr. Shea, of Newfoundland, be the Joint Secretaries of the Conference.

And the question of concurrence being put thereon, the same was resolved in the affirmative.

It was moved by the Honourable Mr. John A. Macdonald, seconded by the Honourable Mr. Tupper :—

That the sittings of the Conference be held on each day (Sundays excepted) from eleven o'clock in the forenoon to four o'clock in the afternoon.

And the question of concurrence being put thereon, the same was resolved in the affirmative.

It was moved by the Honourable Mr. Palmer, seconded by the Honourable Mr. Dickey :—

That in taking the votes on all questions to be decided by this Conference, except questions of order, each Province or Colony, by whatever number of delegates represented, shall have one vote, and that in voting Canada be considered as two Provinces.

And after debate the further consideration of the same was postponed until to-morrow.

It was moved by the Honourable Mr. John A. Macdonald, seconded by the Honourable Mr. Tilley :—

That the best interests and present and future prosperity of British North America will be promoted by a Federal Union under the Crown of Great Britain, provided such union can be effected on principles just to the several Provinces.

And during debate,—

The hour of four o'clock ensuing, the Chairman declared the Conference continued until to-morrow.

TUESDAY, 11th OCTOBER, 1864.

The Chairman took the chair at eleven o'clock a.m., when the members were convened.*

The Honourable Mr. McDougall stated that the Joint Secretaries of the Conference having met, had arrived at the conclusion that, to enable them to give their undisturbed attention to the

* All save Mr. Carter, absent through indisposition, and Mr. Whelan.

matters of the Conference, they thought it advisable that an Executive Secretary should be appointed, and that they accordingly recommended that Mr. Hewitt Bernard, Chief Clerk of the Crown Law Department of Upper Canada, should be appointed as such Executive Secretary.

And the question of concurrence being then put, the same was resolved in the affirmative.

The Conference resumed the consideration of the motion :—

That in taking the votes on all questions to be decided by this Conference, except questions of order, each Province or Colony, by whatever number of delegates represented, shall have one vote, and that in voting Canada be considered as two Provinces.

And after debate,—

The question of concurrence being put thereon, the same was unanimously resolved in the affirmative.

It was moved by the Honourable Mr. John A. Macdonald, seconded by the Honourable Mr. Tilley, that the order of the proceedings in Conference shall be as follows :—

(1) Free individual discussion and suggestion to be allowed.

(2) That all motions and the discussions and votes thereon be in the first place as if in Committee of the Whole.

(3) That after vote put no discussion be allowed.

(4) That each Province may retire for consultation after vote put.

(5) That after the scheme is settled in Committee of the Whole, all the resolutions be reconsidered, as if with Speaker in the chair.

(6) That just before the breaking up of the Conference, the Minutes be carefully gone over and settled, with the view of determining what is to be submitted to the Imperial and Provincial Governments, and what to be published for general information.

And the question of concurrence being put thereon, the same was resolved in the affirmative.

The Conference resumed the further consideration of the motion :—

That the best interests and present and future prosperity of British North America will be promoted by a Federal Union under the Crown of Great Britain, provided such union can be effected on principles just to the several Provinces.

And after debate,—

The question of concurrence being put thereon, the same was unanimously resolved in the affirmative.

It was moved by the Honourable Mr. Brown, seconded by Mr. Archibald :—

That in the Federation of the British North American Provinces the system of government best adapted under existing circumstances to protect the diversified interests of the several Provinces and secure efficiency, harmony and permanency in the working of the Union, would be a General Government, charged with matters of common interest to the whole country ; and Local Governments for each of the Canadas and for the Maritime Provinces, charged with the control of local matters in their respective sections, provision being made for the admission into the Union on equitable terms of the North West Territory, British Columbia and Vancouver.

And during debate,—

The hour of four o'clock ensuing, the Chairman declared the Conference continued until to-morrow.

WEDNESDAY, 12TH OCTOBER, 1864.

The Chairman took the chair at eleven o'clock a. m., when the members were convened.*

The Honourable Mr. Carter and the Honourable Mr. Whelan severally rose and stated that they had been unable to attend at the sitting yesterday, but that they cordially supported the resolutions passed on that day, and desired to be considered as having severally voted therefor.

The Chairman laid before the Conference the following letter from Mr. S. P. Day and others, requesting information of the proceedings of the Conference for publication through the press :—

To The Honourable Sir Etienne P. Taché,

&c., &c., &c.,

Chairman of the Intercolonial Conference.

Sir,—The undersigned, representatives of English and Canadian newspapers, find that it would be impossible for them satisfactorily to discharge their duties if an injunction of secrecy be imposed on the Conference and stringently carried into effect. They therefore beg leave to suggest whether, while the remarks of individual members of your body are kept secret, the propositions made and the treatment they meet with, might not advantageously

* All save Colonel Gray, of Prince Edward Island, absent through indisposition.

be made public, and whether such a course would not best accord with the real interests committed to the Conference. Such a kind of compromise between absolute secrecy and unlimited publicity is usually, we believe, observed in cases where an European Congress holds the peace of the world and the fate of nations in its hands.

And we have thought that the British American Conference might perhaps consider this precedent not inapplicable to the present case. Such a course would have the further advantage of preventing ill-founded and mischievous rumours regarding the proceedings from obtaining currency.

We have the honour to be, Sir,

Your very obt. humble servants,

S. PHILLIPS DAY,
CHARLES LINDSEY,
B. CHAMBERLIN.

It was resolved,—

That the same be referred to the Secretaries of the Conference to prepare an answer declining the proposition made.

The Conference then resumed the consideration of the motion :—

That in the Federation of the British North American Provinces, the system of government best adapted, under existing circumstances, to protect the diversified interests of the several Provinces and secure efficiency, harmony and permanency in the working of the Union, would be a General Government, charged with matters of common interest to the whole country ; and Local Governments for each of the Canadas and for the Maritime Provinces, charged with the control of local matters in their respective sections, provision being made for the admission into the Union on equitable terms of the North-West Territory, British Columbia and Vancouver.

And after debate,—

The question of concurrence being put thereon, the same was unanimously resolved in the affirmative.

The Honourable Mr. Shea rose and suggested that it would tend to the despatch of business before the Conference if the several resolutions intended to be moved were prepared in advance by a committee composed of the delegates of Canada, and

It was unanimously resolved :—

That the Conference should adjourn for such purpose.

The Chairman, therefore, declared the Conference continued until to-morrow morning.

THURSDAY, 13TH OCTOBER, 1864.

The Chairman took the chair at eleven o'clock a.m., when the members were convened.

It was moved by the Honourable Mr. Brown, seconded by the Honourable Mr. Henry :—

That the proposed Union shall at present embrace the following Provinces :

Upper Canada,
Lower Canada,
Nova Scotia,
New Brunswick,
Newfoundland, and
Prince Edward Island.

And after debate,—

The question of concurrence being put thereon, the same was unanimously resolved in the affirmative.

It was moved by the Honourable Mr. Fisher, seconded by the Honourable Mr. Dickey :—

That the constitution of the General and Local Governments shall be framed upon the British model so far as is consistent with our colonial condition, and with a view to the perpetuation of our connection with the Mother Country.

It was then moved in amendment by the Honourable Mr. Tupper, seconded by the Honourable Mr. Mitchell :—

That while it is the avowed desire of this Conference to perpetuate the connection with the parent state by every means in our power, it is not judicious to fetter our actions by the passage of a resolution of a simple declaratory character, and which may embarrass our action in the selection of the best means of providing for the general and local government of the country.

It was then moved in amendment to the said proposed amendment by the Honourable Mr. Tilley, seconded by Mr. Archibald :—

That in framing a Constitution for the General Government, the Conference, with a view to the perpetuation of our connection with the Mother Country, and to the promotion of the best interests of the people of these Provinces, desire to follow the model of the British Constitution, so far as our circumstances will permit.

And after debate,—

The question of concurrence was put thereon, and the Conference divided; and the names of the Provinces were taken down as follows :—

CONTENTS.

Canada.. 2
New Brunswick 1
Newfoundland 1

4

NON-CONTENTS.

Nova Scotia 1
Prince Edward Island 1

2

The amendment to the amendment accordingly passed in the affirmative.

It was then moved by the Honourable Mr. John A. Macdonald, seconded by Colonel the Honourable John Hamilton Gray, (of Prince Edward Island) :—

That there shall be a General Legislature for the Federated Provinces composed of a Legislative Council and Legislative Assembly.

And after debate,—

The question of concurrence being put thereon, the same was unanimously resolved in the affirmative.

The following reply to the letter of Mr. S. P. Day and others was read and ordered to be sent :—

CONFERENCE CHAMBER, PARLIAMENT HOUSE,

OCTOBER 13, 1864.

GENTLEMEN,—I am desired to inform you that Sir Etienne P. Taché, Chairman of the Conference of Delegates from the several British North American Provinces, has laid before the Conference your letter of the 11th instant, in which you suggest whether, whilst the remarks of individual members of the Conference are kept secret, the propositions made and the treatment they meet with may not be advantageously made public, and whether such a course would not best accord with the real interests committed to the Conference.

I am to say that, whilst the members of the Conference fully appreciate the motives by which you are actuated in your communication, and are equally sensible of the deep interest naturally felt by the people of the several British North American Provinces in the objects of the Conference, they cannot but feel that it is inexpedient, at the present stage of the proceedings, to furnish information which must, of necessity, be incomplete; and that no communication of their proceedings can properly be made until they are enabled definitely to report the issue of their deliberations to the Governments of the respective Provinces.

I have the honour to be, gentlemen,

Your very obedient servant,

For the Secretaries of the Conference,

H. BERNARD,
Executive Secretary.

It was moved by the Honourable Mr. John A. Macdonald, seconded by the Honourable Mr. Mowat :—

That for the purpose of forming the Legislative Council, the Federated Provinces shall be considered as consisting of three divisions. 1st, Upper Canada ; 2nd, Lower Canada ; and 3rd, the four Maritime Provinces, and each division shall be represented in the Legislative Council by an equal number of members.

It was moved in amendment by the Honourable Mr. Tilley, seconded by the Honourable Mr. Dickey :—

That the Legislative Council in the Federal Legislature be composed as follows :

Upper Canada 24
Lower Canada... 24
Nova Scotia, New Brunswick, Newfoundland, and Prince Edward Island.. 32
                                                              —
                                                              80

And during debate,—

The hour of four o'clock ensuing, the Chairman declared the Conference continued until to-morrow.

FRIDAY, 14th OCTOBER, 1864.

The Chairman took the chair at eleven o'clock a.m., when the members were convened*.

The Conference resumed consideration of Mr. Tilley's amendment to the motion of Mr. John A. Macdonald respecting the composition of the Legislative Council.

And after debate thereon arising, the amendment was by permission of the Conference withdrawn.

It was moved in amendment by the Honourable Mr. Tupper :—

That for the purpose of forming the Legislative Council the Federated Provinces shall be considered as consisting of three divisions: 1st, Upper Canada; 2nd, Lower Canada; 3rd, Nova Scotia, New Brunswick and Prince Edward Island, with equal representation in the Legislative Council, and the Island of Newfoundland, to which additional representatives shall be allotted.

And during debate,—

The hour of four o'clock arriving, the Chairman declared the Conference continued until to-morrow.

SATURDAY, 15th OCTOBER, 1864.

The Chairman took the chair at eleven o'clock a.m., when the members were convened.

It was moved by the Honourable Mr. John A. Macdonald :—

That on and after Monday next the Conference commence its sittings at ten o'clock a.m., and sit until two o'clock p.m., and that it re-assemble at 7.30 p.m., and sit until adjourned on motion.

And the question of concurrence being put thereon, the same was resolved in the affirmative.

The Conference then resumed consideration of the amendment of the Honourable Mr. Tupper to the motion of the Honourable Mr. John A. Macdonald respecting the composition of the Legislative Council.

* All save Colonel Gray, of Prince Edward Island, absent through indisposition.

And after debate,—

It was moved in amendment to the said proposed amendment by the Honourable Mr. Fisher :—*

That for the purpose of representation in the Legislative Council, the Confederation shall be divided into three divisions :—Upper Canada, Lower Canada, and the Maritime Provinces, including Newfoundland, and that the apportionment amongst them shall be as follows :—Upper Canada, 30; Lower Canada, 30; Nova Scotia, 10; New Brunswick, 10; Newfoundland, 5; Prince Edward Island, 5.

And during debate,—

And at the hour of half-past two p.m., a motion for adjournment being carried, the Chairman declared the Conference continued until Monday, the 17th instant.

MONDAY, 17TH OCTOBER, 1864.

The Chairman took the chair at ten o'clock a.m., when the members were convened.†

The resolution passed on the 12th instant was amended to read as follows :—

That in the Federation of the British American Provinces the system of government best adapted under existing circumstances to protect the diversified interests of the several Provinces and secure efficiency, harmony and permanency in the working of the Union, would be a General Government, charged with matters of common interest to the whole country ; and Local Governments for each of the Canadas and for the Provinces of Nova Scotia, New Brunswick and Prince Edward Island, charged with the control of local matters in their respective sections, provision being made for the admission into the Union on equitable terms of Newfoundland, the North-West Territory, British Columbia and Vancouver.

The Conference resumed consideration of the amendment of the Honourable Mr. Fisher respecting the constitution of the Legislative Council.

And after debate thereon arising, the amendment was, by permission of the Conference, withdrawn.

The Conference resumed consideration of the amendment of the Honourable Mr. Tupper to the motion of the Honourable Mr.

* After this date the names of the seconders are not given.
† All save Messrs. McGee, Palmer and Henry.

John A. Macdonald respecting the composition of the Legislative Council.

And after debate,—

And the same being amended, the question of concurrence was put thereon, and it was resolved:—

That for the purpose of forming the Legislative Council the Federated Provinces shall be considered as consisting of three divisions:—1st, Upper Canada; 2nd, Lower Canada; 3rd, Nova Scotia, New Brunswick and Prince Edward Island, with equal representation in the Legislative Council.

It was moved by the Honourable Mr. John A. Macdonald:—

That Upper Canada be represented in the Legislative Council by 24 members, Lower Canada by 24 members, and the three Maritime Provinces by 24 members, of which Nova Scotia shall have 10, New Brunswick 10, and Prince Edward Island 4 members.

And the question of concurrence being put thereon, the same was unanimously resolved in the affirmative.

It was moved by the Honourable Mr. John A. Macdonald:—

That the Colony of Newfoundland, having sent a deputation to this Conference, be now invited to enter into the proposed Confederation, with a representation in the Legislative Council of four members.

And the question of concurrence being put thereon, the same was unanimously resolved in the affirmative.

And the foregoing resolution having been communicated to the Newfoundland delegates, the invitation was accepted, the right being reserved by them to press their claims for an increased representation in the Legislative Council.

And the hour of two o'clock p.m. ensuing, the Chairman declared the Conference continued until half-past seven o'clock in the evening.

And at half-past seven o'clock p.m. the Chairman took the chair, when the members were convened.*

It was moved by the Honourable Mr. John A. Macdonald:—

That the members of the Legislative Council shall be appointed by the Crown under the Great Seal of the General Government and shall hold office during life.

And during debate,—

And at the hour of twelve o'clock noon, a motion for adjournment being carried, the Chairman declared the Conference continued until to-morrow.

*All save Messrs. Campbell, McGee, Pope and Henry.

TUESDAY, 18TH OCTOBER, 1864.

The Chairman took the chair at ten o'clock a.m., when the members were convened.

The Conference resumed consideration of the motion before them respecting the mode of appointment of members of the Legislative Council.

And after debate,—

The question of concurrence being put thereon, the same was unanimously resolved in the affirmative.

It was proposed by the Honourable Mr. John A. Macdonald:—

That the members of the Legislative Council shall be British subjects, by birth or naturalization, of the full age of thirty years, shall possess a real property qualification of four thousand dollars over and above all incumbrances, and be worth that amount over and above their debts and liabilities.

And after debate,—

The question of concurrence being put thereon, the same was unanimously resolved in the affirmative.

And the hour of two o'clock p.m. ensuing, the Chairman declared the Conference continued until half-past seven o'clock in the evening.

And at half-past seven o'clock in the evening the Chairman took the chair, when the members were convened.

It was moved by the Honourable Mr. Tupper:—

That the members of the Legislative Council for the General Government shall in the first instance be selected from the Legislative Councils of the various Provinces, with the exception of Prince Edward Island, so far as a sufficient number be found qualified and willing to serve.

It was moved in amendment by the Honourable Mr. McCully:—

That it shall be competent for each Province to provide in this Conference its own method for selecting the members of the Legislative Council at its first formation.

And after debate,—

The said amendment was by leave of the Conference withdrawn.

It was moved in amendment by the Honourable Mr. Coles :—

That the first nomination for the upper branch of the united Legislature shall be open to all duly qualified persons in each Province or Colony.

And at the hour of half-past eleven o'clock p.m., a motion for adjournment being carried, the Chairman declared the Conference continued until to-morrow.

WEDNESDAY, 19th OCTOBER, 1864.

The Chairman took the chair at ten o'clock a.m., when the members were convened.

The Conference resumed consideration of the motion of the Honourable Mr. Tupper respecting the selection of members of the Legislative Council, and of the motion of the Honourable Mr. Coles in amendment thereto.

And after debate,—

And the question of concurrence being put on the amendment of the Honourable Mr. Coles, the Conference divided, and the names of the Provinces were taken down as follows :—

CONTENTS.

Prince Edward Island............................ 1

NON-CONTENTS.

Canada 2
Nova Scotia...... 1
New Brunswick 1
Newfoundland 1
                                                  ——
                                                   5

So it passed in the negative.

And the question of concurrence being put on the motion of the Honourable Mr. Tupper, the Conference divided, and the names of the Provinces were taken down as follows :—

CONTENTS.

Canada 2
Nova Scotia 1
New Brunswick 1
Newfoundland 1
　　　　　　　　　　　　　　　　　　　　　　─
　　　　　　　　　　　　　　　　　　　　　　5

NON-CONTENTS.

Prince Edward Island............................... 1

So it passed in the affirmative.

It was moved by the Honourable Mr. Galt :—

That in the first instance, the members to be chosen for the Legislative Council of the United Provinces, excepting Prince Edward Island, shall be chosen by lot from the existing members of the Legislative Councils of the several Maritime Provinces, and of those sitting in Canada from Upper and Lower Canada respectively.

And after debate,—

And the question of concurrence being put thereon, the Conference divided, and the names of the Provinces were taken down as follows :—

CONTENTS.

Canada 2

NON-CONTENTS.

Nova Scotia 1
New Brunswick 1
Newfoundland 1
　　　　　　　　　　　　　　　　　　　　　　─
　　　　　　　　　　　　　　　　　　　　　　3

Prince Edward Island did not vote.

So the motion passed in the negative.

It was moved by the Honourable Mr. Shea :—

That such first selection shall be made by the Local Government of each Province, so far as a sufficient number be found as aforesaid ; and in case such sufficient number cannot be found, then the Local Government shall name for appointment other duly qualified parties to make up the deficiency ; provided that the Government of Canada

POPE CON.—2

shall select for both sections of Canada, and that the Government of Prince Edward Island shall name for appointment the whole number of the Legislative Councillors allotted to it.

And after debate,—

The motion of the Honourable Mr. Shea was by leave of the Conference withdrawn.

It was moved by Mr. Archibald :—

That in the selection of members of the first Federal Legislative Council, each Province shall be governed by such rules now to be agreed upon as are considered by the Conference most suitable to the circumstances of the particular Provinces.

It was moved in amendment by the Honourable Mr. Mc-Cully :—

That the Legislative Council shall, in the first instance, be chosen in Canada by ballot, and in the other Provinces by the Executive Governments.

And after debate,—

The said motion of Mr. Archibald and the proposed amendment of the Honourable Mr. McCully were by leave of the Conference withdrawn.

It was moved by the Honourable Mr. McCully :—

That the members of the first Legislative Council in the Federal Legislature shall be appointed by the Crown at the recommendation of the Federal Executive Government, upon the nomination of the respective Local Governments, and that in such nomination due regard be had to the claims of the members of the Legislative Council of the Opposition in each Province, so that all political parties be as nearly as possible fairly represented.

And after debate,—

And the question of concurrence being put on the motion of the Honourable Mr. McCully, the same was unanimously resolved in the affirmative.

The Honourable Peter Mitchell, a delegate from New Brunswick, rose and stated his regret that private business imperatively required him to leave the Conference and to return to New Brunswick, and he requested leave of absence accordingly.

It was unanimously resolved,—

That leave of absence be granted to the Honourable Mr. Mitchell for the residue of the sittings of the Conference.

And the hour of two o'clock ensuing, the Chairman declared the Conference continued until half-past seven o'clock in the evening.

And at half-past seven o'clock the Chairman took the chair, when the members were convened.

It was moved by the Honourable Mr. Brown :—

That the basis of representation in the House of Commons shall be population, as determined by the official census every ten years ; and that the number of members at first shall be 200—distributed as follows :—

Upper Canada	82
Lower Canada	65
Nova Scotia	19
New Brunswick	15
Newfoundland	7
Prince Edward Island	5

That each section shall distribute its representatives in such electoral divisions as it deems best ;

That until the official census of 1881 has been made up, there shall be no change in the numbers of the representatives from the several sections ;

That immediately after the completion of the census of 1881, and immediately after every decennial census thereafter, the representation in each section shall be re-adjusted on the basis of population ;

That for the purpose of such re-adjustments, Lower Canada shall always be assigned sixty-five members, and each of the other sections shall at each such re-adjustment receive, for the ten years then next succeeding, the number of members to which it will be entitled on the same ratio of representation to population as Lower Canada will enjoy according to the census then just taken by having sixty-five members.

That no reduction shall be made in the number of members returned by any section, unless its population shall have decreased relatively to the whole population of the whole federation to the extent of five *per centum* or over ;

That in computing at each decennial period the number of members to which each section is entitled, no fractional parts shall be considered, unless when exceeding one-half the number entitling to a member, in which case a member shall be given for each such fractional part ;

That the number of members may at any time be increased by the Federal Parliament—regard being had to the proportionate rights then existing.

And after debate,—

And the question of concurrence being put on the motion of

the Honourable Mr. Brown, the Conference divided, and the names of the Provinces were taken down as follows :—

CONTENTS.

Canada... 2
Nova Scotia.................................... 1
New Brunswick................................. 1
Newfoundland................................... 1
                                    —
                                    5

NON-CONTENTS.

Prince Edward Island........................... 1

So it passed in the affirmative.

And the hour of ten o'clock p.m. ensuing, and a motion for adjournment being carried, the Chairman declared the Conference continued until to-morrow.

THURSDAY, 20TH OCTOBER, 1864.

The Chairman took the chair at ten o'clock a.m., when the members were convened.

It was moved by the Honourable Mr. John A. Macdonald :—

That the Legislature of each Province shall divide such Province into the proper number of constituencies and define the boundaries of each of them.

And the question of concurrence being put thereon, the same was unanimously resolved in the affirmative.

It was moved by the Honourable Mr. John A. Macdonald :—

That there shall be a session of the Legislative Council and Assembly once at least in every year, so that a period of twelve calendar months shall not intervene between the last sitting of the Legislative Council and Assembly in one session and the first sitting of the Legislative Council and Assembly in the next session. And every Legislative Assembly shall continue for five years from the day of the return of the writs choosing the same, and no longer; subject nevertheless to be sooner prorogued or dissolved by the Governor.

And after debate,—

And the question of concurrence being put on the above motion, the same was unanimously resolved in the affirmative.

It was moved by the Honourable Mr. John A. Macdonald :—

That until provision shall otherwise be made by the Legislature of the Federated Provinces, all the laws which, at the date of the proclamation constituting such Confederation, are in force in the Provinces respectively relating to the qualification and disqualification of any person to be elected or to sit or vote as a member of the Assembly in the said Provinces respectively, and relating to the qualification or disqualification of voters, and to the oaths to be taken by voters, and to returning officers and the powers and duties thereof, and the proceedings at elections, and the period during which such elections may be continued, and relating to the trial of controverted elections, and the proceedings incident thereto, and to the vacating of seats of members, and the issuing and execution of new writs in case of any seat being vacated otherwise than by a dissolution, shall respectively be applied to elections of members to serve in the Legislative Assembly of the Federated Provinces, for places situate in those Provinces respectively for which such laws were passed.

And the question of concurrence being put thereon, the same was unanimously resolved in the affirmative.

It was moved by the Honourable Mr. John A. Macdonald :—

That the Executive authority or Government shall be vested in the Sovereign of the United Kingdom of Great Britain and Ireland, and be administered according to the well understood principles of the British Constitution by the Sovereign personally or by representative duly authorized.

And the question of concurrence being put thereon, the same was unanimously resolved in the affirmative.

It was moved by the Honourable Mr. John A. Macdonald :—

That the Sovereign or representative of the Sovereign shall be Commander-in-Chief of the Land and Naval Militia Forces.

And the question of concurrence being put thereon, the same was unanimously resolved in the affirmative.

It was moved by the Honourable Mr. Brown :—

That in the Local Government there shall be but one Legislative Chamber.

And after debate,—

The said motion was by leave of the Conference withdrawn.

And the hour of two o'clock p.m. arriving, the Chairman declared the Conference continued until half-past seven o'clock p.m.

And at half-past seven o'clock p.m. the Chairman took the chair, when the members were convened.

It was moved by the Honourable Mr. McCully :—

That with a view of reducing the expenses of the Local Governments, it shall be left to each Province to recommend the reconstruction of its local constitution in such a way as shall be most acceptable to its own Legislature ; provided that in such reconstruction nothing be contained inconsistent with the constitution of the Federal Government.

And the question of concurrence being put on the motion of the Honourable Mr. McCully, the same was unanimously resolved in the affirmative.

It was moved by the Honourable Mr. John A. Macdonald :—

That for each of the Provinces there shall be an executive officer, styled the Lieutenant-Governor, who shall be appointed by the Governor-General in Council under the Great Seal of the Federated Provinces during pleasure, such pleasure not to be exercised before the expiration of the first five years except for cause, such cause to be communicated in writing to the Lieutenant-Governor immediately after the exercise of the pleasure as aforesaid, and also by message to both Houses of the General Legislature within the first week of the first session afterwards.

And after debate,—

And the question of concurrence being put on the motion of the Honourable Mr. Macdonald, the same was unanimously resolved in the affirmative.

And at ten o'clock p.m., a motion for adjournment being carried, the Chairman declared the Conference continued until tomorrow.

FRIDAY, 21st OCTOBER, 1864.

The Chairman took the chair at ten o'clock a.m., when the members were convened.

It was moved by the Honourable Mr. John A. Macdonald :—

That it shall be competent for the General Legislature to make laws for the peace, welfare and good government of the Federated Provinces (saving the sovereignty of England), and especially laws respecting :—

1. Trade and commerce.
2. The imposition or regulation of duties of customs on imports and exports.
3. The imposition or regulation of excise duties.

4. All or any other modes or systems of taxation.

5. Currency and coinage.

6. The borrowing of money on the public credit.

7. Banking and the issue of paper money.

8. The law relating to bills of exchange and promissory notes.

9. The rate of interest.

10. Legal tender.

11. Weights and measures.

12. Postal service.

13. Bankruptcy and insolvent laws operating as a discharge of the debtor.

14. Beacons and lighthouses.

15. Ocean navigation and shipping.

16. Sea fisheries.

17. Patents of invention and discovery.

18. Copy Rights.

19. Telegraphic communication and the incorporation of telegraph companies.

20. Naturalization.

21. Marriage and divorce.

22. The taking of the census.

23. Militia—Military and naval service and defence.

24. Immigration.

25. Agriculture.

26. The criminal law (except the constitution of Courts of Criminal Jurisdiction).

27. Roads, bridges, lines of steam or other ships, railways, canals and other works connecting any two or more of the Provinces together or extending beyond the limits of any one Province.

28. All such works as shall, although lying wholly within any one Province, be specially declared by the Acts authorizing them to be for the general advantage.

29. The establishment of a general Court of Appeal for the Federated Provinces.

30. Subsidies or grants in aid of the Local Governments.

31. The public debt and public property.

32. And generally respecting all matters of a general character, not specially and exclusively reserved for the Local Governments and Legislatures.

And after debate,—

It was moved in amendment by the Honourable Mr. McCully :—

That item number 25, " Agriculture," be struck out of the resolution before the Conference.

And the Conference divided upon the amendment of the

Honourable Mr. McCully, and the names of the Provinces were taken down as follows :—

CONTENTS .... None

NON-CONTENTS.

Canada 2
Nova Scotia 1
New Brunswick 1
Newfoundland 1
Prince Edward Island 1
                                          ——
                                           6

So it passed in the negative.

It was moved by the Honourable Mr. Tilley to strike from item number 27 the words "Roads and Bridges." And the question of concurrence being put thereon, the same was unanimously resolved in the affirmative.

And after further debate,—

And the adoption by the Honourable Mr. John A. Macdonald of certain amendments to his motion, the question of concurrence was put thereon, and the same was resolved in the affirmative as follows :—

That it shall be competent for the General Legislature to make laws for the peace, welfare and good government of the Federated Provinces (saving the sovereignty of England), and especially laws respecting,—

1. Trade and commerce.
2. The imposition or regulation of duties of Customs on imports and exports.
3. The imposition or regulation of excise duties.
4. All or any other modes or systems of taxation.
5. Currency and coinage.
6. The borrowing of money on the public credit.
7. Banking and the issue of paper money.
8. The law relating to bills of exchange and promissory notes.
9. Interest.
10. Legal tender.
11. Weights and measures.
12. Postal service.
13. Bankruptcy and insolvency.
14. Beacons, buoys and lighthouses.

15. Navigation and shipping.

16. Sea fisheries.

17. Patents of invention and discovery.

18. Copy Rights.

19. Telegraphic communication and the incorporation of telegraph companies.

20. Naturalization and aliens.

21. Marriage and divorce.

22. The census.

23. Militia—Military and naval service and defence.

24. Immigration.

25. Agriculture.

26. The Criminal Law (except the constitution of Courts of Criminal Jurisdiction).

27. Lines of steam-ships or other ships, railways and canals connecting any two or more of the Provinces together.

28. Lines of steam-ships between the Federated Provinces and other countries.

And at the hour of half-past four o'clock p.m., a motion for adjournment being carried, the Chairman declared the Conference continued until to-morrow at twelve o'clock noon.

SATURDAY, 22ND OCTOBER, 1864.

The Chairman took the chair at twelve o'clock, when the members were convened.

It was moved by the Honourable Mr. Galt :—

1. That the Confederation shall be vested at the time of the union with all cash, bankers' balances, and other cash securities of each Province.

2. That the Confederation shall be vested with the public works and property of each Province, to wit :—

Canals ;

Public harbours ;

Lighthouses ;

Steamboats, dredges and public vessels ;

River and lake improvements ;

Railroads, mortgages, and other debts due by railroad companies ;

Military roads ;

Public buildings, custom houses and post offices, except such as may be set aside for the use of the Local Legislatures ;

Property transferred by the Imperial Government and known as ordnance property ;

Armouries, drill sheds, military clothing and munitions of war ;

Lands set apart for public purposes.

3. The several Provinces shall remain each vested with all public property therein, except such as is hereinbefore vested in the Confederation, subject to the right of the Confederation to assume any lands or public property required for fortifications or the defence of the country.

4. The Confederation shall assume all the debts and liabilities of each Province.

The debt of Canada, not specially assumed by Upper and Lower Canada respectively, shall not exceed at the time of the union $62,500,000.

New Brunswick and Nova Scotia shall be at liberty to prosecute the works already authorized by their Legislatures within five years from this date; provided the total amount of their liabilities does not exceed for—

Nova Scotia	$8,000,000	
New Brunswick	7,000,000	

Newfoundland and Prince Edward Island, not having incurred debts equal to those of the other Provinces, shall be entitled to receive by half-yearly payments in advance from the Confederation the interest at five per cent. on the difference between the actual amount of their respective debts at the time of the union, and the average amount of indebtedness per head of the population of Canada, Nova Scotia and New Brunswick.

5. In consideration of the transfer to the General Legislature of the powers of taxation, a grant in aid of each Province shall be made, equal to an amount of 80 cents per head of the population, as established by the census of 1861; Newfoundland being estimated at 130,000 inhabitants. Such aid to be in full settlement of all future demands upon the General Legislature for local purposes, and to be payable half yearly in advance to each Province.

6. The position of New Brunswick being such as to entail large immediate charges upon her local revenues, it is agreed that for the period of ten years from the time when the union takes effect, an additional allowance of $63,000 per annum shall be made to that Province.

7. In consideration of the surrender to the Confederation of all the territorial rights of Newfoundland, it is agreed that an annual payment shall be made to that Province of $150,000.

8. All engagements that may be entered into by Canada with the Imperial Government for the defence of the country shall be assumed by the Confederation.

And after debate,—

And at the hour of five o'clock p.m., and a motion for adjournment being carried, the Chairman declared the Conference continued until Monday morning at ten o'clock.

MONDAY, 24th OCTOBER, 1864.

The Chairman took the chair at ten o'clock a.m., when the members were convened.

It was moved by the Honourable Mr. Mowat:—

That it shall be competent for the Local Legislatures to make laws respecting—

1. Agriculture.
2. Education.
3. Emigration.
4. The sale and management of public lands, excepting lands held for general purposes by the General Government.
5. Property and civil rights, excepting those portions thereof assigned to the General Legislature.
6. Municipal institutions.
7. Inland fisheries.
8. The construction, maintenance and management of penitentiaries and of public and reformatory prisons.
9. The construction, maintenance and management of hospitals, charities and eleemosynary institutions.
10. All local works.
11. The administration of justice and the constitution, maintenance and organization of the courts, both of civil and criminal jurisdiction.
12. The establishment of local offices, and the appointment, payment and removal of local officers.
13. The power of direct taxation.
14. Borrowing money on the credit of the Province.
15. Shop, saloon, tavern and auctioneer licenses.
16. Private and local matters.

And after debate,—

And the hour of 2 o'clock p.m. ensuing, the Chairman declared the Conference continued until half-past seven p.m.

And at half-past seven o'clock p.m., the Chairman took the chair, when the members were convened.

It was moved by the Honourable Mr. Coles in amendment to the motion of the Honourable Mr. Mowat:—

That the Local Legislatures shall have power to make all laws not given by this Conference to the General Legislature expressly.

And the question of concurrence being put on the said amendment, the same was unanimously resolved in the negative.

It was moved by Mr. Archibald in amendment to the motion of the Honourable Mr. Mowat:—

That it is inexpedient to name in the constitution the subjects to be entrusted to the Local Legislatures.

And the question of concurrence being put thereon, the same was resolved in the negative.

And the question of concurrence being put on so much of the motion of the Honourable Mr. Mowat as is embraced between the initial word "That," down to and including the word "agriculture," the same was resolved in the affirmative.

And at the hour of eleven o'clock p.m., a motion for adjournment being carried, the Chairman declared the Conference continued until to-morrow.

TUESDAY, 25th OCTOBER, 1864.

The Chairman took the chair at ten o'clock a.m., when the members were convened.

The Conference resumed debate on the motion of the Honourable Mr. Mowat, which was discussed clause by clause.

It was moved by the Honourable Mr. McGee that the following words be added to item 2, " Education ":—

Saving the rights and privileges which the Protestant or Catholic minority in both Canadas may possess as to their denominational schools at the time when the Constitutional Act goes into operation.

Agreed to.

It was moved by Colonel Gray (Prince Edward Island):—

That item number 7 be amended to read "Sea coast and inland fisheries."

Agreeed to.

It was moved by Mr. Archibald that the following item be added to the motion of the Honourable Mr. Mowat:—

" 17. The incorporation of private or local companies, except such as relate to matters assigned to the Federal Legislature."

Agreed to.

And after further debate,—

And the adoption of certain verbal amendments, the question of concurrence being put on the motion of the Honourable Mr.

Mowat (with the exception of item number 11, the consideration of which was postponed), the same was resolved in the affirmative as follows :—

That it shall be competent for the Local Legislatures to make laws respecting : —

Education, saving the rights and privileges which the Protestant or Catholic minority in both Canadas may possess as to their denominational schools at the time when the Constitutional Act goes into operation.

Immigration.

The sale and management of public lands, excepting lands belonging to the General Government.

Property and civil rights, excepting those portions thereof assigned to the General Legislature.

Municipal institutions.

Sea coast and inland fisheries.

The establishment, maintenance and management of penitentiaries and of public and reformatory prisons.

The construction, maintenance and management of hospitals, asylums, charities and eleemosynary institutions.

Local works.

The establishment and tenure of local offices, and the appointment and payment of local officers.

Direct taxation.

Borrowing money on the credit of the Province.

Shop, saloon, tavern and auctioneer licenses.

The incorporation of private or local companies, except such as relate to matters assigned to the Federal Legislature.

And generally all matters of a private or local nature.

It was moved by—

That the Local Legislature of each Province may afterwards, from time to time, alter the electoral districts of the Province for the purposes of representation in the House of Commons, and distribute the number of representatives to which the Province is entitled, in any manner such Legislature may think fit.

And the question of concurrence being put thereon, the same was resolved in the affirmative.

It was moved by the Honourable Mr. John A. Macdonald :—

That the power of respiting, reprieving, commuting and pardoning prisoners convicted of crimes, and of remitting of sentences in whole or in part, which belongs of right to the Crown, shall be administered by the Lieutenant-Governor of each Province in Council, subject to any instructions he may from time to time receive from the General Government, and subject to any provisions that may be made in this behalf by the General Legislature.

And the question of concurrence being put thereon, the same was resolved in the affirmative.

And the hour of two o'clock p.m. ensuing, the Chairman declared the Conference continued until half-past seven o'clock in the evening.

And at half-past seven o'clock p.m. the Chairman took the chair, when the members were convened.

It was moved by—

That the Local Legislature shall have power to provide for inflicting punishment by fine, penalties, imprisonment, or otherwise, for the breach of laws passed in relation to any subject within their jurisdiction.

That in regard to all subjects over which jurisdiction belongs to both the General and Local Governments, the laws of the Federal Parliament shall control and supersede those made by the Local Legislature, and the latter shall be void so far as they are repugnant to or inconsistent with the former.

And the question of concurrence being put thereon, the same was resolved in the affirmative.

It was moved by—

That all lands, mines, minerals and royalties vested in Her Majesty in the Provinces of Upper Canada, Lower Canada, Nova Scotia, New Brunswick and Prince Edward Island, for the use of such Provinces, shall belong to the Local Government of the territory in which the same are so situate ; subject to any trusts that may exist in respect to any of such lands or to any interest of other persons in respect of the same.

All sums due from purchasers or lessees of such lands, mines or minerals at the time of the union, shall also belong to the Local Governments.

And after debate,—

It was resolved that further consideration of the same should be postponed.

It was moved by the Honourable Mr. Mowat that :—

1. It shall be competent for the General Legislature to pass laws respecting—
    1. The Indians.
    2. Ferries between any Province and a foreign country or between any two Provinces.
    3. For the regulation and incorporation of fire and life insurance companies.
    4. Respecting savings banks.
2. It shall also be competent for the General Legislature to pass—
    Inspection laws, and
    Laws relating to quarantine.

3. The General Government and Legislature shall have all powers necessary or proper for performing the obligations of the Province as part of the British Empire to foreign countries, arising under treaties between Great Britain and such countries.

4. All Courts, Judges and Officers of the several Provinces shall aid, assist and obey the General Government in the exercise of its rights and powers under this Act, and for such purposes shall be held to be Judges and Officers of the General Government.

5. The General Government may also, from time to time, establish additional Courts, and appoint other Judges and Officers, when the same shall appear necessary or for the public advantage, in order to the due execution of the laws, rights and obligations of the General Government.

6. All bills for appropriating any part of the public revenue, or for imposing any new tax or impost, shall originate in the House of Commons or the Local Assembly, as the case may be.

7. The House of Commons or Legislative Assembly shall not originate or pass any vote, resolution, address or bill for the appropriation of any part of the public revenue, or of any tax or impost to any purpose, not first recommended to the House or Assembly by message of the Governor-General, during the session in which such vote, resolution, address or bill is passed.

8. Any bill of the General Legislature may be reserved in the usual manner for Her Majesty's assent, and any bill of the Local Governments may in like manner be reserved for the consideration of the General Government.

9. Any bill passed by the General Legislature shall be subject to disallowance by Her Majesty within two years, as in the case of bills passed by the said Provinces hitherto, and in like manner any bill passed by a Local Legislature shall be subject to disallowance by the General Government within one year after the passing thereof.

And after debate,—

And the insertion of certain verbal amendments, the question of concurrence was put on the first seven items of the motion of the Honourable Mr. Mowat, and the same was resolved in the affirmative.

And after further debate,—

And the question of concurrence being put on the eighth and ninth items, the same was resolved in the affirmative.

It was moved, by the Honourable Mr. Mowat* that :—

The North-West Territory, British Columbia and Vancouver shall be admitted into the Union on such terms and conditions as Parliament shall deem equitable, and as shall receive the assent of Her Majesty ; and in the case of the Province of British Columbia or Vancouver, as shall be agreed to by the Legislature of such Province.

And the question of concurrence being put thereon, it was resolved that further consideration of the same should be postponed.

* It is not quite certain from the papers that this resolution was moved by Mr. Mowat.

Attention was called to the minutes of the 13th October instant, by which it appeared that Nova Scotia and Prince Edward Island had voted against the motion :—

That in framing the Constitution for the General Government, the Conference, with a view to the perpetuation of our connection with the Mother Country, and to the promotion of the best interests of the people of these Provinces, desire to follow the model of the British Constitution so far as our circumstances will permit.

It was moved by—

That with the view of explaining the vote of Nova Scotia and Prince Edward Island in the negative on that resolution, the amendment proposed on that occasion be entered on the minutes as being expressive of the views of Nova Scotia and Prince Edward Island on the subject, and which led to their vote in the negative on the main motion, and which amendment is as follows :—

That while it is the avowed desire of this Conference to perpetuate the connection with the parent state by every means in our power, it is not judicious to fetter our actions by the passage of a resolution of a simple declaratory character, and which may embarrass our action in the selection of the best means of providing for the general and local Government of the country.

And the question of concurrence being put thereon, the same was resolved in the affirmative.

And at the hour of twelve o'clock midnight, a motion for adjournment being carried, the Chairman declared the Conference continued until to-morrow morning at eleven o'clock.

WEDNESDAY, 26TH OCTOBER, 1864.

The Chairman took the chair at twelve o'clock noon, when the members were convened.

It was moved by the Honourable Mr. John A. Macdonald :—

That the Judges of the Courts of Record in each Province shall be appointed and paid by the General Government, and their salaries shall be fixed by the General Legislature.

That the Judges of the Court of Admiralty now receiving salaries shall be paid by the General Government.

That the Judges of the Superior Courts shall hold their offices during good behaviour, and shall be removable only on the address of both Houses of the General Legislature.

And the question of concurrence being put on the motion of the Honourable Mr. Macdonald, the same was resolved in the affirmative.

It was moved by—

That the General Legislature shall have power to pass statutes for rendering uniform all or any of the laws relative to property and civil rights in Upper Canada, Nova Scotia, New Brunswick, Prince Edward Island and Newfoundland, and for rendering uniform the procedure of all or any of the Courts in these Provinces ; but not to go into operation in any Province until sanctioned by the Legislature thereof.

And the question of concurrence being put thereon, the same was resolved in the affirmative.

It was moved by—

That subject to any future action of the respective Local Governments in respect thereof, the seat of the Local Government in Upper Canada shall be in Toronto ; of Lower Canada, Quebec ; and the seats of the Local Governments in the other Provinces shall be as at present.

And the question of concurrence being put thereon, the same was resolved in the affirmative.

It was moved by the Honourable Mr. John A. Macdonald :—

That the seat of the Government of the Confederated Provinces shall be Ottawa, subject to the royal prerogative.

And the question of concurrence being put thereon, the same was unanimously resolved in the affirmative.

It was moved by—

That no lands or property belonging to the General or Local Governments shall be liable to taxation.

And the question of concurrence being put thereon, the same was resolved in the affirmative.

It was moved by the Honourable Mr. Galt :—

That in the General Legislature and in its proceedings, the English and French languages may be both especially employed. And also in the Local Legislature of Lower Canada and in the Federal and Local Courts of Lower Canada.

That the Lieutenant-Governor of each Province shall be paid by the General Legislature.

That in undertaking to pay the salaries of the Lieutenant-Governors, the Conference does not desire to prejudice the claim of Prince Edward Island upon the Imperial Government for the amount now paid for the salary of the Lieutenant-Governor thereof.

And the question of concurrence being put thereon, the same was unanimously resolved in the affirmative.

The Conference then discussed the financial resolutions moved by Mr. Galt on the 22nd instant.

And after further debate,—

And the adoption of certain amendments, the question of concurrence was put upon numbers four, five and six, and the same was resolved in the affirmative as follows:—

The Conference shall assume all the debts and liabilities of each Province.

The debt of Canada not specially assumed by Upper and Lower Canada respectively shall not exceed at the time of the Union $62,500,000

Nova Scotia shall enter into the Confederation with a debt not exceeding... 8,000,000

And New Brunswick.. 7,000,000

But it is expressly provided that in case Nova Scotia or New Brunswick do not incur liabilities beyond those for which their Governments are now bound, and which shall make their respective debts at the date of the Union less than $8,000,000 and $7,000,000 respectively, they shall then be entitled to benefit by the interest at five per cent. on the amount not so incurred, in like manner as is hereinafter provided for Newfoundland and Prince Edward Island. The foregoing resolution being in no respect intended to limit the powers now given to the respective Governments of those Provinces by legislative authority, but to limit the extreme amount of charge to be brought by them against the Confederation; provided always, that the powers so conferred by the respective Legislatures must be exercised within five years from this date or will then lapse.

Newfoundland and Prince Edward Island, not having incurred debts equal to those of the other Provinces, shall be entitled to receive by half-yearly payments in advance from the Confederation the interest at five per cent. on the difference between the actual amount of their respective debts at the time of the Union, and the average amount of indebtedness per head of the population of Canada, Nova Scotia and New Brunswick.

In consideration of the transfer to the General Legislature of the powers of taxation, a grant in aid of each Province shall be made, equal to an amount of eighty cents per head of the population as established by the census of 1861; Newfoundland being estimated at 130,000 inhabitants. Such aid to be in full settlement of all future demands upon the General Legislature for local purposes, and to be payable half-yearly in advance to each Province.

The position of New Brunswick being such as to entail large immediate charges upon her local revenues, it is agreed that for the period of ten years from the time when the Union takes effect, an additional allowance of $63,000 per annum shall be made to that Province, provided that so long as the liability of that Province remains under $7,000,000, a deduction equal to the interest on such deficiency shall be made from the $63,000.

And item number seven having been amended to read as follows:—

That in consideration of the surrender to the Confederation by Newfoundland of all its rights in mines and minerals, and of all the ungranted and unoccupied lands of the Crown, it is agreed that the sum of $150,000 shall each year be paid to that Province by semi-annual payments; provided that the Colony shall retain the right of opening, constructing and controlling roads and bridges through any of the said lands, subject to any laws which the General Legislature may pass in respect of the same.

And the question of concurrence being put thereon, the Conference divided, and the names of the Provinces were taken down as follows:—

CONTENTS.

Canada	2
Nova Scotia	1
New Brunswick	1
Newfoundland	1
	5

NON-CONTENTS.

Prince Edward Island	1

So it passed in the affirmative.

And the question of concurrence being proposed on item number eight, the same was resolved in the affirmative as follows:—

8. That all engagements that may be entered into with the Imperial Government for the defence of the country shall be assumed by the Confederation.

The Chairman laid the following letter before the Conference:—

To THE HONOURABLE SIR E. P. TACHÉ, &c., &c., &c.,

Chairman Intercolonial Conference.

SIR,—The undersigned desire respectfully to learn whether the Conference will instruct its secretary to furnish them for publication with a synopsis of the scheme of Confederation which may result from its deliberations.

The previous objection to furnish information which must have been necessarily incomplete does not appear to apply, after the general plan has been agreed upon, and the undersigned, on that account, feel justified in renewing their application for an official statement of the proceedings of the Conference. They trust the Conference will not deem this renewed application importunate when the natural anxiety of the public to learn the result of its deliberations is considered, especially as an intelligent public opinion can only be formed upon a thoroughly reliable statement of the facts.

And they have the honour to remain, Sir,

Your very obedient humble servants,

CHARLES LINDSEY,
for *Leader*.

B. CHAMBERLIN,
for Montreal *Gazette*

The following answer was read and ordered to be sent :—

CONFERENCE CHAMBER,
Parliament House,
Quebec, 26th Oct., 1864.

GENTLEMEN,—I am desired by Sir Etienne Taché to acknowledge your note, requesting that you may be furnished, for publication, with a synopsis of the scheme of Confederation which may result from the deliberations of the Conference.

I am, in reply, to state that the members of the Conference are of opinion that the reasons given in my former communication as those which induced them to decline your request in respect to ensuring publicity of their proceedings are still applicable ; and that they cannot yet feel themselves justified in giving authorized publication to the results of their deliberations.

I have the honour to be, gentlemen,

Your obedient servant,

For the Secretaries of the Conference,

H. BERNARD,
Executive Secretary.

CHARLES LINDSEY and B. CHAMBERLIN, Esquires.

(The rest is wanting).

THURSDAY P.M., 27th OCTOBER, 1864.

It was moved by—

And resolved :—

That all communications from the several Provinces on the subject of the Confederation be addressed to Sir E. P. Taché, the Premier of the Canadian Government, who shall be the medium of communication between them.

It was moved by the Honourable Mr. Galt :—

That the communications with the North-Western Territory and the improvement required for the development of the trade of the Great West with the seaboard are regarded by this Conference as subjects of the highest importance to the Confederation and should be prosecuted at the earliest possible period, when the state of the federal finances will permit the Legislature to do so.

And the question of concurrence being put thereon, the same was resolved in the affirmative.

(The rest is wanting).

SATURDAY, 29th OCTOBER, 1864.

ST. LAWRENCE HALL, Montreal,

12 o'clock noon.

It was moved by the Honourable Mr. Tupper :—

That, in the absence of Sir E. P. Taché, the Honourable Mr. Cartier do take the chair.

Carried, and Mr. Cartier took the chair.

The following heading of the report was carried :—

Report of resolutions adopted at a conference of delegates from the Provinces of Canada, Nova Scotia and New Brunswick and the Colonies of Newfoundland and Prince Edward Island, held at the City of Quebec, as the basis of a proposed confederation of those Provinces.

(The rest is wanting).

Below are the resolutions as finally adopted by the Conference.[*]

It will be seen that the Minutes record the adoption of all save numbers 10, 13, 15, 16, 34, 35, 54, 55, 56, 57, 58, 59, 68, 70 71 and 72.

They further show that of these No. 10 was moved on the 25th October by Mr. Mowat, and Nos. 54, 55 and 59 on the 22nd October by Mr. Galt.

The original papers also disclose that Nos. 13 and 15 were moved by Mr. McCully, No. 68 by Mr. Tupper and No. 70 by Mr. John A. Macdonald.

Respecting Nos. 16, 34, 35, 56, 57, 58, 71 and 72, there is nothing to indicate on which of the three last sittings of the Conference or by whom they were introduced.

REPORT

Of Resolutions adopted at a Conference of Delegates from the Provinces of Canada, Nova Scotia and New Brunswick, and the Colonies of Newfoundland and Prince Edward Island, held at the City of Quebec, 10th October, 1864, as the Basis of a proposed Confederation of those Provinces and Colonies.

1. The best interests and present and future prosperity of British North America will be promoted by a Federal Union under

---

[*] Between the closing of the Quebec Conference in October, 1864, and the meeting of the Canadian Legislature in January, 1865, certain alterations were made by mutual consent of the delegates in the 24th, 29th and 43rd resolutions, as follows :—

The 24th resolution was changed to read :

24. The Local Legislature of each Province may, from time to time, alter the electoral districts for the purposes of representation in such Local Legislature, and distribute the representatives to which the Province is entitled in such Local Legislature in any manner such Legislature may see fit.

Sub-section 3 of section 29 was changed to read :

3. The imposition or regulation of duties of customs on imports and exports, except on exports of timber, logs, masts, spars, deals and sawn lumber from New Brunswick, and of coal and other minerals from Nova Scotia.

Sub-section 1 of section 43 was changed to read :

1. Direct taxation, and in New Brunswick the imposition of duties on the export of timber, logs, masts, spars, deals and sawn lumber ; and in Nova Scotia on coals and other minerals.

For the correspondence arising out of these changes, see Appendix III.

the Crown of Great Britain, provided such Union can be effected on principles just to the several Provinces.

2. In the Federation of the British North American Provinces the System of Government best adapted under existing circumstances to protect the diversified interests of the several Provinces and secure efficiency, harmony and permanency in the working of the Union,—would be a general Government charged with matters of common interest to the whole Country, and Local Governments for each of the Canadas and for the Provinces of Nova Scotia, New Brunswick and Prince Edward Island, charged with the control of local matters in their respective sections.—Provision being made for the admission into the Union on equitable terms of Newfoundland, the North-West Territory, British Columbia and Vancouver.

3. In framing a Constitution for the General Government, the Conference, with a view to the perpetuation of our connection with the Mother Country, and to the promotion of the best interests of the people of these Provinces, desire to follow the model of the British Constitution, so far as our circumstances will permit.

4. The Executive Authority or Government shall be vested in the Sovereign of the United Kingdom of Great Britain and Ireland, and be administered according to the well understood principles of the British Constitution by the Sovereign personally or by the Representative of the Sovereign duly authorized.

5. The Sovereign or Representative of the Sovereign shall be Commander-in-Chief of the Land and Naval Militia Forces.

6. There shall be a General Legislature or Parliament for the Federated Provinces, composed of a Legislative Council and a House of Commons.

7. For the purpose of forming the Legislative Council, the Federated Provinces shall be considered as consisting of three divisions:—1st, Upper Canada; 2nd, Lower Canada; 3rd, Nova Scotia, New Brunswick and Prince Edward Island, each division with an equal representation in the Legislative Council.

8. Upper Canada shall be represented in the Legislative Council by 24 Members, Lower Canada by 24 Members, and the three

Maritime Provinces by 24 Members, of which Nova Scotia shall have Ten, New Brunswick, Ten, and Prince Edward Island, Four Members.

9. The Colony of Newfoundland shall be entitled to enter the proposed Union, with a representation in the Legislative Council of four Members.

10. The North-West Territory, British Columbia and Vancouver shall be admitted into the Union on such terms and conditions as the Parliament of the Federated Provinces shall deem equitable, and as shall receive the assent of Her Majesty; and in the case of the Province of British Columbia or Vancouver, as shall be agreed to by the Legislature of such Province.

11. The Members of the Legislative Council shall be appointed by the Crown under the Great Seal of the General Government and shall hold Office during Life: if any Legislative Councillor shall, for two consecutive sessions of Parliament, fail to give his attendance in the said Council, his seat shall thereby become vacant.

12. The Members of the Legislative Council shall be British Subjects by Birth or Naturalization, of the full age of Thirty Years, shall possess a continuous real property qualification of four thousand dollars over and above all incumbrances, and shall be and continue worth that sum over and above their debts and liabilities, but in the case of Newfoundland and Prince Edward Island, the property may be either real or personal.

13. If any question shall arise as to the qualification of a Legislative Councillor, the same shall be determined by the Council.

14. The first selection of the Members of the Legislative Council shall be made, except as regards Prince Edward Island, from the Legislative Councils of the various Provinces, so far as a sufficient number be found qualified and willing to serve: such Members shall be appointed by the Crown at the recommendation of the General Executive Government, upon the nomination of the respective Local Governments, and in such nomination due regard shall be had to the claims of the Members of the Legislative

Council of the Opposition in each Province, so that all political parties may as nearly as possible be fairly represented.

15. The Speaker of the Legislative Council (unless otherwise provided by Parliament) shall be appointed by the Crown from among the members of the Legislative Council, and shall hold office during pleasure, and shall only be entitled to a casting vote on an equality of votes.

16. Each of the twenty-four Legislative Councillors representing Lower Canada in the Legislative Council of the General Legislature, shall be appointed to represent one of the twenty-four Electoral Divisions mentioned in Schedule A of Chapter first of the Consolidated Statutes of Canada, and such Councillor shall reside, or possess his qualification in the Division he is appointed to represent.

17. The basis of Representation in the House of Commons shall be Population, as determined by the Official Census every ten years; and the number of Members at first shall be 194, distributed as follows:

Upper Canada.................................... 82
Lower Canada................................... 65
Nova Scotia.................................... 19
New Brunswick.................................. 15
Newfoundland................................... 8
and Prince Edward Island....................... 5

18. Until the Official Census of 1871 has been made up there shall be no change in the number of Representatives from the several sections.

19. Immediately after the completion of the Census of 1871 and immediately after every Decennial Census thereafter, the Representation from each section in the House of Commons shall be re-adjusted on the basis of Population.

20. For the purpose of such re-adjustments, Lower Canada shall always be assigned sixty-five members, and each of the other sections shall at each re-adjustment receive, for the ten years then next succeeding, the number of members to which it will be

entitled on the same ratio of representation to population as Lower
Canada will enjoy according to the Census last taken by having
sixty-five members.

21.   No reduction shall be made in the number of Members
returned by any section, unless its population shall have decreased
relatively to the population of the whole Union, to the extent of
five per centum.

22.   In computing at each decennial period, the number of
Members to which each section is entitled, no fractional parts shall
be considered, unless when exceeding one half the number entitling
to a Member, in which case a member shall be given for each such
fractional part.

23.   The Legislature of each Province shall divide such Province into the proper number of constituencies, and define the
boundaries of each of them.

24.   The Local Legislature of each Province may from time to
time alter the Electoral Districts for the purposes of Representation in the House of Commons, and distribute the representatives
to which the Province is entitled in any manner such Legislature
may think fit.

25.   The number of Members may at any time be increased
by the General Parliament,—regard being had to the proportionate rights then existing.

26.   Until provisions are made by the General Parliament, all
the Laws which, at the date of the Proclamation constituting the
Union, are in force in the Provinces respectively, relating to the
qualification and disqualification of any person to be elected or to
sit or vote as a member of the Assembly in the said Provinces
respectively—and relating to the qualification or disqualification
of voters, and to the oaths to be taken by voters, and to Returning
Officers and their powers and duties,—and relating to the proceedings at Elections,—and to the period during which such Elections
may be continued, and relating to the Trial of Controverted Elections, and the proceedings incident thereto, and relating to the
vacating of seats of Members and to the issuing and execution of
new Writs in case of any seat being vacated otherwise than by a

dissolution,—shall respectively apply to elections of Members to serve in the House of Commons, for places situate in those Provinces respectively.

27. Every House of Commons shall continue for five years from the day of the return of the writs choosing the same, and no longer, subject, nevertheless, to be sooner prorogued or dissolved by the Governor.

28. There shall be a Session of the General Parliament once at least in every year, so that a period of twelve calendar months shall not intervene between the last sitting of the General Parliament in one Session and the first sitting thereof in the next session.

29. The General Parliament shall have power to make Laws for the peace, welfare and good Government of the Federated Provinces (saving the Sovereignty of England), and especially Laws respecting the following subjects:—

1. The Public Debt and Property.

2. The Regulation of Trade and Commerce.

3. The imposition or regulation of Duties of Customs on Imports and Exports, except on Exports of Timber, Logs, Masts, Spars, Deals and Sawn Lumber, and of Coal and other Minerals.

4. The imposition or regulation of Excise Duties.

5. The raising of money by all or any other modes or systems of Taxation.

6. The Borrowing of Money on the Public Credit.

7. Postal Service.

8. Lines of Steam or other Ships, Railways, Canals and other works, connecting any two or more of the Provinces together or extending beyond the limits of any Province.

9. Lines of Steamships between the Federated Provinces and other Countries.

10. Telegraphic Communication and the incorporation of Telegraph Companies.

11. All such works as shall, although lying wholly within any Province, be specially declared by the Acts authorizing them to be for the general advantage.

12. The Census.

13. Militia—Military and Naval Service and Defence.

14. Beacons, Buoys and Lighthouses.

15. Navigation and Shipping.

16. Quarantine.

17. Sea Coast and Inland Fisheries.

18. Ferries between any Province and a Foreign Country, or between any two Provinces.

19. Currency and Coinage.

20. Banking, Incorporation of Banks, and the issue of paper money.

21. Savings Banks.

22. Weights and Measures.

23. Bills of Exchange and Promissory Notes.

24. Interest.

25. Legal Tender.

26. Bankruptcy and Insolvency.

27. Patents of Invention and Discovery.

28. Copy Rights.

29. Indians and Lands reserved for the Indians.

30. Naturalization and Aliens.

31. Marriage and Divorce.

32. The Criminal Law, excepting the Constitution of Courts of Criminal Jurisdiction, but including the procedure in Criminal matters.

33. Rendering uniform all or any of the laws relative to property and civil rights in Upper Canada, Nova Scotia, New Brunswick, Newfoundland and Prince Edward Island, and rendering uniform the procedure of all or any of the Courts in these Provinces: but any Statute for

> this purpose shall have no force or authority in any Province until sanctioned by the Legislature thereof.

34. The Establishment of a General Court of Appeal for the Federated Provinces.

35. Immigration.

36. Agriculture.

37. And Generally respecting all matters of a general character, not specially and exclusively reserved for the Local Governments and Legislatures.

30. The General Government and Parliament shall have all powers necessary or proper for performing the obligations of the Federated Provinces, as part of the British Empire, to Foreign Countries, arising under Treaties between Great Britain and such Countries.

31. The General Parliament may also, from time to time, establish additional Courts, and the General Government may appoint Judges and Officers thereof, when the same shall appear necessary or for the public advantage, in order to the due execution of the laws of Parliament.

32. All Courts, Judges and Officers of the several Provinces shall aid, assist and obey the General Government in the exercise of its rights and powers, and for such purposes shall be held to be Courts, Judges and Officers of the General Government.

33. The General Government shall appoint and pay the Judges of the Superior Courts in each Province, and of the County Courts in Upper Canada, and Parliament shall fix their salaries.

34. Until the Consolidation of the Laws of Upper Canada, New Brunswick, Nova Scotia, Newfoundland and Prince Edward Island, the Judges of these Provinces appointed by the General Government, shall be selected from their respective Bars.

35. The Judges of the Courts of Lower Canada shall be selected from the Bar of Lower Canada.

36. The Judges of the Court of Admiralty now receiving salaries shall be paid by the General Government.

37. The Judges of the Superior Courts shall hold their offices during good behaviour, and shall be removable only on the Address of both Houses of Parliament.

LOCAL GOVERNMENT.

38. For each of the Provinces there shall be an Executive Officer, styled the Lieutenant-Governor, who shall be appointed by the Governor-General in Council, under the Great Seal of the Federated Provinces, during pleasure : such pleasure not to be exercised before the expiration of the first five years, except for cause : such cause to be communicated in writing to the Lieutenant-Governor immediately after the exercise of the pleasure as aforesaid, and also by message to both Houses of Parliament, within the first week of the first Session afterwards.

39. The Lieutenant-Governor of each Province shall be paid by the General Government.

40. In undertaking to pay the salaries of the Lieutenant-Governors, the Conference does not desire to prejudice the claim of Prince Edward Island upon the Imperial Government for the amount now paid for the salary of the Lieutenant-Governor thereof.

41. The Local Government and Legislature of each Province shall be constructed in such manner as the existing Legislature of such Province shall provide.

42. The Local Legislatures shall have power to alter or amend their constitution from time to time.

43. The Local Legislatures shall have power to make Laws respecting the following subjects :—

    1. Direct Taxation and the imposition of Duties on the Export of Timber. Logs, Masts, Spars, Deals and Sawn Lumber, and of Coals and other Minerals.

    2. Borrowing Money on the credit of the Province.

    3. The establishment and tenure of local Offices, and the appointment and payment of local Officers.

    4. Agriculture.

    5. Immigration.

6. Education; saving the rights and privileges which the Protestant or Catholic minority in both Canadas may possess as to their Denominational Schools, at the time when the Union goes into operation.

7. The sale and management of Public Lands, excepting Lands belonging to the General Government.

8. Sea coast and Inland Fisheries.

9. The establishment, maintenance and management of Penitentiaries, and of Public and Reformatory Prisons.

10. The establishment, maintenance and management of Hospitals, Asylums, Charities and Eleemosynary Institutions.

11. Municipal Institutions.

12. Shop, Saloon, Tavern, Auctioneer and other licenses.

13. Local Works.

14. The Incorporation of private or local Companies, except such as relate to matters assigned to the General Parliament.

15. Property and civil rights, excepting those portions thereof assigned to the General Parliament.

16. Inflicting punishment by fine, penalties, imprisonment or otherwise for the breach of laws passed in relation to any subject within their jurisdiction.

17. The Administration of Justice, including the Constitution, maintenance and organization of the Courts, both of Civil and Criminal Jurisdiction, and including also the Procedure in Civil Matters.

18. And generally all matters of a private or local nature, not assigned to the General Parliament.

44. The power of respiting, reprieving and pardoning Prisoners convicted of crimes, and of commuting and remitting of sentences in whole or in part, which belongs of right to the Crown, shall be administered by the Lieutenant-Governor of each Province in Council, subject to any instructions he may from time to time receive from the General Government, and subject to any provisions that may be made in this behalf by the General Parliament.

MISCELLANEOUS.

45. In regard to all subjects over which jurisdiction belongs to both the General and Local Legislatures, the laws of the General Parliament shall control and supersede those made by the Local Legislature, and the latter shall be void so far as they are repugnant to or inconsistent with the former.

46. Both the English and French languages may be employed in the General Parliament and in its proceedings, and in the Local Legislature of Lower Canada, and also in the Federal Courts and in the Courts of Lower Canada.

47. No lands or property belonging to the General or Local Government shall be liable to taxation.

48. All Bills for appropriating any part of the Public Revenue, or for imposing any new Tax or Impost, shall originate in the House of Commons or House of Assembly, as the case may be.

49. The House of Commons or House of Assembly shall not originate or pass any Vote, Resolution, Address or Bill for the appropriation of any part of the Public Revenue, or of any Tax or Impost to any purpose, not first recommended by Message of the Governor-General, or the Lieutenant-Governor, as the case may be, during the Session in which such Vote, Resolution, Address or Bill is passed.

50. Any Bill of the General Parliament may be reserved in the usual manner for Her Majesty's Assent, and any Bill of the Local Legislatures may in like manner be reserved for the consideration of the Governor-General.

51. Any Bill passed by the General Parliament shall be subject to disallowance by Her Majesty within two years, as in the case of Bills passed by the Legislatures of the said Provinces hitherto, and in like manner any Bill passed by a Local Legislature shall be subject to disallowance by the Governor-General within one year after the passing thereof.

52. The Seat of Government of the Federated Provinces shall be Ottawa, subject to the Royal Prerogative.

53. Subject to any future action of the respective Local Governments, the Seat of the Local Government in Upper Canada shall be Toronto: of Lower Canada, Quebec; and the Seats of the Local Governments in the other Provinces shall be as at present.

PROPERTY AND LIABILITIES.

54. All Stocks, Cash, Bankers' Balances and Securities for money belonging to each Province, at the time of the Union, except as hereinafter mentioned, shall belong to the General Government.

55. The following Public Works and Property of each Province shall belong to the General Government, to wit :—

1. Canals;
2. Public Harbours;
3. Light Houses and Piers:
4. Steamboats, Dredges and Public Vessels;
5. River and Lake Improvements;
6. Railway and Railway Stocks, Mortgages and other Debts due by Railway Companies;
7. Military Roads;
8. Custom Houses, Post Offices and other Public Buildings, except such as may be set aside by the General Government for the use of the Local Legislatures and Governments;
9. Property transferred by the Imperial Government and known as Ordnance Property;
10. Armouries, Drill Sheds, Military Clothing and Munitions of War: and
11. Lands set apart for Public Purposes.

56.   All lands, mines, minerals and royalties vested in Her Majesty in the Provinces of Upper Canada, Lower Canada, Nova Scotia, New Brunswick and Prince Edward Island, for the use of such Provinces, shall belong to the Local Government of the territory in which the same are so situate: subject to any trusts that may exist in respect to any of such lands or to any interest of other persons in respect of the same.

57.   All sums due from purchasers or lessees of such lands, mines or minerals at the time of the Union, shall also belong to the Local Governments.

58.   All assets connected with such portions of the public debt of any Province as are assumed by the Local Governments, shall also belong to those Governments respectively.

59.   The several Provinces shall retain all other Public Property therein, subject to the right of the General Government to assume any Lands or Public Property required for Fortifications or the Defence of the Country.

60.   The General Government shall assume all the Debts and Liabilities of each Province.

61.   The Debt of Canada not specially assumed by Upper and Lower Canada respectively, shall not exceed at the time of the Union.............$62,500,000

Nova Scotia shall enter the Union with a debt not exceeding   8,000,000

And New Brunswick, with a debt not exceeding..   7,000,000

62.   In case Nova Scotia or New Brunswick do not incur liabilities beyond those for which their Governments are now bound and which shall make their debts at the date of Union less than $8,000,000 and $7,000,000 respectively, they shall be entitled to interest at 5 per cent. on the amount not so incurred, in like manner as is hereinafter provided for Newfoundland and Prince Edward Island; the foregoing resolution being in no respect intended to limit the powers given to the respective Governments of those Provinces by Legislative authority, but only to limit the

maximum amount of charge to be assumed by the General Government. Provided always that the powers so conferred by the respective Legislatures shall be exercised within five years from this date or the same shall then lapse.

63. Newfoundland and Prince Edward Island, not having incurred Debts equal to those of the other Provinces, shall be entitled to receive by half-yearly payments in advance from the General Government the Interest at five per cent. on the difference between the actual amount of their respective Debts at the time of the Union, and the average amount of indebtedness per head of the Population of Canada, Nova Scotia and New Brunswick.

64. In consideration of the transfer to the General Parliament of the powers of Taxation, an annual grant in aid of each Province shall be made, equal to 80 cents per head of the Population as established by the Census of 1861, the population of Newfoundland being estimated at 130,000. Such aid shall be in full settlement of all future demands upon the General Government for local purposes, and shall be paid half-yearly in advance to each Province.

65. The position of New Brunswick being such as to entail large immediate charges upon her local revenues, it is agreed that for the period of ten years from the time when the Union takes effect, an additional allowance of $63,000 per annum shall be made to that Province. But that so long as the liability of that Province remains under $7,000,000, a deduction equal to the interest on such deficiency shall be made from the $63,000.

66. In consideration of the surrender to the General Government by Newfoundland of all its rights in Mines and Minerals, and of all the ungranted and unoccupied Lands of the Crown, it is agreed that the sum of $150,000 shall each year be paid to that Province by semi-annual payments; provided that that Colony shall retain the right of opening, constructing and controlling Roads and Bridges through any of the said Lands, subject to any Laws which the General Parliament may pass in respect of the same.

67. All engagements that may, before the Union, be entered into with the Imperial Government for the Defence of the Country shall be assumed by the General Government.

68. The General Government shall secure, without delay, the completion of the Intercolonial Railway from Rivière-du-Loup through New Brunswick to Truro, in Nova Scotia.

69. The communications with the North-Western Territory, and the improvements required for the development of the Trade of the Great West with the Seaboard, are regarded by this Conference as subjects of the highest importance to the Federated Provinces, and shall be prosecuted at the earliest possible period that the state of the Finances will permit.

70. The Sanction of the Imperial and Local Parliaments shall be sought for the Union of the Provinces, on the principles adopted by the Conference.

71. That Her Majesty the Queen be solicited to determine the rank and name of the Federated Provinces.

72. The proceedings of the Conference shall be authenticated by the signatures of the Delegates, and submitted by each Delegation to its own Government, and the Chairman is authorized to submit a copy to the Governor-General for transmission to the Secretary of State for the Colonies.

DISCUSSIONS IN CONFERENCE

OF THE

DELEGATES FROM THE PROVINCES

OF

BRITISH NORTH AMERICA.

OCTOBER, 1864.

CONFERENCE CHAMBER, PARLIAMENT HOUSE, QUEBEC,

OCTOBER 11TH, 1864.

The discussion was resumed on Mr. Palmer's motion of yesterday :—

> That in taking the votes on all questions to be decided by this Conference, except questions of order, each Province or Colony, by whatever number of delegates represented, shall have one vote, and that in voting Canada shall be considered as two Provinces.

Mr. John A. Macdonald proposed that Upper and Lower Canada should be considered as two Provinces for voting purposes.

Mr. Palmer concurred.

Mr. Haviland suggested that it should be in writing. (It is understood that any question of order is to be settled by the poll of each).

Mr. *Fisher*—In the event of differences arising between the delegates of any one Province, some public notice should be taken of it.

Mr. *Coles*—I think that unnecessary, as occurring in a confidential conference.

Mr. Palmer's motion unanimously agreed to.

Mr. John A. Macdonald moved, seconded by Mr. Tilley, the adoption of the following rules regulating the proceedings of the Conference :—

1. That free and individual discussion and suggestion be allowed.

2. That all motions and the discussions and votes thereon be in the first place as if in Committee of the Whole.

3. That after vote put, no discussion be allowed.

4. That each Province may retire for consultation after vote put.

5. That after the scheme is settled in Committee of the Whole, all the resolutions be reconsidered as if with Speaker in the chair.

6. That just before the breaking up of the Conference, the Minutes be carefully gone over and settled, with the view of determining what is to be submitted to the Imperial and Provincial Governments, and what is to be published for general information.

Mr. Chandler—I beg to suggest that in cases where the delegates of one Province disagree, the names of the dissentients should be inserted in the Minutes, and also whether the vote was unanimous or not.

Mr. John A. Macdonald—I am willing provisionally to adopt the suggestion of Mr. Chandler, but I think the whole question should be carefully reconsidered at the eventual revise of the minutes.

Resolutions unanimously agreed to.

The discussion was resumed upon the motion of Mr. John A. Macdonald :—

That the best interests and present and future prosperity of British North America will be promoted by a Federal Union under the Crown of Great Britain, provided such union can be effected on principles just to the several Provinces.

The opening remarks of Mr. Macdonald in speaking to this resolution do not seem to have been recorded. Proceeding, he said :—

The various States of the adjoining Republic had always acted as separate sovereignties. The New England States, New York State and the Southern States had no sympathies in common. They were thirteen individual sovereignties, quite distinct the one from the other. The primary error at the formation of their constitution was that each state reserved to itself all sovereign rights, save the small portion delegated. We must reverse this process by strengthening the General Government and conferring on the

Provincial bodies only such powers as may be required for local purposes. All sectional prejudices and interests can be legislated for by local legislatures. Thus we shall have a strong and lasting government under which we can work out constitutional liberty as opposed to democracy, and be able to protect the minority by having a powerful central government. Great caution, however, is necessary. The people of every section must feel that they are protected, and by no overstraining of central authority should such guarantees be overridden. Our constitution must be based on an Act of the Imperial Parliament, and any question as to overriding sectional matters determined by " Is it legal or not ?" The judicial tribunals of Great Britain would settle any such difficulties should they occur.

Is this the time for union ? Now is the time, or we may abandon the idea in despair. Canada has not (*sic*) adopted union as a solution of her political difficulties ; but, failing any general union, she cannot remain as at present, and if we come to no decision here, we Canadians must address ourselves to the alternative and reconstruct our Government. Once driven to that, it will be too late for a general federation. We cannot, having brought our people to accept a Canadian federation, propose to them the question of a larger union. It is stated that in England federation will be considered as showing a desire for independence. I believe the people of England are strongly bent on keeping up her position as a mighty empire, which can only be done by helping her Colonies, Goldwin Smith, the Manchester school and the *Times*—the property of Robert Lowe, a recreant colonist—to the contrary notwithstanding. The colonial question has never been fairly represented to the people of England. The English newspapers were alive to the designs of Russia on Australia, a favoured colony of England, for which the Manchester school would fight. The British North American colonies are not so profitable as Australia from a money point of view ; but, if organized as a confederacy, our increased importance would soon become manifest. Our present isolated and defenceless position is, no doubt, a source of embarrassment to England. If it were not for the weakness of Canada, Great Britain might have joined France in acknowledging the Southern Confederacy. We must, therefore, become important, not only to England, but in the eyes of foreign states, and espe-

cially of the United States, who have found it impossible to
conquer four millions of Southern whites. Our united population
would reach that number. For the sake of securing peace to ourselves and our posterity we must make ourselves powerful. Our
population is increasing in geometrical progression. The burdens
of the United States and the re-action after the war will direct the
emigrating population of Great Britain to British America and
from the United States to a freer country—free from taxation and
less likely to be convulsed by war. There must be a new state of
things in the United States before matters settle into their normal
condition.

A question or objection sometimes raised to the proposed
union is that of increased expense. This, I think, will be comparatively small, in fact scarcely appreciable. Take the expenses
of the Governments as they exist to-day, five in number. You will
find that they aggregate a very considerable amount. With one
general Government the expense would be very much less. After
the first two or three sessions the General Legislature, unembar-
rassed by local matters, will take very much less time. The expenses of the subordinate legislatures will be small. Each
local government will be relieved of its provincial debts. I hope
one of the first things under the new system will be the issue of a
commission to enquire into the laws. We should have one statutory law throughout, except in Lower Canada, where the civil law
prevails. The great security for peace is to convince the world of
our strength by being united.

To Nova Scotia and New Brunswick Canada holds out the
Intercolonial road intimately bound up with the question of
union. As Mr. Tilley says, it is "absolutely necessary." When
the Intercolonial road was first proposed it was considered as a
great commercial work. We had then no Grand Trunk Railway,
at least but very slight communication with the seaboard. So
long as there is no war Canada can communicate (with the Lower
Provinces) through the States. Commercially the value of the
Lower Provinces has decreased to Canada, but in military respects
they are very essential. The Intercolonial road must be a political
consequence of a political union. If it were thought by the Canadian Parliament that this union should not take place, it would be

difficult to induce that body to support the plan of an Intercolonial road. I think it should be in any event, and would support and vote for it : but it would be a matter of great difficulty to carry.

It is impossible to have a Zollverein. We must continue to have hostile tariffs unless we have a political union.

A great evil in the United States is that the President is a despot for four years. He is never considered as being the father of his people. It was otherwise with Washington, who did not escape slander. Every President is the leader of a party, and obliged to consider himself as bound to protect the rights of a majority. Under the British Constitution, with the people having always the power in their own hands and with the responsibility of a Ministry to Parliament, we are free from such despotism. These weaknesses in the United States Constitution have not only attracted our attention, but also that of Confederate States, who endeavour to avoid them by having lengthened terms for their President. With them great questions are not settled in committees as in the United States, but they allow Ministers to appear on the floor of the House to defend their measures. They have cut the wings of the President as leader of a party by providing that no Government employee shall be dismissed without cause—that is, that the right shall not be capriciously exercised.

As regards the constitution of our Legislature. In order to have no local jealousies and all things conciliatory, there should be a different system in the two chambers. With the Queen as our Sovereign, we should have an Upper and a Lower House. In the former the principle of equality should obtain. In the Lower House the basis of representation should be population, not by universal suffrage, but according to the principles of the British Constitution. In the Upper House there should be equality in numbers. The population of Upper Canada is 1,400,000 : Lower Canada, 1,200,000 ; Lower Provinces, 750,000. The rate of increase of population in Canada must be greater in future than in the Maritime Provinces. We considered at Charlottetown that Upper Canada should have twenty members, Lower Canada twenty, and the Maritime Provinces twenty. If not politically united they should still have the same aggregate representation.

With respect to the mode of appointments to the Upper House, some of us are in favour of the elective principle. More are in favour of appointment by the Crown. I will keep my own mind open on that point as if it were a new question to me altogether. At present I am in favour of appointment by the Crown. While I do not admit that the elective principle has been a failure in Canada, I think we had better return to the original principle and in the words of Governor Simcoe endeavour to make ours "an image and transcript of the British Constitution."

We have to consider what is desirable: and then what is practicable. We cannot ask each Legislature to relinquish its Upper House. It would be hazardous to the project of union. My proposition to Canada is this. In our Legislative Council there are seventy-two members. In the event of its being decided that in the new body Upper Canada shall be represented by twenty members and Lower Canada by twenty members, let the members in each section meet and ballot or elect, as representative peers in Scotland (the latter is perhaps the better plan), the councillors to the new body, who should at once receive their appointment under the Great Seal, for life; those not elected, to be a portion of the Local Legislature. The latter would have their own social position and be active members of the body politic. A large qualification should be necessary for membership of the Upper House, in order to represent the principle of property. The rights of the minority must be protected, and the rich are always fewer in number than the poor.

Each Province shall adjust its own constituencies. We should not embarrass ourselves with the qualification of the voter. Each Province should send its representatives on the present system of each, and the question of the qualification should be reserved for the consideration of the whole Government united.

Mr. Brown—What as to raising the suffrage?

Mr. John A. Macdonald—The system I propose is that which was in the Union Act of Upper and Lower Canada. The preliminary question for us to consider, is what powers should be reserved to the General Legislature and what given to the Local Legislatures. That must be considered before we enter upon the subject of the constitution. We should keep before us the principles of the British Constitution. It (our constitution) should be a mere skeleton and framework that would not bind us down. We have now all the elasticity which has kept England together.

Motion unanimously agreed to.

AFTERNOON SESSION.

Sir Etienne Taché stated that he was unavoidably obliged to leave the chair to meet His Excellency the Governor-General, and he requested Colonel Gray, of Prince Edward Island, to take the chair during his absence, which the latter accordingly did.

Mr. Dickey—What authority from the Home Government have we to consider this subject?

Mr. John A. Macdonald quoted despatch from the Duke of Newcastle to the Earl of Mulgrave, Lieutenant-Governor of Nova Scotia, dated 6th July, 1862.*

Mr. Brown moved, seconded by Mr. Archibald :—

That in the Federation of the British North American Provinces, the system of government best adapted under existing circumstances to protect the diversified interests of the several Provinces and secure efficiency, harmony and permanency in the working of the Union, would be a General Government, charged with matters of common interest to the whole country; and Local Governments for each of the Canadas and for the Maritime Provinces, charged with the control of local matters in their respective sections ; provision being made for the admission into the Union on equitable terms of the North-West Territory, British Columbia and Vancouver.

Mr. Fisher—I should have preferred a legislative union if it were feasible.

Mr. Brown—It must be a federal and not a legislative union. That is the main object of my motion, together with the inclusion of the North-West Provinces. The latter opens up a wide question. The population of the Red River Settlement is now 12,000 and we must look forward to the day of settlement and occupation of that country. The inclusion of British Columbia and Vancouver Island is rather an extreme proposition, but it would be wrong to exclude them in the formation of the scheme. The Americans are encroaching. A large portion of the land at Saskatchewan might be formed into a Crown Colony or be in the

* See Appendix V.

Union. The people of Upper Canada in going into the Union would feel strongly that that country should be secure to us. To make communication less difficult there should be a winter route.

Mr. Fisher—I think we should lay this matter before each Legislature, but not press it next session.

Mr. McCully—Is it necessary that this question should be submitted to the people? In New Brunswick (?) men of large minds approve of it and think it should be proceeded with at once. But there is another class between them and the mass of the people who hesitate and halt and doubt the propriety of taking a step like this. More intelligent people, like delegates, should take the matter into their own hands and not wait to educate their people up to it.

Adjourned at four o'clock p.m.

WEDNESDAY, 12TH OCTOBER, 1864.

The discussion on Mr. Brown's motion of yesterday was resumed.

Mr. Palmer—I do not oppose the motion generally. But our discussion is in advance of the propositions contained therein. I call attention to the acquisition of the North-West. Our powers as delegates are strictly defined, and we should confine our deliberations to our own Provinces. Is it right or politic to embrace a consideration of the Hudson's Bay Territories, including Mr. Brown's reference to the American views as to acquiring possession of it. Should we introduce any allusion to it?

Mr. Carter—I should have heartily concurred in the vote of yesterday had I been here, and regret my absence. As regards the motion before the chair, I like the grandeur and magnitude of the scheme. But I do not see that anyone is justified in speaking of taking in the Hudson's Bay Territories.

Mr. Whelan—I was absent yesterday, but do not desire to withhold my adhesion from the great and glorious principle involved in the motion of yesterday. I do not fear a small colony like Prince Edward Island being involved. We are forming a constitution for a country larger than Europe in extent. There is an apprehension abroad in the Lower Provinces that Canada desires to swamp and extinguish their provincial character. Such ought not to be objected to. It is desirable that our mere provincial character should be lost and that we should form one great country.

Mr. Brown's motion carried unanimously.

The Honourable Mr. Shea rose and suggested that it would tend to the despatch of business before the Conference if the several resolutions intended to be moved were prepared in advance by a committee composed of the delegates of Canada.

Mr. Shea's suggestion was agreed to, and the Conference accordingly adjourned for such purpose.

WEDNESDAY, 19TH OCTOBER, 1864.

The Conference resumed consideration of the motion of the Hon. Mr. Tupper respecting the selection of members of the Legislative Council, and of the motion of the Hon. Mr. Coles in amendment thereto. (See pp. 15, 16.)

Mr. Fisher—Canada should not prescribe the mode of selection, but leave the matter to the Local Legislatures.

Mr. Tupper—This would be imposing an irritating subject on the Local Legislatures. The Legislatures will say this must be settled before the question of Confederation.

Mr. Chandler concurred.

Mr. McCully—One of the arguments that will be most useful to commend this project of Confederation to the people of the Lower Provinces is that it will not involve additional expenditure but decrease the expenses of the Local Governments. I agree with Mr. Tupper.

Mr. Coles—I differ from him. We should not dictate the course to be taken. Leave it open to all duly qualified persons in the Province. Excepting Prince Edward Island will not satisfy me ; it will place us in difficulty.

Mr. Henry—If we are limited to choose from the present Legislative Councils in the Lower Provinces, we are violating sound principles. It will follow that we cannot have fresh men for ten or twelve years. Each Government should choose its own men in its own way. We should not limit ourselves.

Mr. Tupper—Nova Scotia will be abundantly satisfied by choosing ten Legislative Councillors out of the present men. We can select representative lawyers, merchants, and professors of different creeds out of them. But this should be confined to first selection.

Mr. Coles' amendment defeated, Prince Edward Island alone voting for it.

Mr. Tupper's amendment carried, Prince Edward Island voting against it.

Mr. Galt moved :—

That in the first instance the members to be chosen for the Legislative Council of the United Provinces, excepting Prince Edward Island, shall be chosen by lot from the existing members of the Legislative Councils of the several Maritime Provinces, and of those sitting in Canada, from Upper and Lower Canada respectively.

And that as vacancies occur in the representation from any Province, they shall be filled by the persons whose names shall have been drawn next in priority to those first selected until the whole number shall be exhausted.

Mr. Fisher—I object to the motion. I feel we have been overridden by Canada in this. It overrides the Assembly and makes the Legislative Council the greatest power. Why tie down other Provinces, if Prince Edward Island is excepted ? Canada should give the Local Legislatures the power to choose. As it is, it will add greatly to the difficulties of New Brunswick. It makes the Legislative Councils the controlling power.

Mr. Tupper—I rise to a question of order. No discussion is allowed after the vote is taken. The point alluded to has already been decided.

(From what follows it appears that Mr. Brown here made some remarks adverse to the motion of Mr. Galt, which have not been recorded).

Mr. Tepper—I agree with Mr. Brown that the Legislative Council should be chosen from all parties. This motion will prevent that.

The Canadian delegates retired. On returning,

Mr. Galt—I have decided to drop the last paragraph of my motion as follows :—

And that as vacancies occur in the representation from any Province, they shall be filled by the persons whose names shall have been drawn next in priority to those first selected until the whole number shall be exhausted.

My motion will therefore read :—

That in the first instance the members to be chosen for the Legislative Council of the United Provinces, excepting Prince Edward Island, shall be chosen by lot from the exisiting members of the Legislative Councils of the several Maritime Provinces, and of those sitting in Canada, from Upper and Lower Canada respectively.

Mr. Galt's motion lost. Contents—Canada, two. Non-contents—Nova Scotia, New Brunswick, Newfoundland, three. Prince Edward Island did not vote.

The Hon. Mr. Shea moved :—

That such first selection shall be made by the Local Government of each Province so far as a sufficient number be found as aforesaid, and in case such sufficient number cannot be found, then the Local Government shall name for appointment other duly qualified parties to make up the deficiency. Provided that the Government of Canada shall select for both sections of Canada, and that the Government of Prince Edward Island shall name for appointment the whole number of the Legislative Councillors allotted to it.

Mr. Brown—Although approved by the Canadian delegates by a majority vote, I think the motion very objectionable. It was carried by nine to three, but I cannot agree to it.*

Mr. McCully—If a question of delicacy in a coalition government, how much more so must it be in the case of Governments not formed on the coalition principle. Some modification of the principle stated in the motion is necessary. Due regard should be had to the claims of the Opposition so that political parties may be equally represented in the Legislative Council.

Mr. Tupper—Canada has a combination of parties. But in the Lower Provinces it is otherwise, and both parties are entitled to be fairly represented. If Nova Scotia is called on to appoint ten members it shall be done by fair representation of all parties, but that should be the result of conference, though not necessary to publish the fact.

* There is apparently some confusion in the notes at this place. These remarks of Mr. Brown may refer to Mr. Galt's motion, for the consideration of which the Canadian delegates withdrew. At the same time it is evident from his subsequent remarks, that he strongly opposed Mr. Shea's motion. What adds to the difficulty of interpretation of the record of this part of the debate is the fact that the motion of Mr. Shea is in the handwriting of Mr. John A. Macdonald, and may therefore, equally with that of Mr. Galt, represent the views of the majority of the Canadian delegates against which Mr. Brown protested.

Col. Gray (New Brunswick)—A course to suit one Government will not suit another. Let Canada carry her own plan as she pleases, and let each of the other Provinces do the same. After the first batch is over we fall into the rule prescribed by the Federal constitution. I would leave the first selections to the Local Governments, it would be to their interests to get good men. Local partisanship will not come up in the Legislative Council of the Federal Government, and, therefore, the best men will be chosen. No broad principle can be laid down that is suitable to all. I would propose that mode of first choice shall be settled, and prescribed by the Local Legislatures. The interests of both sides will be regarded. The Canadian Government can thus carry their own plan through their Legislature.

The motion of the Hon. Mr. Shea was by leave of the Conference withdrawn.

Mr. Archibald moved :—

That in the selection of members of the first Federal Legislative Council, each Province shall be governed by such rules now to be agreed upon as are considered by the Conference most suitable to the circumstances of the particular Provinces.

Mr. McCully—This is the same as my amendment of last night. The Conference exhibits evidence that on fundamental principles the Provinces are not prepared for Federation. My argument is that, if you leave the selection to the Local Legislatures, it will prove a bone of contention and jeopardize the Federation. The Legislatures are under no restraint as to the composition of the Legislative Council. The Executive would not be so. I beg to move in amendment to the motion of Mr. Archibald :—

That the Legislative Council shall in the first instance be chosen in Canada by ballot, and in the other Provinces, by the Executive Governments.

Mr. Brown—I appealed to the other Provinces to aid my views because Canada has decided by a majority, but contrary to the views of my party. We say we could not leave to the Executive the choice of Legislative Councillors. A conflict might arise in the Cabinet before the choice was made, and a party administration might be formed.

Mr. John A. Macdonald—But that exists in Nova Scotia and New Brunswick at this time.

Mr. Brown—But the plan could not be carried in Canada.

Mr. John A. Macdonald—Arrangements can be made as to consultation between parties in case of a party Government. But we should not have a different system in the different Provinces. It is of great importance that all should follow the same mode.

Mr. Tupper—An essential point is that the Executive Governments should appoint the first Legislative Council.

The motion of Mr. Archibald and amendment of the Hon. Mr. McCully were withdrawn.

Mr. McCully—Before the Legislative Council can be formed there must be an Executive. I am content to take that the Government of each Province shall appoint subject to the approval of the Executive Council of the whole Federal Government. I accordingly move :—

> That the members of the first Legislative Council in the Federal Legislature shall be appointed by the Crown at the recommendation of the Federal Executive Government upon the nomination of the respective Local Governments. And that in such nomination due regard be had to the claims of the members of the Legislative Council of the Opposition in each Province, so as that all political parties be as nearly as possible fairly represented.

Mr. Tupper—How do you construct the Executive before the Legislative Council ?

Mr. John A. Macdonald—An Executive Council for the Federal Government must be the first thing. It will be in its nature provisional. After the elections the party not having support must go out.

Mr. Tilley—I think this is an additional guarantee to the minority that party shall be represented. Anything to the contrary would be a direct breach of the will of the Conference.

Mr. Coles—How is the minority to know of the proposed appointments ?

Mr. John A. Macdonald—The Federal Government will be bound to see that the parties are appointed under this understanding before their appointments are ratified.

Mr. Brown—I think Mr. McCully's proposal is an amelioration of the evil under which we should labour if Mr. Shea's motion had carried. But I think it still objectionable. I press on the Conference that each Province should be allowed to take its own mode of selection.

Mr. Archibald—It is desirable to have one plan for the whole. The Maritime Provinces will probably adopt the same system, and Canada should agree to one.

Mr. Fisher—Canada has forced us into a false position by requiring the choice to be made from the existing Legislative Councillors.

Mr. John A. Macdonald—I must deny on the part of Canada any attempt to coerce other Governments. The other Provinces took the same view.

Mr. McDougall—I disagree with the shape which the question is in before the Conference. Two questions were submitted to Canada. Mr. Brown asks the other Provinces to assist the minority of the Canadian delegation. That I think wrong. The proper course for the minority of the Canadian Government will be to discuss the matter afterwards among themselves and endeavour to change their colleagues' opinions.

Mr. Brown—It was understood that we should vote by Provinces, but it was also understood that every individual member should speak against the decision of his own Province.

Mr. McDougall—Is it the meaning of the resolution that the Federal Government can displace any member of the Legislative Council appointed in breach of agreement?

Mr. John A. Macdonald—It is the understanding that the Federal Government shall be a Court of Equity to see that the understanding of fairness as to party is carried out.

Mr. McCully's motion was unanimously agreed to.

Mr. Brown moved a resolution defining the representation in the House of Commons. (See pp. 19, 41).

Mr. Galt—In reference to Mr. Brown's motion, I propose 225 members instead of 200. If we divide 225, according to population, I calculate it would give :—

Upper Canada	99
Lower Canada	74
Nova Scotia	21
New Brunswick	17
Newfoundland	8
Prince Edward Island	6

225

We should commence with the census of 1861, and re-adjust after each subsequent census. We have supposed that the population of Lower Canada, being tolerably equable in its character, would afford the best basis. But having respect to the rapid increase of Upper Canada, we think the Lower Provinces should not be reduced if they do not increase in the same ratio. Therefore, the Lower Provinces would have the same as they have now unless in the very improbable case of any one falling off by five per cent. or more—that is a decrease relatively to the whole Federation.

Mr. Brown—We thought it best not to take the census of 1861, but the proportionate increase in five years thence and change in 1881, but this may not be intelligible. It may be better to take the census of 1861. In that case the figures in the motion will be as follows :—

Upper Canada	82
Lower Canada	65
Nova Scotia	19
New Brunswick	15
Newfoundland	7
Prince Edward Island..	5
	193

Mr. Tupper—That is better, as the public in the other case have no data.

Mr. Brown—In the apportionment, if a fractional part, we don't allow it : if over one-half, we allow one.

Mr. Johnson—But if you have quadrennial Parliaments, you may by increase of population have to increase your members in the Assembly at an improper time.

Mr. Tilley—And to alter your electoral divisions.

Mr. Brown—After the census of 1871, we shall adopt the same rule. The practical result will be that while Lower Canada certainly will not be less and the Lower Provinces may increase in population, they cannot decrease in the number of representatives. It keeps the House within a reasonable limit. It is now to start with one in 17,000. It will afterwards vary. There is just one difficulty. Messrs. Galt and Cartier think the number too small. They think the House should number 216.

In that event, Mr. Galt proposes that Lower Canada shall get 73, and the rest in proportion, so as to get, on the basis of the census of 1861, 216 in the House.

Mr. Coles—1871 is too soon to alter. It should be in 1881.

Mr. Galt—Upper Canada will not consent to that, and it must be so definitely understood.

Mr. Tilley—We have fourteen counties, some with four representatives, others with two, and the City of St. John, two. Twenty-one, the number stated in the printed motion, would better answer us. I agree with Mr. Brown's proposition to begin with a goodly number, that it may not be disturbed for some time to come.

Mr. McCully—I advocate the adoption of the measure as it stands. I do not think we should make any local distribution of members.

Mr. Archibald—By accident the proposed arrangement will suit both Nova Scotia and New Brunswick. One member for each county, and one for each metropolis, will give the exact number provided in Mr. Brown's scale of 193.

The several Provinces announced their consent and approval of the scheme of 193 members based on the census of 1861, as precisely suiting the mode in which each could adapt the electoral divisions at present existing to such a state of things.

Mr. Shea, however, argued that inasmuch as the Newfoundland census was taken in 1857, an allowance for the period intervening between that date and 1861 would entitle Newfoundland to another representative. It was conceded by all the Provinces that Newfoundland should have another representative, thus raising its number to eight, and the whole number to 194.

Mr. Brown's motion carried, Prince Edward Island alone voting nay.

Mr. Haviland—Prince Edward Island would rather be out of the Confederation than consent to this motion. We should have no status. Only five members out of 194 would give the Island no position.

Mr. Tilley—That is rather a singular ground of objection, for they have objected to the basis of representation by population. Now it was fully understood at Charlottetown that those who came to the Conference expected representation by population. Some difficulty might have arisen on those points but not on this.

Mr. Palmer—I am not inimical to the grand scheme of Confederation. I believe it will be productive of great benefits. But I take exception to the principle adopted by this resolution. Representation by population is not applicable when a certain number of Provinces are throwing their resources into one Confederation, and giving up their own self-government and individuality. When a colony surrenders that right, she should have something commensurate in the Confederation. The debt of Prince Edward Island is nothing. Our taxation is vastly below that of the other Provinces. Our trade and revenue are rapidly increasing. Why give up so great certainties for an uncertain benefit where we have only a feeble voice? Looking first at the larger Provinces. Canada has secured to herself a greater number of representatives than she had before. It may be said that we may join with the other Maritime Provinces in any matters affecting our common interests, but even then our united strength would still be far below Canada's number of representatives. Not even two or three more members would induce me to give my assent to the scheme. I never understood that any proposition at Charlottetown was to be binding as to representation by population. It was there made by those from Canada and I did not think it necessary to remark on it, as it was a mere suggestion then thrown out by Canada for consideration.

Mr. Shea—The speech just made should have been delivered before we came to this Conference. What has brought us here? What brought about the Conference except the difficulties in Canada over the question of representation by population? We came here from Newfoundland with that understanding. Canada could not give way in such a matter. Prince Edward Island is in a better position than Newfoundland as regards the Legislative Council, as they have an equal number of representatives therein.

Mr. Coles—Newfoundland is the cause of our getting a less representation in the Legislative Council than we should otherwise have had. I understood that this matter was to be settled on the basis of representation by population. I stated lately that I thought our Prince Edward Island Government should not

have sent us here unless to carry out these views stated by the
Canadian Government. The Attorney-General of Prince Edward
Island (Mr. Palmer) now states that the Government cannot ac-
cede to it. I think that we came here prepared for representation
by population, and I regret that the Attorney-General of Prince
Edward Island had not previously stated that he could not ac-
cede to the principle and withdrawn from the Conference.

Mr. Haviland—I am not a member of the Prince Edward
Island Government.   I express only my individual opinion.

Mr. Coles—Then the Government should have instructed
their delegates properly.

Colonel Gray (Prince Edward Island)—My colleagues and
myself feel in a humiliating position.   We feel that a slur has
been cast by Mr. Coles on the Government which I have the
honour to lead.   I came to the Conference understanding fully
the question.   I have never had any conversation with the Attorney-General on the subject. My idea was as clear as the sun
at noonday that we were to treat on the basis of representation
by population. The Attorney-General heard as much as I did at
Charlottetown.   Certainly none of us should have been here unless the members of our delegation had been agreed on the point.
All that I could get for Prince Edward Island I would, but I
fancied we were fully agreed on these points at Charlottetown,
and that our discussion was to be about details.

Mr. Galt—It would be a matter for the greatest regret that
any difficulty should arise over this matter. We request the
Prince Edward Island delegates to reconsider their decision.   It
would be a matter of reproach to us that the smallest colony
should leave us.

Mr. Whelan—I should feel it my duty to-night to vote
against the resolution, but we had better reconsider the matter.
Mr. Haviland and I came here perfectly untrammelled and without any instructions from the Government of Prince Edward Island. We understand that all proceedings were to be *de novo*
and apart from anything which had taken place at Charlottetown.   I thought that Prince Edward Island had not been fairly
treated as to representation in the Legislative Council, but I gave
way on that occasion. I do not think, however, I could say
that I was satisfied with the representation of five in the Federal

House of Commons. We are in an isolated position. Our resources are large, and our people would not be content to give up their present benefits for the representation of five members. It may be said that the Confederation will go on without Prince Edward Island, and that we shall eventually be forced in. Better, however, that, than that we should willingly go into the Confederation with that representation. But if the Government who form the delegation will take the responsibility on them, I may support them.

Adjourned at ten o'clock p.m.

THURSDAY, 20TH OCTOBER, 1864.

Mr. Brown—I desire to ask if the Prince Edward Island delegates will state what their views are on the resolution of last evening.

Mr. Palmer—On making my observations last night I was under the impression with respect to any vote given that the party voting was bound to maintain it. Dr. Tupper had said whoever voted for a proposition could not afterwards oppose it in his Local Legislature, and such appeared to be the general opinion by tacit consent. I could not consent that Prince Edward Island, free of debt comparatively, should come into Federation with the other Provinces indebted largely, especially as nothing had been said or settled as to the relative shares of the burdens to be borne by each. I am told, however, by my colleagues from Prince Edward Island, that the financial questions will follow the present discussion, and that the matter of representation must depend on the financial resolutions. That may alter our position.

Mr. Coles—Every question must stand on its own footing. Why mix up financial matters with representation?

Colonel Gray (Prince Edward Island)—I am instructed by my co-delegates to say that the provision of five members is unsatisfactory. Prince Edward Island is divided longitudinally into three counties, each returning ten members. But they are always opposed to change of representation. We cannot divide the three counties into the five members.

Mr. Brown—Every Province must revise its own electoral divisions to suit the number of its representation.

Mr. Coles—Mr. Galt had proposed six members for Prince Edward Island. I approved that rather than Mr. Brown's motion, because it allows us to give to our three counties two members each.

Mr. Pope—I was absent last night. I was under the impression that it had been clearly laid down at Charlottetown that representation by population was to form the basis of the Lower House. I could not, therefore, have argued for a greater number than our population entitled us to get. I agree in all that has been said by Colonel Gray and Mr. Coles. But the circumstances of Prince Edward Island are such that I hope the Conference will agree to give us such a number as we can divide amongst our three constituencies. Nature, as well as the original settlement of the Island, has made three counties, and it would give rise to much difficulty if we had to adjust five members to the three counties. I cannot ask it as a matter of right, but one of expediency, as one without which it is impossible for us to carry the measure in Prince Edward Island. I, therefore, ask for six members.

Mr. Haviland—I fully agree with Mr. Pope. It would be an insuperable difficulty to us if we had not six members.

Mr. Brown—To give Prince Edward Island five members the total properly should be 205. It is obvious we cannot depart from representation by population. The only thing to do would be to take Prince Edward Island as the basis which would give a House of 230, altogether too large. Give one member to each county and let the whole Island elect the other two, and keep the number five intact ; or let the whole Island elect five. We should have to add thirty-eight members to the House in order to give Prince Edward Island six, as the basis of representation by population.

Mr. A. A. Macdonald—We are not bound by the principle of representation by population laid down at Charlottetown. Our constituents will say and will speak of the increased representation of Canada, and decreased representation of the Lower Provinces.

Mr. Galt—There is no use in asking the Conference to depart from the principle laid down. We could not justify it. If the principle is good it is the same for all, and we could not defend the action of giving 13,000 in Prince Edward Island a member where it requires 17,000 in any other Province for that purpose. It would be indefensible. The difficulty is of a purely local nature. It is impossible for the Conference to depart from the rule of population being the basis of representation.

Mr. McCully—There is another reason. As to the constitution of the Upper House, we looked on that as flexible. If we made the concession perhaps Prince Edward Island might not come in : and, besides, the North-West might require, for some local reason, an increased representation irrespective of population. The rule of representation by population must be rigid and unyielding.

Mr. Dickey—Give one member to each county in Prince Edward Island, one to Charlottetown, and one elected by the whole Island. Members elected for the Federal Legislature would not be elected for local purposes, but are representatives of the whole Island. It is a question for Canada. We (Nova Scotia) would concede the six members though it would place us in difficulty.

Mr. Haviland—There is no solution in the above proposition.

Mr. Pope—Religious feeling in Prince Edward Island runs very high. The Protestants outnumber the Roman Catholics, and in consequence the fifth member as proposed by Mr. Dickey would not represent the Roman Catholics.

Mr. Fisher—I came here convinced that representation by population was settled as the basis upon which the Provinces were to be asked to confederate.

Mr. Coles—Whatever may be the result of this matter, Prince Edward Island should submit.. The question has been settled. Let us go on with the business, and let Prince Edward Island settle for themselves when the question comes before them.

Mr. John A. Macdonald moved :—

That there shall be a session of the Legislative Council and Assembly once at least in every year, so that a period of twelve calendar months shall not intervene between the last sitting of the Legislative Council and Assembly in one session and the first sitting of the Legislative Council and Assembly in the next session. And every Legislative Assembly shall continue for five years from the day of the return of the writs choosing the same and no longer, subject nevertheless to be sooner prorogued or dissolved by the Governor.

He said : There have been only four Parliaments out of eighteen in England which have exceeded five years. The term Parliament is correct, because Parliament is dissolved, but elections take place for Commoners only. I prefer the term " House of Commons," but they do not like it to be used elsewhere than in England as they have prescriptive rights. I desire a clause to the effect that all rights of the Lords or Commons in their legislative capacity shall be provided to the Federal Parliament. It would be necessary to say legislative capacity, as the House of Lords has a judicial capacity. Carried.

Mr. John A. Macdonald moved :—

That the Executive authority or Government shall be vested in the Sovereign of the United Kingdom of Great Britain and Ireland, and be administered according to the well understood principles of the British Constitution by the Sovereign personally or by representative duly authorized.

Mr. Tupper—Is it meant to leave it to the Queen or to make any suggestion as to the appointment of a Viceroy ?

Mr. John A. Macdonald—I think it advisable not to make any suggestion. At least it should not be a constitutional suggestion. Hereafter the Parliament of the Federation may represent a desire for one of the Royal Family as Viceroy.

Mr. McCully—I assume that we should continue to be governed by a Governor-General.

Mr. Macdonald's motion carried.

Mr. Brown—As to Local Governments, we desire in Upper Canada that they should not be expensive, and should not take up political matters. We ought not to have two electoral bodies. Only one body, members to be elected once in every three years. Should have whole legislative power—subject to Lieutenant-Governor. I would have Lieutenant-Governor appointed by General Government. It would thus bring these bodies into harmony with the General Government. In Upper Canada executive officers would be Attorney-General, Treasurer, Secretary, Commissioner of Crown Lands, and Commissioner of Public Works. These would form the Council of the Lieutenant-Governor. I would give Lieutenant-Governor veto without advice, but under certain vote he should be obliged to assent. During recess Lieutenant-Governor could have power to suspend executive officers. They might be elected for three years or otherwise. You might safely allow County Councils to appoint other officers than those they now do. One Legislative Chamber for three years, no power of dissolution, elected on one day in each third year. Lieutenant-Governor appointed by Federal Government. Departmental officers to be elected during pleasure, or for three years. To be allowed to speak but not to vote.

Mr. Cartier—I entirely differ with Mr. Brown. It introduces in our local bodies republican institutions.

Mr. Brown moved :—

That in the Local Government there shall be but one Legislative Chamber.

Sir E. Taché—This motion is made merely to elicit opinion of conference.

Mr. Tilley—New Brunswick differs with Mr. Brown. They propose to keep the existing things as they are, so far as consistent with expense. They propose Lieutenant-Governor, five departmental officers, with seats in House.

Mr. Dickey—Before details, settle principles. Will conference take present Local Governments as models ?

Mr. Fisher—I am opposed to Mr. Brown's views. I approve of the present system of Local Legislatures. I agree with Mr. Brown that the Lieutenant-Governor should be appointed by the Federal Government.

Mr. Carter—In 1842, we had one Chamber in Newfoundland, partly appointed by Crown and partly by people. It worked well. An object to reduce expense.

Mr. Henry—I think uniformity is very desirable. But you should first consider what is to be left to the Local Legislatures before you proceed to discuss their constitutions.

Mr. McGee—No. Institute your body, then assign its powers.

Mr. Chandler — We are here to form a constitution for Federal Government. Let the Provinces otherwise remain as they are, so far as possible.

Mr. Tupper—I agree with general principles laid down by Mr. Brown that the Governments should be as simple and inexpensive as possible. We should diminish the powers of the Local

Governments, but we must not shock too largely the prejudices of the people in that respect.

Mr. McCully—We must have miniature responsible Governments.

Adjourned at two o'clock p.m.

EVENING SESSION.

Mr. Archibald proposed a resolution to the effect that Lieutenant-Governors should be appointed by the Federal Government for five years ; each Legislature to continue until altered. He said : If the Imperial Act authorizes this, you have then the several governments shorn, however, of such powers as are taken from them by the central authority.

Mr. Chandler—I think we should form only a federal constitution, and we should pass no resolutions or act relative to the Local Governments. Let them retain what they have, and have power to manage their own local concerns. The Imperial Government will never consent to put in an Imperial Act of Parliament that the Crown shall appoint Lieutenant-Governors on the recommendation of the Federal Government. It is perfectly understood that as in case of Legislative Councillors the Crown take the recommendation of the Government and appoint a suitable person.

Mr. McCully—I would make it absolute in the Federal Government to appoint Lieutenant-Governors.

Mr. Chandler— I think the Imperial Government would never acquiesce in that.

Mr. McDougall—From the peculiar position of Canada we must get permission to change.

Mr. Dickey—I agree with Mr. Chandler that the Crown should appoint Lieutenant-Governors directly.

Mr. Brown—One material point is that the choice of the Federal Legislative Councillors will extinguish or largely diminish the Local Legislative Councils. If you have a Local Legislative Council you then embarrass yourselves by reconstructing that body. Mr. McDougall says he is willing to take a Governor and two Chambers as a Local Government and reduce them afterwards. Consider how insignificant are the matters agreed at Charlottetown, to be left to the Local Governments. As to private and local bills, that might be done under the General Incorporation Act.

Mr. John A. Macdonald—The Imperial Act must repeal the several Acts affecting the constitution of the various Colonies. The most artistic way to do this would be to wipe them out and re-enact. The mode adopted in Ireland was by resolutions setting forth " it is fit that such should be done," which were afterwards turned into enactments. I have little doubt that when the system is complete a delegate will have to be sent to the Imperial Government from each Province, charged with the interests of the Province and to express them to the Imperial Government and their views. We should have uniformity as much as possible, but that is only a secondary matter as compared with the passage of the measure.

Mr. McCully—Let Upper Canada try a single Chamber, and if it succeeds the other Provinces can afterwards adopt it.

Mr. McCully's motion carried.

Mr. Dickey—Ought not something to be laid down as to the constitution of the Federal Executive Government ? On the principle now adopted by Upper and Lower Canada, ought not there to be some mode of choosing advisers from the agricultural interests of Upper Canada, the mixed agricultural and maritime interests of Lower Canada, and the great maritime interests of the Lower Provinces ?

Mr. John A. Macdonald—We cannot limit or define the powers of the Crown in such respect. See our Union Act. There is nothing in it about Responsible Government. It is a system which we have adopted. There is not even any resolution on our own journals as to the number of the Executive. The Sovereign may have such number as she pleases. In Canada it was found convenient that both sections of the Province should be represented in the Cabinet, and in time it grew practically into an equal division. The same principle must obtain as to the body of advisers of the Governor-General of the Federation. That must be a provisional cabinet, and it probably will be very few and merely for necessary purposes. The Federal Parliament being elected, the person charged with the formation of the

Ministry will probably increase the number. We must leave such arrangements as to equality in the Cabinet to change or necessity.

Mr. Chandler concurred.

Mr. McCully—But the royal instructions limit the number to nine. It should be an unlimited number, and that point seems generally conceded here.

Mr. Henry—We feel that the first Government at least, should contain a due number from the Lower Provinces. We of the Lower Provinces feel that we may be out-voted by Upper and Lower Canada : but we knew that before we came here, and are willing to run the risk of it.

Mr. John A. Macdonald—I think there may be an expresssion of opinion as suggested by Mr. Dickey. In the formation of the first Executive Council I think the Governor-General should send for one man through whom the writs for election should be issued, and choose his Council afterwards.

Mr. John A. Macdonald moved :—

That for each of the Provinces there shall be an Executive Officer, styled the Lieutenant-Governor, who shall be appointed by the Governor-General in Council, under the Great Seal of the Federated Provinces, during pleasure ; such pleasure not to be exercised before the expiration of the first five years, except for cause ; such cause to be communicated in writing to the Lieutenant-Governor immediately after the exercise of the pleasure as aforesaid, and also by message to both Houses of the General Legislature, within the first week of the first session afterwards.

He said : The office must necessarily be during pleasure. The person may break down, misbehave, etc. The term of Governors and Lieutenant-Governors is usually six years; but I have fixed it at five years, that being the duration of our Parliaments. The Lieutenant-Governor will be a very high officer. He should be independent of the Federal Government, except as to removal for cause, and it is necessary that he should not be removable by any new political party. It would destroy his independence. He should only be removable upon an address from the Legislature.

Mr. Macdonald's motion carried.

Mr. John A. Macdonald proceeded to read his several proposed resolutions as to the powers of the Federal and Local Governments.

Mr. McCully—Suppose a Local Legislature should pass a law on a subject in respect of which they have no authority. In New Zealand no laws of Local Legislatures are of effect until approved by the Governor-General.

Mr. John A. Macdonald—If it be clearly an excess in the opinion of the Governor-General and his law officers, it will be disallowed by the Queen.

Adjourned at 10 o'clock p.m.

FRIDAY, 21ST OCTOBER, 1864.

Mr. John A. Macdonald moved resolution defining the powers of the General Legislature (see pp. 22, 24, 43).

Mr. Galt—I propose that we take up the subjects seriatim.

(2) As to duties of Customs on Imports and Exports. New Brunswick has a duty on timber. As proceeds of lands will belong to the Local Government, it will be necessary to consider this point as regards New Brunswick. An export duty on timber must be on timber of public and private lands, and none could therefore be imported at Quebec ; and a question may arise as to the export of coal from Nova Scotia. These questions, however, affect territorial revenues.

Mr. Tilley—The export duty was imposed in New Brunswick on timber because the stumpage dues took so much to collect. Private land owners did not object to it, as few export timber from private lands.

Mr. McCully—I understood that mines and minerals were to be under Local Legislatures. Therefore as to coal in Nova Scotia, the General Government should not be at liberty to put an export duty on coal.

Mr. Tupper—Nova Scotia will rely on the Local Government for its royalty on coal, to meet its expenses. If the General Government have the right to impose a duty on coal, it will add to the revenue of the General Government, to the prejudice of the Local Government.

Mr. Galt—You are assuming that the General Government will impose a duty on coal, whereas the fact is that the General

Government should be in a position to protect the Federation by avoiding a policy injurious to Federation.

Mr. Henry—It is not an export duty on coal in Nova Scotia. It is a royalty, as it is paid by consumers in the Province. (Further consideration of number two reserved).

(3) Excise Duties.

(4) Taxation.

Mr. Tupper proposed to restrict the latter to general taxation.

Mr. John A. Macdonald objected—You could not then tax shares, because it would be a general tax, or impose harbour dues for the same reason on any particular harbour.

(7) Banking.

Mr. Galt—Existing charters of banks will be reserved. In Canada they all expire in 1870, when the subject may be reconsidered.

(15) Ocean Navigation and Shipping.

Colonel Gray (New Brunswick)—I would suggest some insertion providing for safety of passengers, and provisions respecting proper machinery and inspection, etc.

(25) Agriculture.

Mr. McCully—It is said this is concurrent. But I think such an arrangement will be found to be unworkable. It will lead to a conflict between the two jurisdictions. I think Upper and Lower Canada would prefer it being for Local Governments.

Mr. Palmer—I think it should be local. But I apprehend that would not prevent the General Government from taking subjects of agriculture under their care in respect to grants of money locally.

Mr. Brown—I do not think you can make it local and yet expect that the General Government can give moneys to the Local Governments. But if you put it under the General Government you may have the advantage of one Bureau of Agriculture, a Model Farm, etc. But I am willing that it should be local, only in that event not to look for money from the General Government.

Mr. Coles—I think it should be retained for the General Government. There should be a Minister of Agriculture in the Federal Government.

Mr. Tupper—I approve of some things being of a concurrent character. We should confine the jurisdiction neither to one nor the other exclusively. The same remark applies to Immigration, which is intimately connected with the Crown Lands, and these are under the Local Government.

Mr. McGee—The General Government may draw attention to this country for settlement. The only permanent attraction we can offer is cheap land, free institutions, etc. I propose that the Local Legislatures should be bound to let immigrants have lands as hitherto. Immigrants should feel that they came to British America as a whole, and that they are free to choose lands where they like.

Mr. Dickey—The Local Governments have as great an interest as the Federal Government in promoting immigration.

Mr. Henry—The General Government ought to have the control of agriculture. If conflict likely to arise, I would rather withdraw it from the Local Legislature ; but I do not fear any clashing between the two powers. We ought to keep up a Bureau of Agriculture in our Confederation.

Mr. Mowat—The items of Agriculture and Immigration should be vested in both Federal and Local Governments. Danger often arises where there is exclusive jurisdiction, and not so often in cases of concurrent jurisdiction. In municipal matters the county and township council often have concurrent jurisdiction.

Mr. McCully—I take another view. The concurrent jurisdiction is the ground of the difficulties in the United States.

Mr. Mowat—That is because there is a doubt whether there is a concurrent jurisdiction or not.

Mr. McCully—I beg to move that item number 25, " Agriculture," be struck out of the resolution before the Conference.— Lost on a division. all the Provinces voting nay.

(26) Criminal Law.

Mr. John A. Macdonald—We should discuss the appointment of the judiciary, and as to local and supreme judiciary. In whom should the appointment be vested ?

Mr. Tupper – It is of especial value to have a common system of jurisprudence. That is impossible on account of Lower Canada. But as near as possible it should be attempted.

Mr. John A. Macdonald – I am glad to hear that Mr. Tupper and Mr. McCully's views accord with mine. We may have one statutory law, one system of courts, one judiciary, and eventually one bar.

Mr. Mowat – I quite concur in the advantages of one uniform system. It would weld us into a nation. We must, however, provide that the Judges should be appointed and paid by the General Government. But if Lower Canada is excepted, she will still have a voice in deciding for the other Provinces.

(27) Roads and Bridges.

Mr. Tilley – I move to strike out from item 27 of Mr. Macdonald's motion the words " Roads and Bridges."

Agreed to.

After further slight amendments, Mr. Macdonald's motion carried.

Adjourned at half-past four p.m.

SATURDAY, 22ND OCTOBER, 1864.

Mr. Galt moved a series of financial resolutions. (See pp. 25, 26.)

He said : It is very desirable that no question should arise on account of which any Province could complain of injustice. Any Province being less indebted than another, whether through good fortune or good management, should benefit by it. Future liabilities of Confederation must be presumed to be for the benefit of all. We must start, therefore, on a fair basis. It is therefore proposed that certain principles should be laid down. The admission of the principle embodied in number one involves the concession of number two, and then you must proceed to draw the line prescribed by number three.

All works of an intercolonial character, and which have created debt to be borne by Confederation, and not being in private corporations or towns, should be vested in the Confederation, i.e. (as is suggested by Attorney-General Macdonald), harbours.

As to railroads. In Canada we are not proprietors of any railroads, but have lent large sums to them. Buildings for accommodation of Local Legislatures as distinguished from residences of Lieutenant-Governors should be left to the Local Government.

The first three resolutions cover all the property to be taken by the General Government, and the subsequent resolutions show what changes shall be adopted by the Confederation.

I propose five per cent. as the rate of interest. It is impossible for us at this moment to determine the debts and liabilities of the several Provinces. This can only be ascertained when the functions of the Local Legislatures cease in that respect. At that time we can ascertain the amount and debit each Province.

The debt of Canada is different from that of the other Provinces, as it enters as two Provinces. A previous subdivision must be made between Upper and Lower Canada. This subdivision must be done by the Canadian Legislature. In the case of New Brunswick we find an actual debt existing and liabilities which between this time and the passing of the Act of Union may become liabilities of the Confederation. Further liabilities might be incurred, and it is therefore essential that a rule should be laid down and that if, supporting the principle of equality, any one Province goes into such expense it must be on its own account. There should be an officer, not a political officer, to audit the affairs of the Provinces. The honourable gentleman then went on to explain the apportionment of the debt, but his remarks are so imperfectly reported as scarcely to be intelligible.

Mr. Tilley—This scheme gives Newfoundland and Prince Edward Island everything. Takes over railways which cost us a very large sum of money and gives us nothing in return. The Grand Trunk stock is of no value, yet we find it put down as an asset ; and as to Canal tolls, the policy of the Canadian Government is not to look to them. You have fixed the population of New Brunswick as inferior to that of Nova Scotia, which is the case, but it ought not to be immovable but to vary in its increase. The increase of the population will lessen the per capita tax.

Colonel Grey (New Brunswick)—Our railway is productive and yields three per cent. It is only the difference between that and five per cent. which should be charged.

Mr. Tupper—It is wrong to assume assets to be of equal value when they are not so.

The remainder of the debate is not reported.

Adjourned at five o'clock p.m.

MONDAY, 24TH OCTOBER, 1864.

Mr. Mowat moved a series of resolutions defining the powers of the Local Legislatures.

Mr. Chandler—I object to the proposed system. You are adopting a Legislative Union instead of a Federal. The Local Legislatures should not have their powers specified, but should have all the powers not reserved to the Federal Government, and only the powers to be given to the Federal Government should be specified. You are now proceeding to destroy the constitutions of the Local Governments, and to give them less powers than they have had allowed them from England, and it will make them merely large municipal corporations. This is a vital question, which decides the question between a Federal and Legislative Union, and it will be fatal to the success of Confederation in the Lower Provinces.

Mr. Tupper—I have heard Mr. Chandler's argument with surprise. Powers—undefined—must rest somewhere. Those who were at Charlottetown will remember that it was fully specified there that all the powers not given to Local should be reserved to the Federal Government. This was stated as being a prominent feature of the Canadian scheme; and it was said then that it was desirable to have a plan contrary to that adopted by the United States. It was a fundamental principle laid down by Canada, and the basis of our deliberations. Mr. Chandler says that it gives a Legislative instead of a Federal Union. I think that a benefit. Is the Federal Government to be one of mere delegates? We have provided for a legislative representation and for the representation of every section of all the Provinces. Such a costly Government ought to be charged with the fullest powers. It will be easier for every one of the remotest settlers in Nova Scotia and New Brunswick to reach the Federal Legislature than the present Local Legislatures. If it were not for the peculiar condition of Lower Canada, and that the Lower Provinces have not municipal systems such as Upper Canada, I should go in for a Legislative Union instead of a Federal. We propose to preserve the Local Governments in the Lower Provinces because we have not municipal institutions. If Conference limit the powers of the General Legislature, I feel that the whole platform is swept away from us.

Mr. Coles—I did not understand that this was laid down as a basis at Charlottetown. I thought there the only thing specified was representation by population in the Lower House. I agree with Mr. Chandler's view.

Mr. Haviland—I disagree with Messrs. Chandler and Coles. I understand the basis of our scheme, so as to avoid difficulties of the United States, is to give limited powers to Local Legislatures.

Colonel Gray (N.B.).—Mr. Coles' memory is short. (Quotes from Mr. Macdonald's speech at Charlottetown and from Mr. Brown's, that Federal Government was to have general powers and limited as to local). Whatever conclusion we may now arrive at, such was the basis of the Canadian scheme.

Mr. Chandler—My argument is not met as to merits, but as to what was laid down at Charlottetown. We all agree that Local Government should have local powers, we differ as to whether such powers should be defined.

Mr. Tupper—Under Mr. Chandler's view, the Governor-General would be less than the Lieutenant-Governor and the Federal Government less than the Local.

Mr. Dickey—I propose a Supreme Court of Appeal to decide any conflict between general and state rights. I am rather inclined to agree with Mr. Chandler. Immense interests omitted in Mr. Mowat's motion.

Mr. Brown—This matter received close attention of Canadian Government. I should agree with Mr. Chandler were it not that we have done all we can to settle the matter with sufficient powers to Local Legislatures. I would let the courts of each Province decide what is Local and what General Government jurisdiction, with appeal to the Appeal or Superior Court.

Mr. McCully—I refer to New Zealand Act, which is evidently framed to meet difficulty. It strangely defines what the Local government shall not do. In 53rd clause, General Assembly to make laws, etc., for government of New Zealand, and shall control and supersede those of Local Governments repugnant thereto. Mr. Brown will land us in position of United States by referring matter of conflict of jurisdiction to courts. You thus set them over the General Legislature.

Mr. John A. Macdonald—New Zealand constitution was a Legislative Union, ours Federal. Emigrants went out under different guarantees. Local charters jarred. In order to guard these, they gave the powers stated to Local Legislatures, but the General Government had power to sweep these away. That is just what we do not want. Lower Canada and the Lower Provinces would not have such a thing. There is no analogy between New Zealand and ourselves in such respects. Our courts now can decide where there is any conflict between the Imperial and Canadian statutes. I think the whole affair would fail, and the system be a failure, if we adopted Mr. Chandler's views. It would be adopting the worst features of the United States. We should concentrate the power in the Federal Government, and not adopt the decentralization of the United States. Mr. Chandler would give sovereign power to the Local Legislatures, just where the United States failed. Canada would be infinitely stronger as she is than under such a system as proposed by Mr. Chandler. It is said that the tariff is one of the causes of difficulty in the United States. So it would be with us. Looking at the agricultural interests of Upper Canada, manufacturing of Lower Canada, and maritime interests of Lower Provinces, in respect to a tariff, a Federal Government would be a mediator. No general feeling of patriotism exists in the United States. In occasions of difficulty each man sticks to his individual State. Mr. Stephens, the present Vice-President, was a strong Union man, yet, when the time came, he went with his State. Similarly we should stick to our Province and not be British Americans. It would be introducing a source of radical weakness. It would ruin us in the eyes of the civilized world. All writers point out the errors of the United States. All the failings prognosticated by De Tocqueville are shown to be fulfilled.

Mr. Johnson—Enumerate for Local Governments their powers, and give all the rest to General Government, but do not enumerate both.

Mr. Palmer—Easier to define what are general than what are local subjects, but we cannot define both. We cannot meet every possible case or emergency.

Mr. Henry—We should not define powers of General Legislature. I would ask Lower Canada not to fight for a shadow. Give a clause to give general powers (except such as given to Local Legislatures) to Federal Legislature. Anything beyond that is hampering the case with difficulties. If we are to have Confederation let us have one on the principles suggested by Attorney-General Macdonald. In the United States there is no power to settle the constitutionality of an Act. Hereafter we shall be bound by an Imperial Act, and our judges will have to say what is constitutional under it as regards general or local legislation.

Mr. Dickey—Why should not Imperial statutes give the powers they did to New Zealand General Government?

Mr. Chandler—My plan is not precisely the same as in the United States, because the Government does not in the United States appoint the Lieutenant-Governors and the Legislative Councillors. If my plan is not adopted, I should have elective Legislative Councillors.

Colonel Gray, N. B.—The power flows from imperial Government. We propose to substitute the Federal Government for the Imperial Government. But the Federal Government is itself subordinate to the Imperial Government. And as to the policy of the thing, I think it best to define the powers of the Local Governments, as the public will then see what matters they have reserved for their consideration, with which matters they will be familiar, and so the humbler classes and the less educated will comprehend that their interests are protected.

TUESDAY, 25TH OCTOBER, 1864.

Mr. Mowat moved (a series of resolutions respecting the powers of the General Legislature, see pp. 30, 31).

Mr. Fisher—I object to inspection laws being included in the list. Many laws as to inspection of fish, flour, etc., are local, and steamboats may be so also.

Mr. Tupper—I would approve of the General Legislature having the regulation of inspection of steamboats.

It was agreed to strike out of item number one of the resolution moved by the Hon. Mr. Mowat the words, "3. For the regulation and incorporation of Fire and Life Insurance Companies." And from item number two the words, "Inspection laws and laws relating to." And the question of concurrence being put on the eighth item,

Mr. Johnson—I object to this clause. It is too great a restriction.

Mr. Chandler concurred in Mr. Johnson's objection.

Colonel Gray, N. B.—I fully agree with the observations of Messrs. Johnson and Chandler.

Mr. McCully—I think the clause as drawn is desirable.

Mr. Chandler—But your Courts will decide whether the Local Legislatures exceed their powers, and why require a second veto.

Eighth and ninth resolutions agreed to.

RESOLUTIONS

Adopted by the Canadian Legislature on the 11th August, 1866, providing for the Local Governments and Legislatures of Lower and Upper Canada respectively, when the Union of the Provinces of British North America is effected.

RESOLVED :—

1. That by the 38th paragraph of the resolution of this House, passed on the third day of February, 1865, for presenting an humble address to Her Majesty, praying that she may be graciously pleased to cause a measure to be submitted to the Imperial Parliament, for the purpose of uniting the Colonies of Canada, Nova Scotia, New Brunswick, Newfoundland, and Prince Edward Island, in one Government, with provisions based on the resolutions which were adopted at a Conference of Delegates from the said Colonies, held at the City of Quebec, on the 10th of October, 1864, it is provided that " for each of the Provinces there " shall be an Executive Officer, styled the Lieutenant Governor, " who shall be appointed by the Governor General in Council, " under the Great Seal of the Federated Provinces, during plea- " sure ; such pleasure not to be exercised before the expiration of " the first five years, except for cause : such cause to be communi- " cated in writing to the Lieutenant Governor immediately after " the exercise of the pleasure as aforesaid, and also by message " to both Houses of Parliament, within the first week of the first " session afterwards ;" and that by the 41st paragraph of the same resolution it is provided that " the Local Government and Legis- " lature of each Province shall be constructed in such manner as " the existing Legislature of each such Province shall provide :" and it is further now resolved, that in the opinion of this House the appointment of the first Lieutenant Governor shall be provisional, and that he should hold office strictly during pleasure.

2. That under and subject to the Constitution of the Federated Provinces, the executive authority of the Lieutenant

Governor of Lower Canada and Upper Canada respectively shall be administered by each of such officers according to the well understood principles of the British Constitution.

3. The Great Seal of each Province of Lower Canada and Upper Canada shall be the same or of the same design, in each of the said Provinces, as that used in the said Provinces respectively at the time of the existing Union, until altered by the Local Government.

4. That there shall be a Local Legislature for Lower Canada, composed of two Chambers, to be called the Legislative Council and the Legislative Assembly of Lower Canada.

5. That there shall be a Local Legislature for Upper Canada, which shall consist of one Chamber, to be called the Legislative Assembly of Upper Canada.

6. That the Legislative Council of Lower Canada shall be composed of twenty-four members, to be appointed by the Crown, under the Great Seal of the Local Government, who shall hold office during life ; but if any Legislative Councillor shall, for two consecutive Sessions of Parliament, fail to give his attendance in the said Council his seat shall thereby become vacant.

7. That the Members of the Legislative Council of Lower Canada shall be British subjects by birth or naturalization, of the full age of thirty years, shall possess a continuous real property qualification, in Lower Canada, of four thousand dollars over and above all incumbrances, and shall continue worth that sum over and above their debts and liabilities.

8. That if any question shall arise as to the qualification of a Legislative Councillor in Lower Canada, the same shall be determined by the Council.

9. That the Speaker of the Legislative Council of Lower Canada (unless otherwise provided by the Local Parliament) shall be appointed by the Crown, from among the Members of the Legislative Council, and shall hold office during pleasure, and shall only be entitled to a casting vote on an equality of votes.

10. That each of the twenty-four Legislative Councillors of Lower Canada shall be appointed to represent one of the twenty-four Electoral Divisions thereof, mentioned in Schedule A of the first chapter of the Consolidated Statutes of Canada, and such Councillor shall reside or possess his qualification in the Division he is appointed to represent.

11. That the Legislative Assembly of Lower Canada shall be composed of the sixty-five Members to be elected to represent the sixty-five Electoral Divisions into which Lower Canada is now divided, under Chapter 2 of the Consolidated Statutes of Canada, Chapter 75 of the Consolidated Statutes for Lower Canada, and the Act 23 Victoria, Chapter 1, or of any other Act, amending the same, in force at the time when the Local Government shall be constituted, as well for representation in the Local Legislature thereof, as in the House of Commons of the Federated Provinces: Provided that it shall not be lawful to present to the Lieutenant Governor for assent any Bill of the Legislative Council and Assembly of Lower Canada, by which the limits of the electoral divisions mentioned in the schedule hereto annexed, marked A, may be altered, unless the second and third readings of such Bill in the Legislative Assembly shall have been passed with the concurrence of the majority of the members for the time being of the said Legislative Assembly, representing the electoral divisions mentioned in said Schedule marked A, and the assent shall not be given to such Bill unless an Address has been presented by the Legislative Assembly to the Lieutenant Governor that such Bill has been so passed.

12. That the Legislative Assembly of Upper Canada shall be composed of eighty-two Members, to be elected to represent the eighty-two constituencies in Upper Canada, such constituencies being identical, whether for representation in the Local Legislative Assembly or for representation in the House of Commons of the Federated Provinces, and which constituencies shall consist of the divisions and be bounded as is provided in the schedule hereunto annexed, marked B.

13. That until other provisions are made by the Local Legislature of Lower and Upper Canada respectively, changing the same in either of the said Provinces, all the laws which at the date of the Proclamation, constituting the separate Provinces of Lower Canada and of Upper Canada, shall be in force in each of the said Provinces respectively, relating to the qualification and disqualification of any person to be elected or to sit or vote as a Member of the Assembly of the Province of Canada, and relating to the qualification and disqualification of voters, and to the oaths to be taken by voters, and to Returning Officers and their powers and duties, and relating to the proceedings at elections and to the period

during which such elections may be continued, and relating to the trial of controverted elections and the proceedings incident thereto, and relating to the vacating of the seats of members and to the issuing and execution of new writs in case of any seat being vacated otherwise than by a dissolution, shall respectively apply to elections of Members to serve in the said the Legislative Assembly of Lower Canada and in the said the Legislative Assembly of Upper Canada.

14. That the Legislative Assembly of Lower Canada and the Legislative Assembly of Upper Canada respectively, shall continue for four years from the day of the return of the writs for choosing the same and no longer, subject nevertheless to either the said the Legislative Assembly of Lower Canada, or the said the Legislative Assembly of Upper Canada, being sooner prorogued or dissolved by the Lieutenant-Governor of either of the said Provinces respectively.

15. That there shall be a session of the Legislature of each of the said Provinces once at least every year, so that a period of twelve months shall not intervene between the last sitting of the Local Legislature in one session, and the first sitting thereof in the next session.

16. That it is expedient that any Act of the Imperial Parliament which may be passed for the Union of the Colonies of British North America, should contain a provision that the division and adjustment of the debts, credits, liabilities, properties and assets of the Provinces of Upper and Lower Canada, should be referred to the arbitrament of three arbitrators, one to be chosen by the Local Government of Upper Canada, the other by the Local Government of Lower Canada, and the third by the General Government ; it being further provided that the selection of the arbitrators shall not take place until after the General Parliament for British North America and Local Legislatures for Upper and Lower Canada have been elected—and that the third arbitrator shall not be a resident in either Upper or Lower Canada.

SCHEDULE A.

Same as the second Schedule of the B. N. A. Act.

RESOLUTION ADOPTED ON THE TENTH OF AUGUST, 1866.

Resolved,

" That it is expedient that at the first Election for the District of Algoma, both for the General and Local Legislatures, all persons otherwise qualified except in respect to real property, who are householders, shall have the right to vote at the said Election."

SCHEDULE B.

Same as the first Schedule of the B. N. A. Act down to and inclusive of the 82nd clause.

MINUTES

OF THE PROCEEDINGS IN CONFERENCE OF THE DELEGATES FROM THE PROVINCES OF CANADA, NOVA SCOTIA AND NEW BRUNSWICK, HELD IN LONDON, DECEMBER, 1866.

London, Tuesday, 4th December, 1866,

The following gentlemen assembled at the Conference Chamber in the Westminster Palace Hotel, London, on Tuesday, the 4th day of December, 1866, at the hour of twelve o'clock noon:—

CANADA.

The Honourable John A. Macdonald.
G. E. Cartier.
A. T. Galt.
W. McDougall.
W. P. Howland.
H. L. Langevin.

NOVA SCOTIA.

The Honourable Charles Tupper.
William A. Henry.
J. W. Ritchie.
Jonathan McCully.
A. G. Archibald.

NEW BRUNSWICK.

The Honourable S. L. Tilley.
J. M. Johnson.
P. Mitchell.
Charles Fisher.
R. D. Wilmot.

It was proposed by the Honourable Mr. Tupper, and seconded by the Honourable Mr. Tilley,
And resolved,—

That the Honourable John A. Macdonald be Chairman of the Conference.

It was proposed by the Honourable Mr. McCully, and seconded by the Honourable Mr. Fisher,

And resolved,—

That Lieutenant-Colonel Hewitt Bernard be appointed Secretary of the Conference.

It was resolved,—

That in taking the votes on all questions to be decided by this Conference, except questions of order, each Province by whatever number of delegates represented, shall have one vote, and that in voting, Canada be considered as two Provinces.

The Conference then entered upon the consideration of the Resolutions of the Conference held at Quebec in the year 1864.

And at a quarter past 5 o'clock p.m., a motion for adjournment being carried, the Chairman declared the Conference continued until 11 o'clock a.m. to-morrow.

WEDNESDAY, 5TH DECEMBER, 1866.

The Conference met at 11 o'clock a.m., all the members being present.

The Honourable Mr. Tupper laid before the Conference a Resolution of the House of Assembly of Nova Scotia of 17th April, 1866, as follows :—

WHEREAS, in the opinion of this House, it is desirable that a Confederation of the British North American Provinces should take place :

RESOLVED THEREFORE, That His Excellency the Lieutenant-Governor be authorized to appoint delegates to arrange with the Imperial Government a scheme of union which will effectually ensure just provision for the rights and interests of this Province ; each Province to have an equal voice in such delegation, Upper and Lower Canada being for this purpose considered as separate Provinces.

The Honourable Mr. Tilley laid before the Conference a Resolution of the House of Assembly of New Brunswick of 30th June, 1866, as follows :—

"RESOLVED, That an humble address be presented to His Excellency the Lieutenant-Governor, praying that His Excellency will be pleased to appoint Delegates, to unite with Delegates from the other Provinces in arranging with the Imperial Government for the Union of British North America, upon such terms as will secure the just rights and interests of New Brunswick, accompanied with provision for the immediate construction of the Inter-Colonial Railway, each Province to have an equal voice in such Delegation, Upper and Lower Canada to be considered as separate Provinces."

The Conference then proceeded with the consideration of the Quebec Resolutions.

And at a quarter to five o'clock, p.m., the Chairman declared the Conference continued until eleven o'clock a.m. to-morrow.

THURSDAY, 6TH DECEMBER, 1866.

The Conference met at 11 o'clock, a.m., and proceeded with the consideration of the Quebec Resolutions.

It was resolved,—

That the Honourable Messrs. Galt, Howland, Henry and Tilley be appointed a Committee to consider the 54th of the Quebec Resolutions, and matters of Finance generally, and to report thereon.

And at half-past four o'clock p.m., the chairman declared the Conference continued until eleven o'clock a.m., to-morrow.

FRIDAY, 7TH DECEMBER, 1866.

The Conference met at eleven o'clock, a.m., and having further taken into consideration the Quebec Resolutions, adjourned at the hour of two o'clock p.m., until Tuesday next, the 11th instant, at 11 o'clock a.m.

TUESDAY, 11TH DECEMBER, 1866.

The Conference continued until to-morrow at one o'clock p.m.

WEDNESDAY, 12TH DECEMBER, 1866.

The Conference continued until to-morrow at eleven o'clock a.m.

THURSDAY, 13TH DECEMBER, 1866.

The Conference met at eleven o'clock, a.m. and at the hour of half-past two o'clock p.m. adjourned until to-morrow at eleven o'clock, a.m.

FRIDAY, 14TH DECEMBER, 1866.

The Conference met at the hour of eleven o'clock.   The following letter from the Right Honourable C. B. Adderley was read :—

Downing Street, 13th December, 1866.

Sir.—I am directed by the Earl of Carnarvon to acknowledge the receipt of your letter of the 4th of this month, reporting that the Delegates from Canada, Nova Scotia and New Brunswick had formed themselves into a Conference for the purpose of arranging the terms of the Confederation of those Provinces.

I am, Sir,

Your obedient servant,

C. B. ADDERLEY.

The Honourable John A. Macdonald, etc., etc.

The Conference then continued the consideration of the Quebec Resolutions, and at the hour of three o'clock p.m. adjourned until Monday next, the 17th instant, at 12 o'clock noon.

MONDAY, 17TH DECEMBER, 1866.

The Conference met at eleven o'clock a.m. and continued the consideration of the Quebec Resolutions, and at five o'clock, adjourned until to-morrow at eleven o'clock a.m.

TUESDAY, 18TH DECEMBER, 1866.

The Conference met at eleven o'clock a.m., and continued the consideration of the Quebec Resolutions, and at five o'clock p.m. adjourned until to-morrow at eleven o'clock a.m.

WEDNESDAY, 19TH DECEMBER, 1866.

The Conference met at the hour of eleven o'clock a.m., and having proceeded with the consideration of the Quebec Resolutions adjourned at five-thirty p.m. until to-morrow at eleven o'clock a.m.

THURSDAY, 20TH DECEMBER, 1866.

The Conference met at the hour of eleven o'clock a.m., and having proceeded with the consideration of the Quebec Resolutions adjourned at four p.m. until to-morrow at noon.

MONDAY, 24TH DECEMBER, 1866.

The Conference met at eleven o'clock a.m. and passed the Resolutions following :—

RESOLUTIONS

ADOPTED AT A

Conference of Delegates from the Provinces of Canada, Nova Scotia and New Brunswick.

HELD AT

THE WESTMINSTER PALACE HOTEL, LONDON,

ON THE

FOURTH DAY OF DECEMBER,

ONE THOUSAND EIGHT HUNDRED AND SIXTY SIX.

1. The best interests and present and future prosperity of British North America will be promoted by a Federal Union under the Crown of Great Britain, provided such Union can be effected on principles just to the several Provinces.

2. In the Confederation of the British North American Provinces, the system of government best adapted under existing circumstances to protect the diversified interests of the several Provinces, and secure efficiency, harmony, and permanency in the working of the Union, is a General Government charged with matters of common interest to the whole country, and Local Governments for each of the Canadas, and for the Provinces of Nova Scotia and New Brunswick, charged with the control of local matters in their respective sections, provision being made for the admission into the Confederation, on equitable terms, of Newfoundland, Prince Edward Island, the North West Territory, and British Columbia.

3. In framing a Constitution for the General Government, the Conference, with a view to the perpetuation of the connec-

tion with the mother country, and the promotion of the best interests of the people of these Provinces, desire to follow the model of the British Constitution, so far as circumstances will permit.

4. The Executive Authority or Government shall be vested in the Sovereign of the United Kingdom of Great Britain and Ireland, and be administered according to the well-understood principles of the British Constitution, by the Sovereign personally, or by the representative of the Sovereign duly authorized.

5. The Sovereign shall be Commander-in-Chief of the Land and Naval Militia Forces.

6. There shall be a General Legislature or Parliament for the Confederation, composed of the Sovereign, a Legislative Council, and a House of Commons.

7. For the purpose of forming the Legislative Council, the Confederation shall be considered as consisting of three divisions :—

First—Upper Canada,

Second—Lower Canada, and

Third—Nova Scotia and New Brunswick.

Each division with an equal representation in the Legislative Council.

8. Upper Canada shall be represented in the Legislative Council by twenty-four Members, Lower Canada by twenty-four Members, and the Maritime Provinces by twenty-four Members, of which Nova Scotia shall have twelve and New Brunswick twelve Members.

9. The Colony of Prince Edward Island, when admitted into the Confederation, shall be entitled to a representation of four Members in the Legislative Council. But in such case the Members allotted to Nova Scotia and New Brunswick shall be diminished to ten each, such diminution to take place in each Province as vacancies occur.

10. The Colony of Newfoundland, when admitted into the Confederation, shall be entitled to a representation in the Legislative Council of four Members.

11. The North West Territory and British Columbia shall be admitted into the Union on such terms and conditions as the

Parliament of the Confederation shall deem equitable, and as shall receive the assent of the Sovereign, and in case of the Province of British Columbia, as shall be agreed to by the Legislature of such Province.

12. The Members of the Legislative Council shall be appointed by the Crown under the Great Seal of the General Government, from among residents of the Province for which they are severally appointed, and shall hold office during life. If any Legislative Councillor shall for two consecutive Sessions of Parliament fail to give his attendance in the said Council, his seat shall thereby become vacant.

13. The Members of the Legislative Council shall be British subjects by birth or naturalization, of the full age of thirty years, shall each possess in the Province for which they are appointed, a continuous real property qualification of four thousand dollars over and above all incumbrances, and shall be and continue worth that sum over and above their debts and liabilities, and shall possess a continuous residence in the Province for which they are appointed, except in the case of persons holding official positions which require their attendance at the seat of Government pending their tenure of office.

14. If any question shall arise as to the qualification of a Legislative Councillor, the same shall be determined by the Legislative Council.

15. The Members of the Legislative Council for the Confederation, shall, in the first instance, be appointed upon the nomination of the Executive Governments of Canada, Nova Scotia, and New Brunswick, respectively, and the number allotted to each Province shall be nominated from the Legislative Councils of the different Provinces, due regard being had to the fair representation of both political parties, but in case any Member of the Local Council so nominated shall decline to accept, it shall be competent for the Executive Committee in any Province to nominate in his place a person who is not a Member of the Local Council.

16. The Speaker of the Legislative Council (unless otherwise provided by Parliament) shall be appointed by the Crown from among the Members of the Legislative Council, and shall hold office during pleasure, and shall only be entitled to a casting vote on an equality of votes.

17. Each of the twenty-four Legislative Councillors repre-

senting Lower Canada in the Legislative Council of the General Legislature, shall be appointed to represent one of the twenty-four electoral divisions mentioned in schedule A of chapter first of the Consolidated Statutes of Canada, and such Councillor shall reside or possess his qualification in the division he is appointed to represent.

18. The basis of representation in the House of Commons shall be population, as determined by the official census every ten years, and the number of Members at first shall be one hundred and eighty-one, distributed as follows :—

Upper Canada - - - Eighty-two.
Lower Canada - - - Sixty-five.
Nova Scotia - - - Nineteen.
New Brunswick - - - Fifteen.

19. Until the first General Election after the official census of One thousand eight hundred and seventy-one has been made up, there shall be no change in the number of representatives from the several sections.

20. Immediately after the completion of the census of One thousand eight hundred and seventy-one, and immediately after every decennial census thereafter, the representation from each Province in the House of Commons shall be readjusted on the basis of population, such readjustment to take effect upon the termination of the then existing Parliament.

21. For the purpose of such readjustments, Lower Canada shall always be assigned sixty-five Members, and each of the other Provinces shall, at each re-adjustment, receive for the ten years then next succeeding, the number of Members to which it will be entitled on the same ratio of representation to population as Lower Canada will enjoy, according to the census then last taken by having sixty-five Members.

22. No reduction shall be made in the number of Members returned by any Province, unless its population shall have decreased relatively to the population of the whole Union to the extent of five per centum.

23. In computing at each decennial period the number of Members to which each Province is entitled, no fractional parts shall be considered, unless when exceeding one-half the number entitling to a Member, in which case a Member shall be given for each such fractional part.

24. The number of Members may at any time be increased by the General Parliament, regard being had to the proportionate rights then existing.

25. Until provisions are made by the General Parliament, all the laws which at the date of the Proclamation constituting the Union are in force in the Provinces respectively relating to the qualification and disqualification of any person to be elected, or to sit or vote as a Member of the Assembly in the said Provinces respectively, and relating to the qualification or disqualification of voters, and to the oaths to be taken by voters, and to Returning Officers, and their powers and duties, and relating to the proceedings at elections, and to the period during which such elections may be continued, and relating to the trial of controverted elections, and the proceedings incident thereto, and relating to the vacating of seats of Members, and to the issuing and execution of new writs in case of any seat being vacated otherwise than by a dissolution, shall respectively apply to elections of Members to serve in the House of Commons of places situate in those Provinces respectively.

26. Every House of Commons shall continue for five years from the day of the return of the writs choosing the same, and no longer : subject, nevertheless, to be sooner prorogued or dissolved by the Governor-General.

27. There shall be a Session of the General Parliament once at least in every year, so that a period of twelve calendar months shall not intervene between the last sitting of the General Parliament in one Session and the first sitting thereof in the next Session.

28. The General Parliament shall have power to make laws for the peace, welfare, and good government of the Confederation (saving the Sovereignty of England), and especially laws respecting the following subjects :—

1. The public debt and property.

2. The regulation of trade and commerce.

3. The raising of money by all or any mode or system of taxation.

4. The borrowing of money on the public credit.

5. Postal service.

6. Lines of steam or other ships, railways, canals, and other works connecting any two or more of the Provinces together, or extending beyond the limits of any Province.

7. Lines of steamships between the Confederated Provinces and other countries.

8. Telegraphic communication and the incorporation of Telegraph Companies.

9. All such works as shall, although lying wholly within any Province, be specially declared by the Acts authorizing them to be for the general advantage.

10. The census and statistics.

11. Militia, military and naval service, and defence.

12. Beacons, buoys, light-houses, and Sable Island.

13. Navigation and shipping.

14. Quarantine.

15. Sea coast and inland fisheries.

16. Ferries between any Province and a foreign country, or between any two Provinces.

17. Currency and coinage.

18. Banking: Incorporation of Banks, and the issue of paper money.

19. Savings Banks.

20. Weights and measures.

21. Bills of exchange and promissory notes.

22. Interest.

23. Legal tender.

24. Bankruptcy and Insolvency.

25. Patents of Invention and Discovery.

26. Copyrights.

27. Indians, and land reserved for the Indians.

28. Naturalization and Aliens.

29. Marriage and Divorce.

30. The Criminal Law, except the Constitution of Courts of Criminal Jurisdiction, but including the procedure in criminal matters.

31. The establishment, maintenance and management of Penitentiaries.

32. Rendering uniform all or any of the laws relative to property and civil rights in Upper Canada, Nova Scotia, and New Brunswick, and rendering uniform the procedure of all or any of the Courts in these provinces ; but any Statute for this purpose shall have no force or authority in any Province until sanctioned by the Legislature thereof, and the power of repealing, amending, or altering such Laws, shall henceforward remain with the General Parliament only.

33. The establishment of a General Court of Appeal for the Confederation.

34. Immigration.

35. Agriculture.

36. And generally respecting all matters of a general character, not specially and exclusively reserved for the Local Legislatures.

29. The General Government and Parliament shall have all powers necessary or proper for performing the obligations of the Confederation as part of the British Empire to Foreign Countries, arising under Treaties between Great Britain and such Countries.

30. The powers and privileges of the House of Commons of the United Kingdom of Great Britain and Ireland shall be held to appertain to the House of Commons of the Confederation, and the powers and privileges appertaining to the House of Lords in its legislative capacity, shall be held to appertain to the Legislative Council.

31. The General Parliament may from time to time establish additional Courts, and the General Government may appoint Judges and Officers thereof, when the same shall appear necessary, or for the public advantage, in order to the due execution of the Laws of such Parliament.

32. All Courts, Judges, and Officers of the several Provinces shall aid, assist, and obey the General Government in the exercise of its rights and powers, and for such purposes shall be held to be Courts, Judges and Officers of the General Government.

33. The General Government shall appoint and pay the salaries of the Judges of the Superior and District and County Courts in each Province, and Parliament shall fix their salaries.

34. Until the consolidation of the Laws of Upper Canada,

Nova Scotia and New Brunswick, the Judges of these Provinces, appointed by the General Government, shall be selected from their respective Bars.

35. The Judges of the Courts of Lower Canada shall be selected from the Bar of Lower Canada.

36. The Judges of the Court of Admiralty shall be paid by the General Government.

37. The Judges of the Superior Courts shall hold their offices during good behaviour, and shall be removable on the address of both Houses of Parliament.

38. For each of the Provinces there shall be an Executive Officer styled the Governor, who shall be appointed by the Governor General in Council, under the Great Seal of the Confederation during pleasure ; such pleasure not to be exercised before the expiration of the first five years, except for cause, such cause to be communicated in writing to the Governor immediately after the exercise of the pleasure as aforesaid, and also by message to both Houses of Parliament, within the first week of the first Session afterwards ; but the appointment of the first Governors shall be provisional, and they shall hold office strictly during pleasure.

39. The Governor of each Province shall be paid by the General Government.

40. The Local Government and Legislature of each Province shall be constructed in such manner as the Legislature of each such Province shall provide.

41. The Local Legislatures shall have power to make laws respecting the following subjects :—

1. The altering or amending their Constitution from time to time.

2. Direct taxation, and, in the case of New Brunswick, the right of levying timber dues by the mode and to the extent now established by law, provided such timber be not the produce of the other Provinces.

3. Borrowing money on the credit of the Province.

4. The establishment and tenure of Local offices, and the appointment and payment of Local officers.

5. Agriculture.

6. Immigration.

7. Education : saving the rights and privileges which the Protestant or Catholic minority in any Province may have by law as to denominational schools at the time when the Union goes into operation.   And in any Province where a system of separate or dissentient schools by law obtains, or where the Local Legislature may hereafter adopt a system of separate or dissentient schools, an appeal shall lie to the Governor General in Council of the General Government, from the acts and decisions of the Local Authorities which may affect the rights or privileges of the Protestant or Catholic minority in the matter of education ; and the General Parliament shall have power in the last resort to legislate on the subject.

8. The sale and management of public lands, excepting lands belonging to the General Government.

9. The establishment, maintenance, and management of public and reformatory prisons.

10. The establishment, maintenance, and management of Hospitals, Asylums, Charities and Eleemosynary Institutions, except Marine Hospitals.

11. Municipal Institutions.

12. Shop, Saloon, Tavern, Auctioneer, and other licenses for Local Revenue.

13. Local works.

14. The Incorporation of Private or Local Companies, except such as relate to matters assigned to the General Parliament.

15. Property and civil rights (including the solemnization of marriage) excepting portions thereof assigned to the General Parliament.

16. Inflicting punishment by fine, penalties, imprisonment or otherwise, for the breach of laws passed in relation to any subject within their jurisdiction.

17. The administration of Justice, including the constitution, maintenance, and organization of the Courts, both of Civil and Criminal jurisdiction, including also the procedure in civil matters.

18. And generally all matters of a Private or Local Nature not assigned to the General Parliament.

42. All the powers, privileges and duties conferred and imposed upon Catholic separate schools and School Trustees in Upper Canada, shall be extended to the Protestant and Catholic Dissentient Schools in Lower Canada.

43. The power of respiting, reprieving, and pardoning prisoners convicted of crimes, and of commuting and remitting of sentences in whole or in part which belongs of right to the Crown, shall, except in capital cases, be administered by the Governor of each Province in Council, subject to any instructions he may from time to time receive from the General Government, and subject to any provisions that may be made in this behalf by the General Parliament.

44. In regard to all subjects over which jurisdiction belongs to both the General and Local Legislatures, the Laws of the General Parliament shall control and supersede those made by the Local Legislature, and the latter shall be void so far as they are repugnant to, or inconsistent with the former.

45. Both the English and French languages may be employed in the General Parliament, and in its proceedings, and in the Local Legislature of Lower Canada, and also in the Federal Courts, and in the Courts of Lower Canada.

46. No lands or property belonging to the General or Local Governments shall be liable to taxation.

47. All Bills for appropriating any part of the public revenue, or for imposing any tax or impost, shall originate in the House of Commons, or House of Assembly, as the case may be.

48. The House of Commons or House of Assembly, shall not originate or pass any vote, Resolution, Address or Bill, for the appropriation of any part of the Public Revenue, or of any tax or impost to any purpose, not first recommended by message of the Governor-General, or the Governor as the case may be during the Session in which such Vote, Resolution, Address, or Bill is passed.

49. Any Bill of the General Parliament may be reserved in the usual manner for Her Majesty's assent, and any bill of the Local Legislatures may, in like manner, be reserved for the consideration of the Governor General.

50. Any Bill passed by the General Parliament shall be subject to disallowance by Her Majesty within two years, as in

the case of Bills passed by the Legislatures of the said Provinces hitherto, and in like manner any Bill passed by a Local Legislature shall be subject to disallowance by the Governor General within one year after the passing thereof.

51. The seat of Government of the Confederation shall be Ottawa, subject to the Royal Prerogative.

52. Subject to any future action of the respective Local Governments, the seat of the Local Governments in Upper Canada shall be Toronto : of Lower Canada, Quebec : and the seats of the Local Governments in the other Provinces shall be as at present.

53. All stocks, cash, bankers' balances, and securities for money belonging to each Province at the time of the Union, except as hereinafter mentioned, shall belong to the General Government.

54. The following Public Works and Property of each Province shall belong to the General Government, to wit :—

1. Canals.

2. Public harbours.

3. Light-houses and piers, and Sable Island.

4. Steamboats, dredges, and public vessels.

5. Rivers and lake improvements.

6. Railways and railway stocks, mortgages, and other debts due by railway companies.

7. Military roads.

8. Custom-houses, post offices, and all other public buildings, except such as may be set aside by the General Government for the use of the Local Legislatures and Governments.

9. Property transferred by the Imperial Government, and known as Ordnance property.

10. Armouries, drill sheds, military clothing, and munitions of war, and lands set apart for general public purposes.

55. All lands, mines, minerals, and royalties vested in Her Majesty in the Provinces of Upper Canada, Lower Canada, Nova Scotia, and New Brunswick, for the use of such Provinces, shall belong to the Local Government of the territory in which the same are so situate : subject to any trusts that may exist in respect to any of such lands or to any interest of other persons in respect of the same.

56. All sums due from purchasers or lessees of such lands, mines, or minerals, at the time of the Union, shall also belong to the Local Government.

57. All assets connected with such portions of the Public Debt of any Province as are assumed by the Local Governments, shall also belong to those Governments respectively.

58. The several Provinces shall retain all other public property therein subject to the right of the General Government to assume any lands or public property required for fortifications or the defence of the country.

59. The General Government shall assume the debts and liabilities of each province.

60. The debt of Canada not specially assumed by Upper and Lower Canada respectively, shall not exceed at the time of the Union sixty-two million five hundred thousand dollars ; Nova Scotia shall enter the Union with a debt not exceeding eight million dollars, and New Brunswick with a debt not exceeding seven million dollars.   But this stipulation is in no respect intended to limit the powers given to the respective Governments of those Provinces by Legislative authority, but only to determine the maximum amount of charge to be assumed by the General Government.

61. In case Nova Scotia or New Brunswick should not have contracted debts at the date of Union equal to the amount with which they are respectively entitled to enter the Confederation they shall receive by half-yearly payments in advance from the General Government, the interest at five per cent. on the difference between the actual amount of their respective debts and such stipulated amounts.

62. In consideration of the transfer to the General Parliament of the powers of taxation, the following sums shall be paid by the General Government to each Province for the support of their Local Governments and Legislatures :—

Upper Canada..	$80,000
Lower Canada..	70,000
Nova Scotia..	60,000
New Brunswick..	50,000
	$260,000

and an annual grant in aid of each Province shall be made, equal to eighty cents per head of the population, as established by the Census of One thousand eight hundred and sixty-one, and in the case of Nova Scotia and New Brunswick, by each subsequent decennial Census until the population of each of those Provinces shall amount to four hundred thousand souls, at which rate it shall thereafter remain. Such aid shall be in full settlement of all future demands upon the General Government for local purposes, and shall be paid half-yearly in advance to each Province ; but the General Government shall deduct from such subsidy all sums paid as interest on the Public Debt of any Province in excess of the amount provided under the sixtieth resolution.

63. The position of New Brunswick being such as to entail large immediate charges upon her local revenues, it is agreed that for the period of ten years from the time when the Union takes effect, an additional allowance of sixty-three thousand dollars per annum shall be made to that Province. But that so long as the liability of that Province remains under seven millions of dollars, a deduction equal to the interest on such deficiency shall be made from the sixty-three thousand dollars.

64. All engagements that may, before the Union, be entered into with the Imperial Government for the defence of the country shall be assumed by the General Government.

65. The construction of the Intercolonial Railway being essential to the consolidation of the Union of British North America, and to the assent of the Maritime Provinces thereto, it is agreed that provision be made for its immediate construction by the General Government, and that the Imperial guarantee for three millions of pounds sterling pledged for this work be applied thereto, so soon as the necessary authority has been obtained from the Imperial Parliament.

66. The communications with the North Western Territory, and the improvements required for the development of the trade of the Great West with the Sea-board, are regarded by this Conference as subjects of the highest importance to the Confederation, and shall be prosecuted at the earliest possible period that the state of the Finances will permit.

67. The sanction of the Imperial Parliament shall be sought for the Union of the Provinces on the principle adopted by this Conference.

68. That Her Majesty the Queen be solicited to determine the rank and name of the Confederation.

69. That a copy of these Resolutions signed by the Chairman and Secretary of the Conference be transmitted to the Right Honourable the Secretary of State for the Colonies.

The Conference adjourned at six o'clock p.m. until Friday, the 28th December, at 12 o'clock noon.

TUESDAY, 4TH DECEMBER, 1866.

At a meeting of the delegates held this day.—Present: Messrs. John A. Macdonald, Cartier, Galt, McDougall, Howland, Tupper, Henry, Ritchie, Archibald, McCully, Tilley, Mitchell, Fisher, Wilmot and Johnson.

The New Brunswick delegates stated that their authority to act was contingent upon their securing the construction of the Intercolonial Railway, and requested the opinion of their co-delegates. All agreed that the road was desirable and that permission or security for its construction by Imperial action should be asked. After a brief discussion as to the form which this aid should take.

Mr. Tupper stated the action had in relation to Prince Edward Island.*

It was agreed that on all questions Canada should have two votes, Nova Scotia and New Brunswick, one each.

The first 29 of the resolutions of the Quebec Conference were then considered.

Adjourned.

WEDNESDAY, 5TH DECEMBER, 1866.

Present.—All the delegates.

Mr. McCully suggested that an intimation of the meeting of the delegates be given to the Colonial Secretary. Agreed to.†

* See Appendix No. VI.
† See Appendix No. VI.

The Quebec Resolutions, beginning with No. 30, were then considered, and the following action had thereon :—

No. 30. Mr. McDougall suggested whether it would be advisable to give power to the General Government to act with foreign Governments. Stand over. (Consular powers).

No. 31. Stand over.
No. 32. Passed.
No. 33. It is suggested that County Courts be established and appointed in all the Provinces.
No. 34. Passed.
No. 35. Passed.
No. 36. Powers be fixed. Imperial Parliament. Passed.
No. 37. Passed.
No. 38. Stand over. (Case of illness).
No. 39. In case of death or absence of Lieutenant-Governor, who to be Administrator ?
No. 40. Out.
No. 41. Passed.
No. 42. Passed.
No. 43.

  (1) Stand over.
  (2) Passed.
  (3) Passed.
  (4) Passed.
  (5) Passed.
  (6) Passed with Mr. Galt's amendment.*

* Mr. Galt moved :—That the following words be added to and form part of the 6th sub-section of the 43rd clause :

"And in any Province where a system of Separate or Dissentient schools by law obtains, or where the Local Legislature may hereafter adopt a system of Separate or Dissentient schools, an appeal shall lie to the Governor in Council of the General Government from the acts and decisions of the local authorities which may affect the rights or privileges of the Protestant or Catholic minority in the matter of education. And the General Parliament shall have power in the last resort to legislate on the subject."

The above amendment is in the handwriting of Mr. Galt. In the left hand corner is the following memorandum in the handwriting of the Chairman (Mr. John A. Macdonald) :—

Nova Scotia—Yes.
New Brunswick—Yes.
Canada—Yes.

Nova

New

Co...

And as any Province where a system of Separate or Dissentient Schools by law obtains or where the local legislature may hereafter adopt a system of Separate or Dissentient Schools an appeal shall lie to the Governor General of the second [Set?] from the acts and decisions of the local authorities which may affect the rights or privileges of the Protestant or Catholic minority in the matter of Education, and the General Parliament shall have power in the last resort to legislate on the subject —

Nova Scotia + Yes —
New Brunswick + Yes
Canada Yes

This is part of the Substitute of 43 Clause

(7) Considered.
(8) Stand.
(9) Passed. (Penitentiary).
(10) Passed (except Marine Hospitals).
(11) Passed.
(12) Passed.
(13) Passed.
(14) Passed.
(15) Passed.
(16) Passed.
(17) Passed.
(18) Stand.

Adjourned.

THURSDAY, 6TH DECEMBER, 1866.

The consideration of the Resolutions of the Quebec Conference was proceeded with.

No. 44. Stand over. Pardoning power to be amended.
No. 45. Passed.
No. 46. Passed.
No. 47. Passed.
No. 48. Passed.
No. 49. Passed.
No. 50. Passed.
No. 51. Passed.
No. 52. Passed.
No. 53. Passed.
No. 54. Passed. Proviso to be put in to omit appropriations of the current year.
No. 55.

    (1) Passed.
    (2) Passed.
    (3) Passed.
    (4) Passed.
    (5) Passed.
    (6) Passed.
    (7) Passed.

(8) and (11) To be further considered in relation to appropriation of public buildings and lands for local or general purposes.

(9) Passed.

(10) Passed.

No. 56. Stand.

No. 57. Stand.

No. 58. Stand.

No. 59. Stand.

No. 60. Passed.

No. 61. Stand.

No. 62. Stand.

No. 63. Out.

No. 64. Stand. Mr. Tilley suggested that the eighty cents be continued as a regular increase until population goes up to half a million.

No. 65. Stand.

No. 66. Out.

No. 67. Stand.

No. 68. Passed.

No. 69. Passed.

No. 70. Passed.

No. 71. Stand.

No. 72. Out.

THURSDAY, 13TH DECEMBER, 1866.

The Resolutions of the Quebec Conference, beginning with number one, were considered.

No. 1. Word " Federal " objected to by Mr. Henry. To be considered.

No. 2. The term " Federation " to be " Confederation " ; " would be " to be " is." The words " Prince Edward Island " to be dropped the first place they occur.

No. 3. Agreed to previously.

No. 4. Agreed to previously.

No. 5. Reserved as to Representative of the Sovereign.

Mr. McDougall—Why assert that the Sovereign is Commander-in-Chief when it is part of the constitution of England?

Mr. Macdonald—I am not prepared to admit that. The Sovereign is not absolutely the Commander-in-Chief of the militia of England except by proclamation.

Mr. McDougall—I am prepared to go the same lengths as is constitutional in England.

Mr. Macdonald—Read it in connection with the third resolution.

Mr. Tupper—Then constitutional advice will be necessary.

Mr. Macdonald—Any powers given by statute to the Sovereign must be exercised constitutionally.

Mr. McCully—If any doubt remain on the point, it would require delegation from the Queen in her Commission to the Governor-General.

It was agreed to strike out the words "or Representative of the Sovereign."

No. 6. Mr. Tupper proposed "Confederation" in lieu of "Federated Provinces." He said the term "Local Legislature" and "Federal Parliament" are used advisedly. The distinction breaks off here.

Mr. Archibald proposed that "Legislature" be designated "Parliament."

Mr. Macdonald proposed that the words "the Sovereign" be inserted immediately after the words "composed of." Agreed to.

No. 7. Mr. Macdonald proposed that the word "Confederation" be substituted for "Federated Provinces," and that the words "Prince Edward Island" be omitted. Agreed to.

No. 8. *Mr. Tupper*—I propose the third division shall stand giving Nova Scotia and New Brunswick the full number, to fall back to the number prescribed as vacancies occur. This is the plan of Messrs. Cartier and Langevin and is reasonable. Omit word "three," give Nova Scotia and New Brunswick twelve each, and add a separate clause like number nine to meet the case of Prince Edward Island.

Mr. Mitchell—Any representation of Prince Edward Island should be taken out of the whole without specifying the number here for them.

Mr. Macdonald—I think we should adhere to the number of four for Prince Edward Island.

Mr. Tupper—I agree with Mr. Mitchell.

Mr. Tilley—It is for the General Government to settle with Prince Edward Island.

Mr. Ritchie—Canada may bring in Prince Edward Island, and in so doing sacrifice the Lower Provinces. Therefore define the number at once.

Mr. Fisher—It would be a great evil to leave the matter open. Prescribe the number now to prevent heartburnings in the future. Prince Edward Island may have two, four or six. Ten each for Nova Scotia and New Brunswick is sufficient. Do not change that number.

Mr. Henry—The entrance of Prince Edward Island would be specially the object of the Lower Provinces. It is safe therefore to run the risk that Canada will not act adversely to the Lower Provinces. It is not the interest of Canada to use power improperly.

Mr. Johnson—You will create a difficulty between Nova Scotia and New Brunswick. The former may want a preponderance.

Mr. Tupper—I move that :—

In case Prince Edward Island is admitted into the union its representation in the Legislative Council shall be four, to be appointed from Nova Scotia and New Brunswick as vacancies occur.

Mr. Mitchell—That does not meet my objection. I think four was originally too large a representation for Prince Edward Island. Discretion should be allowed.

Mr. Wilmot—The number was fixed upon at the Quebec Conference and agreed to by the delegates from Prince Edward Island. It should not now be altered.

Mr. Ritchie—I suggest provision that in no case should Nova Scotia or New Brunswick have fewer than ten.

Mr. Galt—That comes to the same thing.

Mr. Macdonald—It will give confidence to Prince Edward Island to leave it as it is. But you may limit the time. The Confederation Parliament alone can admit Prince Edward Island, and it will be against the interest of the Lower Provinces to cut themselves down to eight each in order to admit of Prince Edward Island having four.

Mr. Cartier referred to the Charlottetown Conference. There it was understood the Lower Provinces were to be accounted as one, but not Newfoundland. They came to Quebec only.

Mr. Tupper moved :—

That the Members of the Legislative Council for the Confederation shall in the first instance be appointed upon the nomination of the Executive Government of Canada, Nova Scotia, and New Brunswick respectively, and the number allotted to each Province shall be nominated from the Legislative Councils of the different Provinces, due regard being had to the fair representation of both political parties ; but in case any member of the Local Council so nominated shall decline to accept, it shall be competent for the Executive Government in any Province to nominate in his place a person who is not a member of the Local Council.

Mr. Archibald moved :—

That the Province of Prince Edward Island when admitted into the Confederation shall be entitled to a representation of four Members in the Legislative Council. But in such case the numbers allotted to New Brunswick and Nova Scotia shall be diminished to ten each, such diminution to take place in each Province as vacancies occur.

Mr. Henry—What we should do is that which will bind some one.

Mr. Galt—Unless specifically provided for, there would be no power to reduce Nova Scotia and New Brunswick afterwards. Resolution as amended carried.

Mr. Henry—Do not say " when," put " if."

Mr. Fisher—All these questions must come up again in the Bill.

Mr. Galt—To the Legislative Council all the Provinces look for protection under the Federal principle. Therefore, we should in this respect define now the extent to which we should settle the constitution of the Upper House.

Mr. Johnson—The Colonial Office took objection to a fixed number. They deprecated a cast iron rule.

Mr. Tupper—True, Mr. Cardwell so said, but I think it desirable to fix it. In the Maritime Provinces we felt that the great preponderance of Canada could only be guarded against by equal representation in the Legislative Council. If an increase could be made by the Crown it might disturb the relative proportions. It may limit the Crown to define the number, but it can't be helped.

Mr. Howland—I did not consider the mode of appointments so much as the number and duration.

Mr. Henry—I oppose the limitation of number. We want a complete work. Do you wish to stereotype an Upper Branch, irresponsible both to the Crown and the people? a third body interposed unaccountable to the other two. The Crown unable to add to their number. The people unable to remove them. Suppose a general election results in the election of a large majority in the Lower House favourable to a measure, but the Legislative Council prevent it from becoming law. The Crown should possess some power of enlargement.

Mr. Tupper—I agree with Mr. Henry; but he does not reflect that this is not a Legislative Union, and we had sectional and local differences. Lower Canada and the Lower Provinces require some guarantee. No addition would be required except in case of a dead-lock, when the Government of the day would appoint men pledged beforehand.

Mr. Fisher—The prerogative of the Crown has been only occasionally used, and always for good. This new-fangled thing now introduced, 72 oligarchs, will introduce trouble. I advocate the principle of the power of the Crown to appoint additional members in case of emergency.

Mr. Tilley—I agree with Dr. Tupper. Our protection is as now settled. The objection was that Upper Canada would swamp the Lower Provinces. What is the Crown? The Government of the day.

Mr. Howland—I admit that if the Government is to be constituted on the Federal principle, the number should be fixed and to represent localities. I am in favour of the Federal principle, and I think that if you have a Federal Parliament you must not give power to the Crown to increase the number of the Legislative Council. Thirty-seven members of that House may say at any time what the Government shall not do, and be accountable to no one. My remedy would be to limit the period of service and vest the appointment in the Local Legislatures. It would then be a true Federal Parliament. Now it is an anomaly. It won't work and cannot be continued. You cannot give the Crown an unlimited power to appoint.

Mr. Archibald—This lies at the root of our whole scheme the spirit of which is that each Province shall be sectionally represented in the Legislative Council. The Upper House may disagree with the House of Commons. Its value will be that of occasional obstruction.

Mr. McCully—There are difficulties on both sides. Is there no escape from them? I feel that we are now touching the very life of the whole scheme. If we err, the whole scheme will come down some time. My views, as we stand to-day, are :— Here we are three Provinces. Dead-lock arises. Necessity for creation of three or four additional members of Upper House imperative. Why not trust the Executive Government to appoint one from Upper Canada, one from Lower Canada, and one from the Maritime Provinces?

Mr. Macdonald—We are all agreed that each of the divisions should be equally represented, and should not be varied. If any addition is made it must be in equal proportions from each division. That is a limit to the prerogative.

Mr. Wilmot—I agree with Messrs. Tilley and Tupper as to the necessity of keeping sectional representatives, but I disapprove of cast-iron rules. Prefer mode of increasing number relatively. Instead of the Crown appointing, I would prefer choice by joint ballot of Local Legislatures.

Mr. Langevin—If you give power to swamp the Legislative Council then you destroy its utility. Lower Canada insists that each of its present divisions shall have a representative in the Council, that is the existing divisions. If you give power to the Central Government to increase the number you change the proportions. This has been settled to the satisfaction of Roman Catholics and Protestants, British and French.

No. 9. Agreed to.

Adjourned.

The consideration of the Resolutions of the Quebec Conference was proceeded with.

No. 10. Agreed to, omitting words " Vancouver Island."

No. 11. Stands.

No. 12. *Mr. Macdonald*—At the Quebec Conference we were all in favour of a higher qualification, but it was reduced to suit Prince Edward Island and Newfoundland. (It was agreed to strike out part referring to Prince Edward Island and Newfoundland).

Mr. Tupper—I move that the word "real" be struck out. I should be willing to strike out the property qualification altogether. If the office were elective, it might be different. If a qualification be thought necessary, then $4,000 is too insignificant for the Parliament of the Confederation. Suppose a man with $50,000 worth of shipping. Should he be ineligible because he had not land worth $4,000 ?

Mr. Fisher—I differ from Mr. Tupper. I would vote for a higher qualification. If a man has $50,000 let him buy land and pay taxes on it.

Mr. Tupper—In Nova Scotia we have no property qualification for the Legislative Assembly.

Mr. Fisher—We have in New Brunswick.

Mr. Wilmot—I think $4,000 too small.

Mr. McDougall—I desire to raise the question whether matters settled at the Quebec Conference can be changed. Canadian delegates are in a different position to those from the Lower Provinces. As to any subject which has not been agitated in the Lower Provinces, do we not lose time by arguing them as they should not be altered ? Is Conference as a whole at liberty to vary these resolutions ?

Mr. Mitchell—I would have taken the same ground. As regards New Brunswick, I look on our position here as not to open and discuss old resolutions, but as to certain and specific objections to that scheme. That is my individual view. Having gone twice to the people on the Quebec scheme, I can say that there are two leading features objectionable to New Brunswick :—

(1) Representation in the Legislative Council.

(2) Financial arrangements.

They also demand more definite mention of the Intercolonial road.

Mr. McCully—We have adopted the Quebec scheme as the backbone, but I think we are here to bring our judgment and maturer reflections to bear upon it. We are tied down to nothing, but should not depart unnecessarily from the Quebec scheme. I will act with the majority of the Conference, although contrary to my own opinion.

Mr. Macdonald—The Maritime delegates are differently situated from us. Our Legislature passed an address to the Queen praying for an Act of Union, on the basis of the Quebec resolutions. We replied to enquiries in our last Session of Parliament that we did not feel at liberty ourselves to vary those resolutions. It is quite understood in Canada, though never reduced to writing, that if any serious objection should be made by the Maritime Provinces, we should be prepared to listen and consider.

Mr. Fisher—I have heard forty objections in New Brunswick to the scheme, but shall act on my own judgment. But this matter will be settled on the basis of the Quebec scheme.

Mr. Ritchie—I entirely concur in the views of Mr. Macdonald. But we of the Maritime Provinces may bring forward matters for discussion. In the Legislature of Nova Scotia it was understood that all matters should be entirely open.

Mr. Johnson—The Quebec scheme should be the basis, but we may agree upon some alterations, and these may necessitate other changes.

Mr. McDougall—I have felt my hands tied and Mr. Howland also.

Mr. Galt—I look on myself as bound by the Quebec scheme as asserted on two occasions in Canada. The real points upon which we might vary them are those which were notoriously ob-

jected to in the Maritime Provinces.　But in a matter of detail
I think we should not depart from Quebec.　I was in favour of
a larger qualification than $4,000, but would not now vary it.

Mr. Howland—We place ourselves in a false position in
every departure from the Quebec scheme.　But in advocating
an alteration on the question objected to by the Colonial Office
(limit of prerogative) I thought we had full power.

Mr. Macdonald—The Conference can now quite understand
our position, and we may now go on.　We are quite free to discuss points as if they were open, although we may be bound to
adhere to the Quebec scheme.

Mr. McCully—I think it might be well to have had a higher
qualification, but not to change now.

Mr. Archibald—I move continuance of property qualification
in the Province for which the member is chosen.　Agreed to.*

No. 13. Agreed to.

No. 14. Stands.

No. 15. Agreed to.

No. 16. Agreed to.

No. 17. 194 reduced to 181.　Prince Edward Island and
　　　　Newfoundland struck out.

No. 18. Agreed to.　"The first general election after" to be
　　　　inserted after "until."

No. 19. Stands.

No. 20. Agreed to.

No. 21. Stands.

No. 22. Agreed to.

No. 23. To be modified.

No. 24. Struck out.　See 41.

No. 25. Stands over.

No. 26. Agreed to.

No. 27. Agreed to.

No. 28. Agreed to.

No. 29. Stands for consideration.

---

* Apparently this concludes the work of the day.　What follows indicates the procedure with respect to the remaining clauses, though the dates on which they were
severally dealt with in Conference are wanting.

ROUGH DRAFT OF CONFERENCE.

BE IT ENACTED by THE QUEEN'S MOST EXCELLENT MAJESTY, by and with the advice and consent of the Lords Spiritual and Temporal and Commons in this present Parliament assembled, and by the authority of the same, as follows:—

1. It shall be lawful for Her Majesty, with the advice of her Privy Council, to declare, or to authorize the Governor-General to declare by proclamation, that the Provinces of Canada, Nova Scotia, and New Brunswick, upon, from, and after a certain day in such proclamation to be appointed, which day shall be within   calendar months next after the passing of this Act, shall, for the purposes hereof, form and be one Province or Confederation, under the name of   and thenceforth the said several Provinces shall constitute and be one Province or Confederation, under the name aforesaid, upon, from, and after the day so appointed, as aforesaid.

GENERAL GOVERNMENT.

2. The Executive Authority or Government, so far as may be necessary for the purposes of this Act, shall be and continue to be vested in the Queen of the United Kingdom of Great Britain and Ireland, to be administered either personally or by representatives upon the principles of the British Constitution.

3. The Queen shall be Commander-in-Chief of the land and naval militia forces.

4. There shall be within the said Confederation a Parliament composed of the Queen, Legislative Council, and a House of Commons.

LEGISLATIVE COUNCIL.

5. There shall be 72 Members in the Legislative Council, and for the purpose of constituting such Legislative Council the Confederation shall be deemed to consist of three divisions, each to have an equal representation, that is to say : first, the Province of Upper Canada, 24 ; second, Lower Canada, 24 ; third, Nova Scotia and New Brunswick, 24 ; being 12 to each.

6. After the admission of Prince Edward Island into the Confederation, the representation of Nova Scotia and New Bruns-

wick in the Legislative Council shall be reduced to ten each, such reduction only to take place on the occurrence of vacancies by death or otherwise.

7. The colonies of Newfoundland and Prince Edward Island, the North Western Territory and British Columbia, shall be admitted into the Confederation on such terms and conditions as the Parliament shall deem equitable, and as shall receive the assent of Her Majesty, and in the case of Newfoundland, Prince Edward Island, and British Columbia as shall be agreed upon by their respective Legislatures, but Newfoundland and Prince Edward Island, when admitted, shall each be entitled to a representation in the Legislative Council of four Members.

8. The Members of the Legislative Council shall be appointed by Her Majesty under the Great Seal of the Confederation, and hold their seats for life, subject to the provisions hereinafter contained for vacating the same. Every person so appointed shall be a British subject of the age of thirty years or upwards, and shall at the time of such appointment reside in the Province for which he is appointed, and shall be seised in fee to his own use of real estate therein of the value of $4,000 over and above all incumbrances, and shall be worth that sum over and above all his debts and liabilities. Provided, in the case of Lower Canada, every person appointed shall be a resident of the said Province, and shall reside or possess his qualification in the Electoral District he is appointed to represent, as is mentioned in Schedule A, Chapter 1, of the Consolidated Statutes of Canada.

9. Nothing hereinafter contained as to the residence of Legislative Councillors shall apply to any person holding an official position which requires his attendance at the seat of Government during the term of his office.

10. If any Legislative Councillor shall, for two successive Sessions of Parliament, fail to give his attendance in the Legislative Council without the permission of the Governor-General, or shall take any oath, or make any declaration or acknowledgment of allegiance, obedience, or adherence to any Foreign Prince or Power, or shall do or concur in or adopt any act whereby he may become a subject or citizen of any Foreign State or Power, or whereby he may become entitled to the rights, privileges, or immunities of a subject or citizen of any Foreign State or Power, or shall cease to reside in the Province for which he is appointed,

or, in the case of Lower Canada, in the Electoral District, as herein
provided, subject to the exception as to Officers of the Government hereinbefore provided, or shall cease to hold the property
qualification hereinbefore mentioned, or shall become bankrupt,
or take the benefit of any law relating to Insolvent Debtors, or
shall become a public defaulter, or be attainted of felony, or of
any infamous crime, his seat in the Legislative Council shall
thereby become vacant.

11. Every Member of the Legislative Council before he shall
sit or vote therein, shall take the oath of allegiance to Her Majesty before the Governor-General, or some person or persons
authorized by him to administer such oath, and shall also make
and subscribe a declaration in writing under his hand, and de-
liver the same to the Clerk of the Council, which declaration shall
be as follows : " I, A. B, do declare and testify that I am by law
duly qualified to be appointed a Member of the Legislative Council of Canada, and that I am duly seised of an estate in fee simple
to my own use, in lands or tenements, in (here set forth the place
where such lands are situate, and a particular description thereof) of the value of $4,000 over and above all incumbrances af-
fecting the same, and that I am worth that sum over and above
all my debts and liabilities, and that I have not collusively or
colourably obtained a title to or become possessed thereof, or of
any part thereof, for the purpose of enabling me to become a
member of the said Legislative Council." And every Member
who shall sit or vote in the Council before making and filing such
declaration as aforesaid, shall be liable for every day he shall
so sit to pay the sum of $500, to be recovered by any person who
shall sue for the same, and whoever shall wilfully, falsely, and
corruptly make any such declaration or affirmation, shall be
guilty of perjury, and suffer the pains and penalties therefor.

12. If any question shall arise as to the right of any person to
hold his seat in the Legislative Council, it shall be heard and determined by the Legislative Council. But it shall be lawful
either for the person respecting whose seat such question shall
have arisen, or for Her Majesty's Attorney-General or other
principal Law Officer of the said Confederation, to appeal from
the determination of the said Council in such case to Her
Majesty, and that the judgment of Her Majesty, with the advice
of Her Privy Council thereon shall be final and conclusive in
the premises.

13. Any Member of the Legislative Council may, by writing under his hand addressed to the Governor-General, resign his seat in the said Legislative Council, and upon such resignation the seat of such Legislative Councillor shall become vacant.

14. The Governor General, unless otherwise provided by Parliament, shall appoint during pleasure one of the Members of the Legislative Council to be Speaker thereof.

15. The presence of at least　　　Members of the Legislative Council, exclusive of the Speaker, shall be necessary to constitute a meeting for the exercise of its powers, and all questions which shall arise therein shall be decided by a majority of voices of the Members present, other than the Speaker ; but when the voices are equal, the Speaker shall have the casting vote.

16. The Legislative Council, or the Members thereof, shall be entitled and exercise as a Branch of the Legislature within the Confederation all the powers and privileges, and be subject to all the responsibilities and duties which the House of Lords in England, or the Members thereof enjoy, or are subject to, except as hirein provided, and also as to what appertains to the judicial functions of the House of Lords.

17. The Governor-General shall in the first instance appoint the Members of the Legislative Council upon the nomination of the Executive Governments of Canada, Nova Scotia and New Brunswick, respectively, to be selected from the Legislative Council of each Province : but if any member of such Legislative Council so nominated shall not accept such nomination, the Executive Government in any Province may nominate in his place a person who is not a member of such Legislative Council.

HOUSE OF COMMONS.

18. The House of Commons shall be constituted upon the basis of representation by population, and shall consist of 181 Members, distributed as follows :—To Upper Canada, 82 ; Lower Canada, 65 ; Nova Scotia, 19 ; and to New Brunswick, 15 ; and after the decennial census of 1871, and every decennial census thereafter, upon the termination by a dissolution or otherwise of the Parliament then existing, the representation from each Province shall be readjusted, and for that purpose Lower Canada shall always be assigned 65 Members, and to each of the other

Provinces at each readjustment shall be assigned the number of Members to which it will be entitled in the same ratio of representation to population as Lower Canada will have.

19. In the computation at each decennial period of the number of Members to which each Province is entitled, no fractional part shall be considered, except in cases when any such fractional part shall exceed one-half of the number which would entitle a Province to a Member on the basis of population, in which case a Member shall be assigned for each such fractional part ; and no reduction shall be made in the number of Members to be returned by any Province unless its population shall have decreased relatively to the population of the whole Union, to the extent of five per centum.

20. The Parliament may at any time increase the number of Members in the House of Commons, but such increase shall be in the proportion to which each Province would be entitled under this Act.

21. Until provision is made by Parliament, all the laws which at the time this Act comes into operation are in force in the Provinces, respectively relating to the qualification and disqualification of persons elected or entitled to sit and vote as Members of the Assembly of the said Provinces respectively, or relating to the qualification or disqualification of Electors, or to the oaths to be taken by Electors, or to returning officers, their powers and duties, or to the proceedings at elections, or to the manner and time of holding and conducting such elections, except as to Electoral Districts, or to the trial of Controverted Elections ; and all proceedings incidental thereto, or relating to the vacating the seat of Members, or to the execution of new writs in case of any seat being vacated otherwise than by a dissolution, shall respectively apply to elections of Members to serve in the House of Commons for those Provinces respectively.

22. The Governor-General shall within   after this Act comes into operation, cause writs to be issued in such form as he may prescribe for the election of Members of the House of Commons, and within   after the return thereof, summon Parliament for the despatch of business, and in case any vacancy should occur in the House of Commons before provision is made by Parliament, such vacancy may be filled, and writs therefor may be issued in like manner.

23. No Member of the House of Commons shall be permitted to sit or vote therein until he shall have taken the oath of allegiance to Her Majesty before the Governor-General, or other person or persons authorised by him to administer such oath.

24. The House of Commons shall, upon their first assembling after every general election, proceed forthwith to elect one of their Members to be Speaker, and in the case of his death, resignation or removal by a vote, shall forthwith proceed to elect another of such Members to be such Speaker, and the Speaker so elected shall preside in the said House of Commons.

25. Upon any general election the House of Commons shall be competent to proceed to the despatch of business at the time appointed by the Governor-General, provided that no more than five of the writs of election shall not have been returned, or that in any of the Electoral Districts the electors shall have failed to elect a Member to serve in the said House of Commons.

26. The presence of at least   Members of the House of Commons, exclusive of the Speaker, shall be necessary to constitute a meeting for the exercise of its powers, and all questions which shall arise in such House of Commons, shall be decided by a majority of voices of such Members as shall be present other than the Speaker, and whenever the voices shall be equal the Speaker shall have the casting voice.

27. The House of Commons, and the Members thereof, subject to the provision of this Act, shall enjoy all the powers, privileges and functions, and be subject to all the duties and responsibilities within the Confederation, as the British House of Commons and the Members thereof.

28. No person, being a Member of the Legislative Council, shall be capable of being elected, or of sitting, or voting as a Member of the House of Commons.

PARLIAMENT.

29. Every Parliament shall continue for five years from the day of the return of the writs under which the Members of the House of Commons shall be elected, and no longer, but subject to be sooner prorogued or dissolved by the Governor-General, and a Session of the Parliament shall be holden at least once in every year, so that a period of twelve calendar months shall not intervene between any two Sessions.

30. The Governor-General may fix such place or places within the Confederation, and such time for holding the first and every other Session of Parliament as he may deem advisable, and from time to time change or vary the same.

31. Whenever any Bill which has been passed by the Legislative Council and House of Commons shall be presented for the assent of Her Majesty to the Governor-General, he shall declare according to his discretion, but subject, nevertheless, to the provisions of this Act, and to such instructions as may from time to time be given in that behalf by Her Majesty, that he assents to such Bill in Her Majesty's name, or that he withholds such assent, or that he reserves the Bill for the signification of Her Majesty's pleasure.

32. No Bill which shall be reserved for the signification of Her Majesty's pleasure shall have any force or authority until the Governor-General shall signify, either by speech or message to the Legislative Council and House of Commons of the Confederation, or by proclamation, that such Bill has been laid before Her Majesty in Council, and that Her Majesty has been pleased to assent to the same, and an entry shall be made in the journals of the Legislative Council and House of Commons respectively of every such message or speech, and a duplicate thereof, duly attested, shall be delivered to the proper officer, to be kept among the records of the Confederation, and no Bill which shall be so reserved as aforesaid shall have any force or authority unless Her Majesty's assent shall have been so signified as aforesaid within the space of two years from the day on which such Bill shall have been presented to the Governor-General as aforesaid.

33. Whenever any Bill which shall have been presented for the assent of Her Majesty to the Governor-General shall have been assented to by him, he shall by the first convenient opportunity transmit an authentic copy thereof to one of Her Majesty's principal Secretaries of State. And Her Majesty may, within two years after such Bill shall have been so received by such Secretary of State, by Order in Council, declare the disallowance of such Bill, and such disallowance, together with a certificate under the hand and seal of such Secretary of State, certifying the day on which such Bill was disallowed as afore-

said, being signified by the Governor-General to the Legislative Council and House of Commons by speech or message or by proclamation, shall make void and annul the same from and after the day of such signification.

34. The Governor-General may disallow any Bill passed by the Local Legislature within one year after the passing thereof, and upon the proclamation thereof by the Governor it shall become null and void ; and no Bill which shall be reserved by the Governor for the consideration of the Governor-General shall have any force or authority until the Governor-General shall signify his assent thereto and proclamation thereof made within the Province by the Governor of the Province for which such Bill has been passed.

APPOINTMENT OF GOVERNORS, ETC.

35. The Governor-General may appoint Governors for the respective Provinces, Judges and other officers authorised by Parliament, and also the Judges of the Superior and District and County Courts in each Province. But the Judges of Lower Canada shall be selected from the bar of that Province, and until the consolidation of the laws of the other Provinces the Judges of these Provinces shall be selected from their respective benches or bars.

POWERS OF PARLIAMENT.

36. The Parliament shall have power to make laws respecting the following subjects :—

1. The Public Debt and Property.
2. The Regulation of Trade and Commerce.
3. The raising of money by all or any mode or system of Taxation.
4. The borrowing of money on the public credit.
5. Postal Service.
6. Lines of Steam or other Ships, Railways, Canals, and other works connecting any two or more of the Provinces together, or extending beyond the limits of any Province.
7. Lines of Steamships between the Confederated Provinces and other countries.

8. Telegraphic Communication and the incorporation of Telegraph Companies.

9. All such works as shall, although lying wholly within any Province, be specially declared by the Acts authorising them to be for the general advantage.

10. The Census and Statistics.

11. Militia—Military and Naval Service and Defence.

12. Beacons, Buoys, Light Houses, and Sable Island.

13. Navigation and Shipping.

14. Quarantine.

15. Sea Coast and Inland Fisheries.

16. Ferries between any Province and a Foreign Country, or between any two Provinces.

17. Currency and Coinage.

18. Banking—Incorporation of Banks and the issue of paper money.

19. Savings Banks.

20. Weights and Measures.

21. Bills of Exchange and Promissory Notes.

22. Interest.

23. Legal Tender.

24. Bankruptcy and Insolvency.

25. Patents of Invention and Discovery.

26. Copy Rights.

27. Indians and Lands reserved for the Indians.

28. Naturalization and Aliens.

29. Marriage and Divorce.

30. The Criminal Law, excepting the Constitution of Courts of Criminal Jurisdiction but including the procedure in Criminal matters.

31. The establishment, maintenance, and management of Penitentiaries.

32. Rendering uniform all or any of the laws relative to property and civil rights in Upper Canada, Nova Scotia, and New Brunswick, and rendering uniform the procedure of all or any of the Courts in these Provinces : but any Statute for this purpose shall have no force or authority in any Province until sanctioned

by the Legislature, and when so sanctioned the power
of amending, altering, or repealing such laws shall
thenceforward be vested in the Parliament only.

33. Immigration.

34. Agriculture.

35. To establish a General Court of Appeal, and in order to
the due execution of the Laws of Parliament additional Courts when necessary.

36. To fix and provide for the salaries and allowances of the
Governors of the several Provinces, and of the Judges
and all other Officers of the Confederation, and of the
Judges of the Superior, and District, and County
Courts, and of the Admiralty Courts, in cases where
the Judges thereof are paid by salaries.

37. And also for the peace, welfare and good government
of the Confederation respecting all matters of a general character, not specially and exclusively herein
reserved for the Legislatures ; and such laws shall
control and supersede any laws in any wise repugnant
thereto or inconsistent therewith which may have
been made prior thereto ; and any law made by any
Legislature in pursuance of the authority hereby conferred upon it in regard to matters and subjects in
which concurrent jurisdiction is hereby given to the
Parliament shall, so far as the same is repugnant to
or inconsistent with any Act passed by the Parliament, be null and void.

37. The Government of the Confederation and the Parliament shall have and exercise all powers necessary or proper for
the performance of the obligations of the Confederation as part
of the British Empire to Foreign Countries arising under treaties between Great Britain and such countries.

LOCAL GOVERNMENTS.

38. For each of the Provinces there shall be an Executive
Officer styled the Governor, who shall be appointed by the
Governor-General under the Great Seal of the Confederation, to
hold office during pleasure, such pleasure, however, not to be
exercised before the expiration of five years from the date of his
appointment, except for cause to be communicated in writing to

the Governor immediately after the exercise of the pleasure as aforesaid, and also by message to both Houses of Parliament within the first week of the first Session thereafter.

39. The Governor, subject to the provisions of this Act and any Act of Parliament, and of such instructions as he may from time to time receive from the Governor-General, shall administer the Government of the Province for which he is appointed upon the principles of the British Constitution. He shall have power from time to time to prorogue or dissolve the Legislature ; he may reserve any Bill passed by the Legislature for the consideration of the Governor-General, and may from time to time, except in capital cases, reprieve or pardon prisoners convicted of crimes, and commute and remit such sentences in whole or in part, which belong of right to the Crown.

40. The Governor-General shall from time to time make provision for the administration of the Government of any Province, during the temporary absence or other inability to discharge the duties of his office of the Governor thereof from any cause.

41. The Local Government and Legislature of each Province shall be constructed subject to the provisions of this Act in such manner as the Legislature shall from time to time provide.

42. The Legislature shall have exclusive power to make laws respecting the following subjects, with the exception of Agriculture and Immigration, in regard to which Parliament shall have concurrent jurisdiction :—

1. The altering and amending their constitution from time to time.

2. Direct Taxation, and reserving to New Brunswick the right to collect the lumber dues provided in Chapter 15, Title III. of the Revised Statutes of that Province, and any amendment thereof, made before or after this Act comes into operation, which does not increase the amount, but excepting therefrom the lumber of any other Province.

3. Borrowing money on the credit of the Province.

4. The establishment and tenure of Local Offices, and the appointment and payment of Local Officers.

5. Agriculture.

6. Immigration.

7. Education—saving the rights and privileges which the Protestant or Roman Catholic minority in any Province at the time when this Act came into operation. And in any Province where a system of separate or dissentient schools by law obtains, or where the Legislature may thereafter adopt a system of separate or dissentient schools, an appeal shall lie to the Governor-General from the acts and decisions of the Local Authorities which affect the rights and privileges of the Protestant or Roman Catholic minority in the matter of education, and the Parliament shall have power, in the last resort, to legislate on the subject.

8. The sale and management of Public Lands, except Lands owned by the General Government.

9. The establishment, maintenance, and management of Public and Reformatory Prisons.

10. The establishment, maintenance, and management of Hospitals, Asylums, Charities, and Eleemosynary Institutions, except Marine Hospitals.

11. Municipal Institutions.

12. Shop, Saloon, Tavern, Auctioneer and other Licenses for Local Revenue.

13. Local Works.

14. The incorporation of private or local companies, except such as relate to matters assigned to the General Parliament.

15. Property and civil rights, including the solemnisation of marriage, excepting those portions thereof assigned to the General Parliament.

16. The infliction of punishment by fine, penalties, imprisonment, or otherwise for the breach of laws passed in relation to any subject within their jurisdiction.

17. The administration of justice, including the constitution, maintenance, and organisation of the Courts—both of Civil and Criminal Jurisdiction, and including also the procedure in Civil Matters.

18. And generally all matters of a private or local nature, not assigned to the Parliament.

43. All the powers, privileges, and duties conferred and imposed upon Roman Catholic separate schools, and school trustees in Upper Canada, shall be extended to the Protestant and Roman Catholic schools in Lower Canada.

MISCELLANEOUS.

44. The English and French languages may both be employed in Parliament, and in its proceedings, and in the Legislature and Courts of Lower Canada, and also in the Courts of the Confederation which may be established under this Act.

45. For the purposes of this Act, Courts, Judges, and Officers of the several Provinces shall be Courts, Judges and Officers of the Confederation.

46. The Judges of the Superior Courts shall hold their offices during good behaviour, and shall be removable on the address of both Houses of Parliament, but not on the address of the Houses of any of the Legislatures.

47. No lands or property of the Confederation or Local Government shall be liable to taxation.

48. All Bills for appropriating any part of the Public Revenue, or for imposing any tax or imposts shall originate in the House of Commons or the House of Assembly, as the case may be.

49. The House of Commons or House of Assembly shall not originate or pass any vote, resolution, address, or bill, for the appropriation of any part of the public revenue or of any tax or impost, to any purpose not previously recommended by message of the Governor-General, or the Governor, as the case may be, during the Session in which such vote, resolution, address, or bill is moved.

50. The seat of Government of the Confederation shall be Ottawa, subject to the Royal prerogative.

51. Subject to any future action of the respective Local Governments, the seat of the Local Government in Upper Canada shall be Toronto, in Lower Canada, in Quebec ; and the seat of the Local Government in the other Provinces shall be as at present.

52. All stocks, cash, bankers' balances and securities for money belonging to each Province at the time this Act comes

into operation, except as hereinafter mentioned, shall become the property and assets of the Confederation.

53. The following works and property of each Province shall become the property of the Confederation :—

1. Canals.

2. Public Harbours.

3. Lighthouses, Piers and Sable Island.

4. Steamboats, Dredges and Public Vessels.

5. River and Lake Improvements.

6. Railways and Railway Stocks, Mortgages and other debts due by Railway Companies.

7. Military roads.

8. Custom Houses, Post Offices, and all other public buildings, except such as may be set aside by the Government of the Confederation for the use of the Local
Governments and Legislatures.

9. Property transferred by the Imperial Government, and
known as Ordnance Property.

10. Armouries, Drill Sheds, Military Clothing and munitions
of war, and land set apart for general public purposes.

54. All lands, mines, minerals and royalties vested in Her Majesty in the several Provinces for the use of the Province, or owned by any such Province, and all sums due therefor at the time this Act comes into operation, shall be and continue to be the property of the Province in which the same are or were situate respectively, subject to any trust or other interest that may exist in respect to any such lands, and subject to the rights of the Government of this Confederation to assume, upon equitable terms, any land or public property required for fortifications or the defence of the country, all public property therein.

55. All assets connected with such portions of the Public Debt of any Province as are assumed by the Local Government, shall continue to be the property of those Governments respectively, not exceeding the amount of such assumptions.

56. When this Act comes into operation, all the debts, liabili-
ties, agreements, and obligations of each Province shall become the debts, liabilities, agreements, and obligations of the Confederation, except as hereinafter provided.

57. For the purposes of the Confederation the debt not specially assumed by each Province respectively, shall, for Canada, not exceed the sum of $62,500,000; Nova Scotia, $8,000,000; and New Brunswick, $7,000,000.

58. If any of the Provinces, at the time this Act comes into operation, shall not have contracted debts equal to the amount hereinbefore mentioned, such Province shall receive, by half-yearly payments in advance from the Government of the Confederation, interest at the rate of five per centum on the difference between the actual amount of their respective debts, and such stipulated amount until such debts shall have been so contracted to such respective amounts; but nothing herein contained shall be construed to prevent any Province from increasing the debt chargeable upon the Confederation at any time until it reaches such amount.

59. In consideration of the transfer of the powers of taxation to the Parliament, the Government of the Confederation shall annually pay to each Province, for local purposes, the following sums:—

Upper Canada	$80,000
Lower Canada	$70,000
Nova Scotia	$60,000
New Brunswick	$50,000

and also a sum equal to eighty cents per head of the population as ascertained by the census of the year 1861; and in the case of Nova Scotia and New Brunswick, at the same rate per head as ascertained by each subsequent decennial census, until the population of each of these Provinces shall amount to four hundred thousand. Such aid shall be paid half-yearly in advance, by warrant of the Governor-General on the Treasury of the Confederation, in favour of the officer appointed in each Province to receive the same, deducting from any such subsidy all sums paid as interest on the Public Debt of any Province in excess of the amount hereinbefore stipulated, and also in like manner annually pay to the Province of New Brunswick the sum of $63,000 for the period of ten years. But so long as the liability of that Province remains under $7,000,000 a deduction shall be made therefrom equal to the interest on such deficiency.

60. All engagements of any of the Provinces made with the Imperial Government for the defence of the country shall be fulfilled by the Government of the Confederation.

61. Quakers and Moravians may affirm in any case where an oath is required.

62. All persons, bodies politic or corporate, acting under any law in force at the time this Act comes into operation, shall continue until others are appointed under the authority of this Act, and all proceedings taken shall continue when not inconsistent with the provisions of this Act, and all penalties and forfeitures may be recovered in the same manner as if this Act had not been passed; and any act done, or any right of action which existed, or had accrued or was accruing when this Act came into operation, shall not be affected thereby, and any offence committed or penalty or forfeiture incurred, or any proceeding thereon or in relation thereto, shall not be affected by the passing of this Act, and judgment may in all cases be pronounced thereafter, and all appointments made, and bonds and securities given by any person or persons, under the authority of any law in force at the time this Act comes into operation, shall not be affected thereby.

63. When this Act comes into operation, and until provision is made therefor by Parliament, all the officers of the several Provinces having duties to discharge connected with the several subjects with which Parliament is empowered to deal, shall thenceforth be and become officers of the Confederation and continue to discharge the duties of their respective offices under the same liabilities, responsibilities, and penalties as are provided by the Acts under the authority of which they have been respectively appointed, or they shall have respectively acted, and all Judges and other officers in the several Provinces shall continue to discharge the duties of their respective offices in the same manner in all respects, and subject to the same liabilities, responsibilities, and penalties as if this Act had not been passed, and all laws in force in the several Provinces at the time this Act comes into operation not inconsistent herewith, shall continue to be in force and authority within each Province until they are altered, amended, or repealed under the authority of this Act.

64. The first appointments of the Governors of the several Provinces shall be provisional, and they shall hold office during pleasure. The Governor-General of Canada and also the respective Governors or other officers administering the Governments of the Provinces of Nova Scotia and New Brunswick respectively,

in office at the time the Act comes into operation, shall be the Governors of Upper and Lower Canada and of Nova Scotia and New Brunswick respectively, and shall continue to exercise the functions and discharge the duties of their respective offices subject to the provisions of this Act until a Governor shall be appointed for each Province, and shall receive the same pay and allowances as they shall be then severally receiving ; and the Government of Canada shall exercise the functions of the Governments of Upper and Lower Canada respectively, and the Governments of Nova Scotia and New Brunswick shall continue to exercise the functions of the Governments of those Provinces respectively until Local Governments are formed under the provisions of this Act. The Legislature of New Brunswick shall continue for the period for which it was elected, unless sooner dissolved, and the Constitution of the said Province, and of Nova Scotia, shall continue as now established, subject to the provisions of this Act until altered or amended under the authority of this Act.

65. Until otherwise provided, the Province of Nova Scotia, for the purposes of the election of Members to serve in Parliament, is hereby divided into eighteen electoral districts, of which the county of Halifax, including the City of Halifax, shall be one, and shall be entitled to elect two Members, and each of the other seventeen counties into which the Province is divided, is hereby constituted an electoral district, and shall be entitled to elect one Member.

66. Unless otherwise provided by the Legislature, for the purpose of the first election of Members to serve in the first Parliament, each of the counties into which the Province of New Brunswick is divided, and the City of Saint John, shall constitute an electoral district, and be respectively entitled to elect a Member.

INTERPRETATION.

67. In the construction of this Act the following rules shall be observed with respect to the following terms, unless otherwise expressly provided for, or such construction would be inconsistent with the manifest intention of the Act, or repugnant to the context—that is to say :—

Her Majesty or the Queen shall include Her Heirs and Successors.

Governor-General shall include the Chief Executive Officer or other Administrator of the Government for the time being appointed by Her Majesty, by whatever name designated, and when any act is herein required to be done by the Governor-General, it shall be meant and intended that such act shall be done by and with the advice and consent of the Executive Council of the Confederation.

Legislature shall mean the Local Legislature of any Province before or after this Act comes into operation.

Governor shall include Administrator of the Government of any Province for the time being, and whenever any act is herein required to be done by the Governor, it shall be meant and intended that such act shall be done by and with the advice and consent of the Executive Council of the Province.

Parliament shall mean the Parliament of the Confederation.

Person may include any body corporate, company or society not corporate.

Every word importing the singular number may extend to several persons or things as well as to one person or thing ; and importing the plural number to one person or thing, as well as to several persons or things ; and importing the masculine gender, to females as well as males.

REPEALING.

68.

and all other Acts and parts of Acts inconsistent herewith or repugnant hereto shall be and are hereby repealed when this Act comes into operation.

British North America.

DRAFT

OF A

BILL

FOR

The Union of the British North American Colonies, and for Government of the United Colony.

(Qu. whether to say the Eastern B. N. A. Colonies.)

WHEREAS the Union of the British North American Colonies for Purposes of Government and Legislation would be attended with great Benefits to the Colonies and be conducive to the Interests of the United Kingdom :

Be it therefore enacted by the Queen's most Excellent Majesty, by and with the Advice and Consent of the Lords Spiritual and Temporal, and Commons, in this present Parliament assembled, and by the authority of the same, as follows :

Preliminary.

1. This Act may be cited as the British North America Act, 1867.   Short Title

[*Here would follow:*

1. *Any Interpretation Clause that may be necessary.*

2. *Clause repealing Imperial and Colonial Acts, if necessary.*]

Union.

2. It shall be lawful for Her Majesty, at any Time not later than   , by Letters Patent under   Declaration of Union.

the Great Seal of the United Kingdom, to declare the Union of the Colonies of Canada, Nova Scotia, and New Brunswick into One Colony, with such name as Her Majesty thinks fit.

Proclamation in Canada. 3. The Governor-General of British North America shall, within   after Receipt by him of the Letters Patent declaring the Union, proclaim the same by Publication thereof in the Government Gazette of Canada, and thereupon the Union shall have full Effect, and the said Three Colonies shall thenceforth form and be One Colony.

[*Qu. as to Mode of Proclamation.*]

Provinces of United Colony.

Division into Four Provinces. 4. The United Colony shall be composed of Four Provinces, namely,—Upper Canada, Lower Canada, Nova Scotia, and New Brunswick, each thereof having the same Limits as it has immediately before the Union.

Governor General.

Governor General of United Colony. 5. There shall be one Governor-General for the United Colony, appointed from Time to Time by Her Majesty, Her Heirs and Successors, by Letters Patent under the Great Seal of the United Kingdom.

Executive Council. 6. The Governor-General of the United Colony may, by Instrument under the Great Seal of the United Colony, constitute an Executive Council, and from Time to Time appoint and remove Members thereof.

The Resolutions say nothing of an Executive Council]

Command-in-Chief of Armed Forces. 7. The Command-in-Chief of all Armed Forces raised in the United Colony, or in any Province, for Service by Land or by Water, shall be vested in Her Majesty, Her Heirs and Successors.

General Legislature.

Houses of Parliament of United Colony. 8. There shall be for the United Colony Two Houses of Parliament styled the Legislative Council and the House of Commons.

Legislative Council.

9. In the Legislative Council the Four Provinces shall be represented as follows, namely,—there shall be for Upper Canada Twenty-four Members, for Lower Canada Twenty-four Members, for Nova Scotia Twelve Members, and for New Brunswick Twelve Members.

Constitution of Legislative Council.

10. The First Members of the Legislative Council shall be the Persons named in the Schedule to this Act who shall be deemed respectively to represent the Province in connexion with which they are named ; and the Representatives of Lower Canada shall be deemed also respectively to represent the Division in connexion with which they are named.

First Legislative Council named in Schedule.

11. A Member of the Legislative Council may, by Writing under his Hand delivered to the Governor-General, resign his Seat.

Resignation of Seat.

12. All the First Members of the Legislative Council shall, subject to the Provisions of this Act, hold their Seats for Ten Years from the Union.

Tenure of Seats of First Members.

13. From and after the end of Ten Years from the Union Members of the Legislative Council shall retire from it according to the following rotation :

Rotation of Members.

(1) At the End of each Year from the Commencement of the Rotation Three of the Representatives of Upper Canada and Three of the Representatives of Lower Canada shall retire :

(2) At the end of the First, the Third, the Fifth, and the Seventh Year from the Commencement of the Rotation Two of the Representatives of Nova Scotia and one of the Representatives of New Brunswick, and at the End of the Second, the Fourth, the Sixth, and the Eighth Year from the Commencement of the Rotation One of the Representatives of Nova Scotia and Two of the Representatives of New Brunswick shall retire :

(3) For the first Seven Years from the Commencement of the Rotation the Representatives to retire shall be determined by Lot :

[Qu. How Lots to be drawn ; by Speaker of Legislative Council ?]

(4) From and after the Expiration of Eight Years from the Commencement of the Rotation, the Representatives to retire shall be such as have for the Time being longest held their Seats.

Capacity for Re-appointment.

14. A Member of the Legislative Council retiring by Rotation shall be capable of Re-appointment.

Disqualification of first and subsequent Members.

15. The Seat of a Member of the Legislative Council, either named in the Schedule to this Act or appointed under this Act, shall become vacant in any of the following Cases :—

(1) If for Two consecutive Sessions of Parliament he fails to give his attendance in the Legislative Council without Leave of Absence granted by Her Majesty or the Governor-General, and signified by the Governor-General to the Legislative Council :

(2) If he takes an Oath or makes a Declaration or Acknowledgment of Allegiance, Obedience, or Adherence to a Foreign Power, or does an Act whereby he becomes a Subject or Citizen, or entitled to the Rights or Privileges of a Subject or Citizen, of a Foreign Power :

(3) If he is adjudged Bankrupt or Insolvent, or applies for the Benefit of any Law relating to Insolvent Debtors, or becomes a public Defaulter :

(4) If he is attainted of Treason or convicted of Felony or of any infamous Crime :

(5) If he ceases to be qualified in respect of Property or of Residence ; provided, that a Member shall not be deemed to have ceased to be qualified in respect of Residence by rea-

son only of his residing at the Seat of Government while holding an Office requiring his Presence there.

16. When a Vacancy happens in the Legislative Council by Retirement by Rotation, Resignation, Death, or otherwise, the Governor-General of the United Colony shall, by Instrument under the Great Seal of the United Colony, appoint to fill the Vacancy a fit Person qualified as follows, namely,— *Qualification of subsequent Members.*

(1) Being a British Subject by Birth or by Naturalization :

(2) Being of the Age of Thirty Years or upwards :

(3) Possessing Real Property in the Province of which he is appointed a Representative, of the clear value of Four thousand Dollars or upwards, above all incumbrances :

(4) Being resident in that Province :

(5) In the case of Lower Canada either possessing his Property Qualification in the Division of which he is appointed Representative or being resident therein.

17. Except in case of Retirement by Rotation a Person appointed to fill a Vacancy in the Legislative Council shall hold the seat as long only as the Person vacating the same would have been entitled to hold it. *Duration of appointment on casual Vacancy.*

18. If before the Union any Person named in the Schedule to this Act declares, by Writing under his hand delivered to the Governor-General of British North America, his refusal to act as a Member of the Legislative Council, or dies, or ceases to be qualified in respect of Property or of Residence, the Governor-General, by Instrument under the Great Seal of Canada, shall appoint to be a Member of the Legislative Council in his Stead a fit Person who would be qualified to be so appointed after the Union, and if Her Majesty thinks fit to confirm such Instrument by Warrant under Her Royal Sign Manual, the Person so appointed shall thereby become *Casual Vacancies before Union.*

a Member of the Legislative Council, and shall be in the same Position with respect of Tenure of Office and otherwise, as if he had been named in the Schedule to this Act.

Questions as to Vacancies. 19. If any Question arises respecting a Vacancy in the Legislative Council, the same shall be referred by the Governor-General to the Legislative Council, and shall be heard and determined by them.

Speaker of Legislative Council. 20. Subject to the Provisions of any Act of the Parliament of the United Colony, the Governor-General of the United Colony may from Time to Time, by Instrument under the Great Seal of the United Colony, appoint a Member of the Legislative Council to be Speaker thereof, and may remove him and appoint another Member in his Stead.

Quorum of Legislative Council. 21. Subject to the Provisions of any Act of the Parliament of the United Colony, the Presence of at least Fifteen Members of the Legislative Council, including the Speaker, shall be necessary to constitute a Meeting for the Exercise of its Powers.

Voting in Legislative Council. 22. Questions arising in the Legislative Council shall be decided by a Majority of Voices, and when the Voices are equal, but not otherwise, the Speaker shall have a Vote.

House of Commons.

Constitution of House of Commons. 23. In the House of Commons the Four Provinces shall, subject to the Provisions of this Act, be represented as follows,—namely, there shall be for Upper Canada Eighty-two Members, for Lower Canada Sixty-five Members, for Nova Scotia Nineteen Members, and for New Brunswick Fifteen Members.

[*The Regulation of Constituencies is to be provided for; there is no Provision on the Subject in the Amended Resolutions. Nos. 23, 24 of the Quebec Resolutions related to the subject, but they would not have operated until after the Union.*

Provisions will also be required as to Quorum, Election of Speaker, and his Vote.

Qu. *Oath of Allegiance to be taken by every Member of either House.*]

24. Subject to the Provisions of any Act of the Parliament of the United Colony, all Laws in force in the several Provinces at the Union relative to the following Matters or any of them, namely,—the Qualifications and Disqualifications of Persons to be elected or to sit or vote as Members of the Assembly or Lower House in the respective Provinces, the Voters at Elections of such Members, the Oaths to be taken by Voters, the Returning Officers, their Powers and Duties, the Proceedings at Elections, the Periods during which Elections may be continued, [the Trial of Controverted Elections, and Proceedings incident thereto, the vacating of Seats of Members, and the issuing and Execution of new Writs in case of Seats vacated otherwise than by Dissolution,]—shall respectively apply to Elections of Members to serve in the House of Commons of the United Colony for Places situate in the respective Provinces.

Continuance of existing Election Laws.

[*This follows No. 25 of the Amended Resolutions, and Sect. 27 of the Canada Union Act of 1840 : but qu. as to the Propriety of the words in Brackets.*]

25. On the Completion of the Official Census of the Population of the United Colony in the Year One thousand eight hundred and seventy-one, and of each subsequent decennial Census, the Representation of the Four Provinces shall be re-adjusted by such Authority, in such Manner, and from such Time, as any Act of the Parliament of the United Colony from Time to Time directs, according to the following Rules :—

Decennial Re-adjustment of Representation.

[*Qu. the Re-adjustment to be made by an independent Authority, as some of the Judges, to be specified in the Imperial Act.*]

(1) Lower Canada shall have the fixed Number of Sixty-five Representatives :

(2) There shall be assigned to each of the other Provinces such a Number of Representatives as will bear the same Proportion to the Num-

ber of its Population (ascertained at such Census) as the Number Sixty-five bears to the Number of the Population of Lower Canada (so ascertained) :

(3) In the Computation of the Number of Representatives for a Province a fractional Part less than One Half of the whole Number requisite for entitling the Province to a Representative shall be disregarded ; but a fractional Part exceeding One Half of that Number shall be equivalent to the whole Number:

(4) On any such Re-adjustment the Number of Representatives of a Province shall not be reduced unless the Proportion which the Number of the Population of the Province bore to the Number of the aggregate Population of the United Colony at the then last preceding Re-adjustment of the Number of Representatives of the Province is ascertained at the then last Census to be diminished by One Twentieth Part or upwards.

Increase of Number of House of Commons, 26. The Number of Members of the House of Commons may be from Time to Time increased by Act of the Parliament of the United Colony, provided the proportionate Representation of the several Provinces prescribed by this Act is not thereby disturbed.

Duration of House of Commons. 27. Every House of Commons shall continue for Five Years from the Day of the Return of the Writs for choosing the House (subject to be sooner dissolved by the Governor-General), and no longer.

Money.

Appropriation and Tax Bills. 28. Bills for appropriating any Part of the Public Revenue of the United Colony, or for imposing any Tax or Impost, shall originate in the House of Commons.

Recommendation of Money Votes. 29. It shall not be lawful for the House of Commons to adopt or pass any Vote, Resolution, Address, or Bill for the Appropriation of any Part of the Public Revenue, or of any Tax or Impost, to any purpose that has not been first recommended to that House by Message of the Governor-General in the Session in which such Vote, Resolution, Address, or Bill is proposed to be adopted or passed.

Royal Assent, &c.

30. Where a Bill passed by the Houses of Parliament of the United Colony is presented to the Governor-General of the United Colony for Her Majesty's Assent, he shall declare according to his Discretion, but subject to the Provisions of this Act and to Her Majesty's Instructions, either that he assents thereto in Her Majesty's Name, or that he withholds Her Majesty's Assent, or that he reserves the Bill for the Signification of Her Majesty's Pleasure.

Royal Assent to Bills, &c.

31. Where the Governor-General assents to a Bill in Her Majesty's Name, he shall by the First convenient Opportunity send an authentic Copy of the Act to One of Her Majesty's Principal Secretaries of State, and if Her Majesty in Council within Two Years after Receipt thereof by the Secretary of State thinks fit to disallow the Act, such Disallowance (with a Certificate of the Secretary of State of the Day on which the Act was received by him) being signified by the Governor-General, by Speech or Message to the Houses of Parliament of the United Colony or by Proclamation, shall annul the Act from and after the Day of such Signification.

Disallowance by Order in Council of Act assented to by Governor.

32. A Bill reserved for the Signification of Her Majesty's Pleasure shall not have any Force unless and until within Two Years from the Day on which it was presented to the Governor-General for Her Majesty's Assent, the Governor-General signifies, by Speech or Message to each of the Houses of Parliament of the United Colony or by Proclamation, that it has received the Assent of Her Majesty in Council.

Signification of Pleasure on Bill reserved.

An entry of every such Speech, Message, or Proclamation shall be made in the Journal of each House, and a Duplicate thereof duly attested shall be delivered to the proper Officer to be kept among the Records of the United Colony.

Annual Session.

Yearly Session of Parliament.

33. There shall be a Session of the Parliament of the United Colony once at least in every Year, so that a Period of Twelve Months shall not intervene between the last Sitting of the Parliament in one Session and the first Sitting thereof in the next Session.

Superintendents of Provinces.

Superintendents of Provinces.

34. For each Province there shall be an Officer, styled the Superintendent, appointed by the Governor-General in Council, by an Instrument under the Great Seal of the United Colony.

Tenure of Office of Superintendent.

35. A Superintendent shall hold Office during the Pleasure of the Governor-General in Council, but any Superintendent appointed after the Commencement of the first Session of the Parliament of the United Colony after the Union shall not be removable within Five Years from his Appointment, except for Cause assigned, which shall be communicated to him in Writing within   after the Order for his Removal is made, and shall be communicated by Message to each of the Houses of Parliament of the United Colony within One Week thereafter if the Parliament is then sitting, and if not then within One Week after the Commencement of the next Sitting of the Parliament.

Salaries of Superintendents.

36. The Salaries of the Superintendents shall be fixed and provided by Act of Parliament of the United Colony.

> [*The first Superintendents will have no Salaries fixed till such an Act is passed.*
>
> *Here will follow Constitutions of Provincial Assemblies; see Note at End of Draft.*]

Distribution of Legislative Powers.

Subjects of exclusive Provincial Legislation.

37. In each Province the Superintendent may, by and with the Advice and Consent of the Provincial Assembly, make Ordinances in relation to Matters coming within the Classes of Subjects next hereinafter enumerated, which Ordinances exclusively (subject to the Provi-

sions of this Act) shall in relation to those Matters have the Force of Law in and for the Province, that is to say,—

(1) The Amendment from Time to Time of the Constitution of the House or Houses of the Provincial Assembly :

(2) Direct Taxation within the Province in order to the raising of a Revenue for Provincial Purposes, including in the case of New Brunswick the levying, by the Mode and to the Extent (if any) established by Law at the Union, Dues on Timber, not being the Produce of any of the Provinces other than New Brunswick :

(3) The borrowing of Money on the sole Credit of the Province for Provincial Purposes :

(4) The Establishment and Tenure of Provincial Offices and the Appointment and Payment of Provincial Officers :

(5) The Management and Sale of the Public Lands belonging to the Province :

(6) The Establishment, Maintenance, and Management of Public and Reformatory Prisons in and for the Province :

(7) The Establishment, Maintenance, and Management of Hospitals, Asylums, Charities, and Eleemosynary Institutions in and for the Province (other than Marine Hospitals) :

(8) Municipal Institutions in the Province :

(9) Shop, Saloon, Tavern, Auctioneer and other Licenses in order to the raising of a Revenue for Provincial Purposes :

(10) Local Works and Undertakings other than such as are of the following Classes :

(a) Lines of Steam or other Ships, Railways, Canals, Telegraphs, and other Works and Undertakings connecting the Province with any other or others of the Provinces, or extending beyond the Limits of the Province :

(b) Lines of Steam Ships between the
Province and any British or Foreign
Country :

(c) Ferries between the Province and any
other or others of the Provinces or between the Province and any British or
Foreign Country :

(d) Such Works as, although situate within
the Province, are before or after their
Execution declared by Act of the Parliament of the United Colony to be for
the general Advantage of the United
Colony or for the Advantage of Two
or more of the Provinces :

(11) The Incorporation of Companies with exclusively Provincial Objects :

(12) The Solemnization of Marriage in the Province:

(13) Property and Civil Rights in the Province :

(14) The Administration of Justice in the Province,
including the Constitution, Maintenance, and
Organization of Provincial Courts, both of
Civil and of Criminal Jurisdiction, and in-
cluding Procedure in Civil Matters in those
Courts :

(15) The Imposition of Punishment by Fine, Penalty,
or Imprisonment for enforcing any Provincial
Ordinance made in relation to any Matter
coming within any of the Classes of Subjects
enumerated in this Section :

(16) Such other Classes of Subjects (if any) as are
from Time to Time added to the Enumeration
in this Section by any Act of the Parliament
of the United Colony.

Legisla-
tive Au-
thority of
Parlia-
ment of
United
Colony.

38. It shall be lawful for Her Majesty, Her Heirs
and Successors, by and with the Advice and Consent of
the Houses of Parliament of the United Colony, to make
laws for the Peace, Order, and good Government of the
United Colony and of the several Provinces, in relation

to all Matters not coming within the Classes of Subjects by this Act assigned exclusively to Provincial Legislation ; and for greater Certainty, but not so as to restrict the Generality of the foregoing Terms of this Section, it is hereby declared that the Legislative Authority of the Parliament of the United Colony extends to all Matters coming within the Classes of Subjects next hereinafter enumerated ; that is to say,—

1. The Public Debt and Property.

2. The Regulation of Trade and Commerce.

3. The raising of Money by any Mode or System of Taxation.

4. The borrowing of Money on the Public Credit.

5. Postal Service.

6. The Census and Statistics.

7. Militia, Military and Naval Service, and Defence.

8. Beacons, Buoys, Lighthouses, and Sable Island.

9. Navigation and Shipping.

10. Quarantine.

11. Sea Coast and Inland Fisheries.

12. Currency and Coinage.

13. Banking, Incorporation of Banks, and the Issue of Paper Money.

14. Savings Banks.

15. Weights and Measures.

16. Bills of Exchange and Promissory Notes.

17. Interest.

18. Legal Tender.

19. Bankruptcy and Insolvency.

20. Patents of Invention and Discovery.

21. Copyrights.

22. Indians, and Lands reserved for the Indians.

23. Naturalization and Aliens.

24. Marriage and Divorce.

25. The Criminal Law, except the Constitution of Courts of Criminal Jurisdiction, but including the Procedure in Criminal Matters.

26. The Establishment, Maintenance, and Management of Penitentiaries.

27. Such Classes of Subjects as are by this Act expressly excepted in the Enumeration of the Classes of Subjects by this Act assigned exclusively to Provincial Legislation.

And any Matter coming within any of the Classes of Subjects enumerated in this Section shall not be deemed to come within the Subject of Property and Civil Rights comprised in the enumeration of the Classes of Subjects by this Act assigned exclusively to Provincial Legislation.

Legislation respecting Education.

39. In each Province the Superintendent may, by and with the Advice and Consent of the Provincial Assembly, make Ordinances in relation to Education in the Province, subject and according to the following Provisions :

(1) Nothing in any such Ordinance shall prejudicially affect any Right or Privilege with respect to Denominational Schools which any Class of Persons have by Law in the Province at the Union :

(2) All the Powers, Privileges, and Duties for the Time being by Law conferred and imposed in Upper Canada on the Separate Schools and School Trustees of Her Majesty's Roman Catholic Subjects shall from Time to Time be extended to the Schools of Her Majesty's Protestant and Roman Catholic Dissentient Subjects in Lower Canada :

(3) Where in any Province a System of Separate or Dissentient Schools for the Time being exists by Law, an Appeal shall lie to the Governor-General in Council from any Act or Decision of any Provincial Authority affecting any Right or Privilege of any Class of Persons in relation to Education :

(4) In case any such Provincial Ordinance as from Time to Time seems to the Governor-General in Council requisite for the due Execution of the Provisions of this Section is not made, or in case any Decision of the Governor-General in Council on any Appeal under this section is not duly executed by the proper Provincial Authority in that Behalf, then and in every such Case, and as far as the Circumstances of each Case require, the Power of the Parliament of the United Colony to make Laws in relation to Education shall, notwithstanding anything in this Act, be unrestricted.

40. Notwithstanding anything in this Act, any Act of the Parliament of the United Colony may make Provision for the Uniformity of all or any of the Laws relative to Property and Civil Rights in Upper Canada, Nova Scotia, and New Brunswick, and of the Procedure of all or any of the Courts in those Three Provinces, and thenceforth the power of the Parliament of the United Colony to make Laws in relation to any Matter comprised in any such Act shall, notwithstanding anything in this Act, be unrestricted ; but any Act of the Parliament of the United Colony making Provision for such Uniformity shall not have effect in any Province unless and until it is approved and adopted by the House or Houses of the Provincial Assembly thereof by Address to the Governor-General of the United Colony. *Legislation for Uniformity of Laws in Three Provinces.*

41. Any Act of the Parliament of the United Colony may, notwithstanding anything in this Act, from Time to Time provide for the Constitution, Maintenance, and Organization of a General Court of Appeal for the United Colony. *General Court of Appeal.*

42. Notwithstanding anything in this Act, any Act of the Parliament of the United Colony may from Time to Time make Provision in relation to Agriculture in all or any of the Provinces, or in relation to Immigration into all or any of the Provinces, and in each Province Provincial Ordinances may make provision in relation *Concurrent Powers of Legislation as to Agriculture and Immigration.*

to Agriculture in the Province or Immigration into the Province ; but any such Provincial Ordinance shall have the Force of Law in and for the Province as long and as far only as it is not repugnant to any Act of the Parliament of the United Colony.

Language.

Use of English and French languages.

43. Either the English or the French Language may be used by any Person in the Debates of the Houses of Parliament of the United Colony, and of the Houses of the Provincial Assembly of Lower Canada, and either or both of those Languages may be used in the respective Records and Journals of those Houses, and either of those Languages may be used by any Person or in any Pleading or Process in or issuing from any Court of the United Colony, and in or from all or any of the Provincial Courts of Lower Canada.

> [Qu. whether, as to Courts of the United Colony, this should not be confined to such of those Courts as sit in Lower Canada.]

Newfoundland and Prince Edward Island.

Admission of other Colonies.

44. It shall be lawful for Her Majesty in Council, on Addresses from the Houses of the Parliament of the United Colony, and from the Houses of the Legislature of the Colony of Newfoundland or of the Colony of Prince Edward Island, to admit the Colony of Newfoundland or the Colony of Prince Edward Island (as the case may be), into the Union on the Terms and Conditions in the Addresses expressed : and the Provisions of any Order in Council in that Behalf shall have Effect as if they had been enacted in this Act.

THE SCHEDULE.

First Members of the Legislative Council of United Colony.

    1. Upper Canada.

    2. Lower Canada.

    [Specifying the Twenty-four Divisions.]

    3. Nova Scotia.

    4. New Brunswick.

[No. 30 of the Amended Resolutions (Powers and Privileges of the Houses) may be provided for by Colonial Legislation.

Nos. 31-7 (Courts, Judges, etc.) might be left for Colonial Legislation, unless there is some special Reason for having them inserted in the Imperial Act.

No. 40 and Parts of Nos. 47-50 relate to the Constitution and Proceedings of the Provincial Governments and Legislatures. It is understood that Draft Clauses on these Subjects are being prepared by the Delegates of the several Colonies, which when completed can be considered in Consultation with them.

Nos. 53-63 (Property and Liabilities) are reserved for further Consideration.

No. 65 (Intercolonial Railway) must be dealt with separately.

All the other Resolutions seem disposed of in this Draft Bill as far as Legislation is requisite.

Are such Provisions considered desirable as ss. 47, 48, of the Canada Union Act of 1840, relating to Continuance of Courts, Commissions, etc., and to Temporary Acts?]

THIRD DRAFT* (OF CONFERENCE).

Dated 2nd February, 1867.

WHEREAS the Provinces of CANADA, NOVA SCOTIA, and NEW BRUSWICK have expressed their desire to form a Federal Union under the British Crown, for the purposes of Government and Legislation, based upon the principles of the British Constitution.

BE IT THEREFORE ENACTED BY THE QUEEN'S MOST EXCELLENT MAJESTY, by and with the advice and consent of the Lords Spiritual and Temporal, and Commons in this present Parliament assembled, and by the authority of the same, as follows:

1. This Act may be cited as "The British North American Act, 1867."

2. The words "the Queen," shall mean Her Majesty, Her Heirs, and Successors, Sovereigns of the United Kingdom of Great Britain and Ireland.

The words "from and after the Union," shall mean from and after the day on which the proclamation, declaring the Union of the Provinces, shall take effect.

The word "Parliament" shall mean the Legislature or Parliament of the United Provinces.

The word "Legislature" shall mean the Local Legislature or Parliament of the several Provinces.

The word "Union," shall mean the Union of the Provinces of Canada, Nova Scotia, and New Brunswick.

The words "Governor General in Council," shall mean the Governor or person administrating for the time being the Government of Canada, acting by and with the advice of the Privy Council thereof.

*The drafts marked respectively: "1st draft, 30th January, 1867," and "2nd draft, 31st January, 1867," are incomplete, but so far as they go contain nothing not included in this draft.

The words "Lieutenant-Governor in Council," shall mean the Lieutenant-Governor or person administering for the time being the Government of either of the Provinces of Ontario, Quebec, Nova Scotia, or New Brunswick, acting by and with the advice of the Executive Council thereof.

3. From and after the Union, all Acts and parts of Acts passed by the Parliament of Great Britain, the Parliament of the United Kingdom of Great Britain and Ireland, the Legislature of Upper Canada, the Legislature of Lower Canada, the Legislature of Canada, the Legislature of Nova Scotia, or the Legislature of New Brunswick, which are repugnant to or inconsistent with the provisions of this Act shall be and the same are hereby repealed : Provided always that the repeal of the said several Acts of Parliament and parts of Acts of Parliament shall not be held to revive or give any force or effect to any enactment which has, by the said Acts, or any of them, been repealed or determined.

4. It shall be lawful for the Queen with the advice of her Privy Council, to declare by proclamation that the said Provinces of Canada, Nova Scotia and New Brunswick upon, from, and after a certain day in such proclamation to be appointed, which day shall be within
calendar months next after the passing of this Act, shall form and be one united dominion, under the name of the Kingdom of Canada, and thenceforth the said Provinces shall constitute and be One Kingdom under the Name aforesaid, upon, from, and after the day so appointed as aforesaid.

5. From and after the Union, Upper Canada and Lower Canada shall be severed, and each shall form a separate Province.

6. From and after the said Union, Upper Canada shall be named and known as the Province of Ontario, and Lower Canada shall be named and known as the Province of Quebec.

THE EXECUTIVE POWER.

7. The Executive Government and authority is and shall be vested in the Queen.

8. The Queen has and shall have the Command-in-Chief of the Land and Naval Militia, and of all Naval and Military Forces whatsoever.

8. The Governor-General may, by instrument under the Great Seal of Canada, constitute an Executive Council, which shall be called the Privy Council of Canada, and he may from time to time appoint and remove Members thereof.

9. All powers, authorities and functions which by any Act of the Parliament of Great Britain, or of the Parliament of the United Kingdom of Great Britain and Ireland, or by any Act of the Legislature of Upper Canada, Lower Canada, Canada, Nova Scotia, or New Brunswick respectively, are vested in, or are authorised or required to be exercised by the respective Governors or Lieutenant-Governors of the said Provinces, with the advice, or with the advice and consent, of the Executive Council of such Provinces respectively, or in conjunction with such Executive Council, or with any number of the Members thereof, or by the said Governors or Lieutenant-Governors individually and alone, shall, in so far as the same are not repugnant to or inconsistent with the provisions of this Act, be vested in and may be exercised by the Governor-General of the Kingdom of Canada, with the advice, or with the advice and consent of, or in conjunction, as the case may require, with the Privy Council, or any Members thereof, as may be appointed by the Queen for the affairs of the Kingdom of Canada, or by the Governor-General of the Kingdom of Canada individually and alone, where the advice, consent, or concurrence of the Privy Council is not required.

THE LEGISLATIVE POWER.

10. From and after the Union, there shall be within and for the Kingdom of Canada, one General Parliament, which shall be composed of the Queen, an Upper Chamber to be called the Senate, and a House of Commons.

SENATE.

11. For the purpose of forming the Senate the Kingdom of Canada shall be considered as consisting of three Divisions :—

(1) Ontario.

(2) Quebec.

(3) The Maritime Provinces of Nova Scotia and New Brunswick ;

And each Division shall have an equal representation in the Senate.

12. Ontario shall be represented in the Senate by twenty-four Members, Quebec by twenty-four Members, and the Maritime Provinces by twenty-four Members, of which Nova Scotia shall have twelve Members, and New Brunswick twelve Members.

13. For the purpose of composing the Senate, it shall be lawful for the Governor-General, before the time to be appointed for the first meeting of the Parliament of Canada, by an instrument or instruments under the Great Seal of Canada, to summon to the Senate such persons as Her Majesty may think fit, subject to the provisions of this Act ; and it shall also be lawful for the Governor-General in like manner to summon to the Senate such other person or persons as Her Majesty shall think fit, subject to the provisions of this Act, and every person who shall be so summoned shall thereby become a Member of the Senate.

QUALIFICATION FOR SENATE.

14. The Senators shall each be of the full age of thirty years, shall each be a natural born subject of the Queen, or her subject naturalized by Act of the Parliament of the United Kingdom of Great Britain and Ireland, or by an Act of any or either or one of the Legislatures of the Provinces of Canada, Upper Canada, Lower Canada, Nova Scotia, or New Brunswick, or by an Act of the Parliament of Canada hereby created, and shall each be legally or equitably seised or entitled as of freehold for his own use and benefit of lands or tenements held in free and common socage, or seised and possessed for his own use and benefit of land or tenements held in fief, franc-allen or roture, in the Province for which he shall be appointed, of the value of four thousand dollars over and above all debts, charges, dues, and incumbrances thereon, and shall each be and continue to be worth the sum last aforesaid over and above his debts and liabilities ; and shall each also possess a continuous residence in the Province for which he is appointed, except during the time that he shall hold an office under the Government, the duties of which will require his continuous attendance at the seat of Government of Canada.

15. In the case of Quebec, each of the twenty-four Senators representing such Province shall be appointed to represent one of the twenty-four Electoral Divisions mentioned in Schedule A.

of Chapter First of the Consolidated Statutes of Canada, and such Senator shall reside or possess his qualification in the Electoral Division he is appointed to represent.

16. If any Money Bill passed by the House of Commons is rejected by the Senate for any one Session, or if any other Bill passed by the House of Commons is rejected by the Senate on three consecutive occasions, and if in such case or cases the Governor-General shall ascertain that such Bill or Bills has or have been carried by the majority of voices from two out of the three divisions of the Kingdom, then and in such case it shall be lawful for Her Majesty to create additional Members of the Senate, preserving the rule of equality between the three Divisions of Upper Canada, Lower Canada, and the Maritime Provinces.

17. In case of such increase on such vote beyond the normal number of seventy-two Members of the Senate, no additions shall thereafter be made until each section shall be represented by twenty-four Members and no more.

18. Whenever after the first appointment a vacancy in the Senate shall take place, it shall be lawful for the Governor-General, in the Queen's Name, by an instrument under the Great Seal of Canada, to summon to the said Senate a person duly qualified according to the provisions of this Act to fill such vacancy.

19. Every Senator shall hold his seat in the Senate for the term of his life, subject to the provisions of this Act.

20. If any Senator shall, for two successive Sessions of Parliament, fail to give his attendance in the Senate, or if he shall take any oath or make any declaration or acknowledgment of allegiance, obedience, or otherwise, to any foreign Prince or Power, or shall do, concur in, or adopt any act whereby he may become a subject or a citizen of any foreign state or power, or whereby he may become entitled to the rights, privileges, or immunities of a subject or citizen of any foreign State or Power, or shall cease to have any of the qualifications required by this Act, or shall become bankrupt or take the benefit of any Act relating to insolvent debtors, or become a defaulter, or be attainted of treason, or be convicted of felony or of any infamous crime, his seat in the Senate shall thereby become vacant.

21. Every Senator shall, before taking his seat, take the oath of Allegiance to The Queen before The Governor-General

or some person or persons authorised by him to make a declaration in Schedule A mentioned.

22. Any person who at the time of the Union is a Member of the Legislative Council of Canada, or of Nova Scotia, or of New Brunswick, and who may accept the office of Senator, shall, by his acceptance, be held to have vacated his seat in such Legislative Council.

23. Any Senator may, by writing under his hand, addressed to the Governor-General, resign his seat in the Senate, and thereupon such seat shall become vacant.

24. If any question respecting a vacancy in the Senate shall arise, the same shall be heard and determined by the Senate.

25. The Governor-General shall have power by an instrument under the Great Seal of the Kingdom, to appoint one Member of the Senate to be Speaker thereof, and to remove him and appoint another in his stead.

26. Subject to alteration by the Parliament of Canada, the presence of at least fifteen Members of the Senate, including the Speaker, shall be necessary to constitute a Meeting for the exercise of its powers.

27. The Speaker shall vote as other Members, and in case of an equality of votes, it shall be held that the decision is in the negative.

HOUSE OF COMMONS.

28. For the purpose of constituting the House of Commons of the Kingdom of Canada, it shall be lawful for the Governor within   months after the Union, and thereafter from time to time, as occasion shall require, in Her Majesty's name and by an instrument or instruments under the Great Seal of Canada to summon and call together a House of Commons in and for Canada.

29. The House of Commons shall consist of one hundred and eighty-one members, of whom eighty-two members shall be elected for Ontario, sixty-five for Quebec, nineteen for Nova Scotia and New Brunswick.

30. Constituencies of Ontario.

31. Constituencies of Quebec.

32. Constituencies of Nova Scotia.

33. Constituencies of New Brunswick.

34. There shall be a General Census of the people of the Kingdom of Canada taken in the year One thousand eight hundred and seventy-one, and decennially afterwards; and immediately after the said census, and immediately after every decennial census thereafter, the representation from each Province in the House of Commons shall be re-adjusted by such authority, in such manner, and from such time, as any Act of the Parliament of Canada from time to time directs, according to the following rules :—

(1) Lower Canada shall have the fixed Number of Sixty-five Representatives :

(2) There shall be assigned to each of the other Provinces such a number of Representatives as will bear the same Proportion to the number of its Population (ascertained at such census) as the Number Sixty-five bears to the Number of the population of Lower Canada (so ascertained).

(3) In the computation of the Number of Representatives for a Province a fractional part less than one-half of the whole number requisite for entitling the Province to a Representative shall be disregarded ; but a fractional part exceeding one-half of that number shall be equivalent to the whole number.

(4) On any such Re-adjustment the Number of Representatives of a Province shall not be reduced unless the Proportion which the Number of the Population of the Province bore to the Number of the aggregate Population of the United Colony at the then last preceding Re-adjustment of the Number of Representatives of the Province is ascertained at the then latest Census to be diminished by One Twentieth Part or upwards.

But such re-adjustment shall not take effect until after the termination of the then existing Parliament.

35. The Number of Members of the House of Commons may be from Time to Time increased by Act of the Parliament of Canada, provided the proportionate Representation of the several Provinces prescribed by this Act is not thereby disturbed.

36. Every House of Commons shall continue for five Years from the Day of the Return of the Writs for choosing the House (subject to be sooner prorogued or dissolved by the Governor-General), and no longer.

37. For the purpose of such Readjustments, Quebec shall always be assigned sixty-five Members, and each of the other Provinces shall, at each Readjustment, receive for the ten years then next succeeding, the number of Members to which it will be entitled on the same ratio of representation to population as Quebec will enjoy, according to the census then last taken by having sixty-five Members.

38. No reduction shall be made in the number of Members returned by any Province, unless its population shall have decreased relatively to the population of the whole of Canada, to the extent of five per centum.

39. In computing at each decennial period the number of Members to which each Province is entitled, no fractional parts shall be considered, unless when exceeding one-half the number entitling to a Member, in which case a Member shall be given for each such fractional part.

40. The number of Members may at any time be increased, regard being had to the proportionate rights then existing.

41. Until provisions are made by the Parliament of Canada, all the laws which at the date of the Proclamation constituting the Union are in force in the Provinces respectively relating to the qualification and disqualification of any person to be elected, or to sit or vote as a Member of the House of Assembly in the respective Provinces, and relating to the qualifications or disqualification of voters, and to the oaths to be taken by voters, and to Returning Officers, and their powers and duties, and relating to the proceedings at elections, and to the period during which such elections may be continued, and relating to the trial of controverted elections, and the proceedings incident thereto, and relating to the vacating of seats of Members, and to the execution of new writs in case of any seat being vacated otherwise than by a dissolution, shall respectively apply to Elections of Members to serve in the House of Commons of Canada.

42. The Senate and House of Commons of Canada, shall be called together for the first time, at some period not later than   calendar months from and after the Union.

43. The House of Commons shall, upon its first assembling, after every general election, proceed forthwith to elect one of its number to be Speaker, and in case of his death, resignation, or removal by a vote of the Commons, the said House of Commons shall forthwith proceed to elect another of their Members to be Speaker : and the Speaker so elected shall preside at all Meetings of the Commons.

44. The presence of at least Twenty Members of the House of Commons, including the Speaker, shall be necessary to constitute a Meeting of the House of Commons for the exercise of its powers, and all questions which shall arise in the Commons shall be decided by the majority of voices of such Members as shall be present, other than the Speaker : and when the voices shall be equal, the Speaker shall have the casting vote.

45. No Senator shall be capable of being elected, or of sitting or voting as a Member of the House of Commons.

MONEY.

46. Bills for appropriating any part of the Public Revenue of Canada or for imposing any Tax or Impost shall originate in the House of Commons.

47. It shall not be lawful for the House of Commons to adopt or pass any vote, resolution, address, or bill for the appropriation of any part of the Public Revenue, or of any Tax or Impost, to any purpose that has not been first recommended to that House by message of the Governor-General in the Session in which such vote, resolution, address, or bill is proposed to be adopted or passed.

ROYAL ASSENT, &c.

48. Where a Bill passed by the Houses of Parliament of Canada is presented to the Governor-General for The Queen's assent, he shall declare according to his discretion, but subject to the provisions of this Act and to Her Majesty's instructions, either that he assents thereto in The Queen's name, or that he withholds The Queen's assent, or that he reserves the Bill for the signification of The Queen's pleasure.

49. Where the Governor-General assents to a Bill in The Queen's name, he shall by the first convenient opportunity send an authentic copy of the Act to one of The Queen's principal Secretaries of State, and if the Queen in Council within two

years after receipt thereof by the Secretary of State thinks fit to disallow the Act, such disallowance (with a certificate of the Secretary of State of the day on which the Act was received by him) being signified by the Governor-General, by speech or message to the Houses of Parliament of Canada, or by proclamation, shall annul the Act from and after the day of such signification.

50. A Bill reserved for the signification of The Queen's pleasure shall not have any force unless and until within two years from the day on which it was presented to the Governor-General for Her Majesty's assent, the Governor-General signifies, by speech or message to each of the Houses of Parliament of Canada, or by proclamation, that it has received the assent of The Queen in Council : an entry of every such speech, message, or proclamation shall be made in the Journal of each House, and a duplicate thereof duly attested shall be delivered to the proper officer to be kept among the records of Canada.

ANNUAL SESSION.

51. There shall be a Session of the Parliament of Canada once at least in every year, so that a period of twelve months shall not intervene between the last sitting of the Parliament in one Session, and the first sitting thereof in the next Session.

POWERS OF PARLIAMENT.

52. It shall be lawful for the Queen, by and with the advice and consent of the Houses of Parliament of Canada, to make laws for the peace, order, and good government of the Kingdom, and of the several Provinces, in relation to all matters not coming within the classes of subjects by this Act assigned exclusively to Provincial Legislation : and for greater certainty, but not so as to restrict the generality of the foregoing terms of this Section, it is hereby declared that the Legislative Authority of the Parliament of Canada extends to all matters coming within the classes of subjects next hereinafter enumerated, that is to say:—

1. The Public Debt and Property.
2. The Regulation of Trade and Commerce.
3. The raising of money by all or any mode or system of Taxation.
4. The borrowing of money on the Public Credit.
5. Postal Service.

6. Lines of Steam or other Ships, Railways, Canals, and other works connecting any two or more of the Provinces together, or extending beyond the limits of any Province.

7. Lines of Steamships between Canada and other countries.

8. Telegraphic Communication and the incorporation of Telegraph Companies.

9. All such works as shall, although lying wholly within any Province, be specially declared by the Acts authorising them to be for the general advantage.

10. The Census and Statistics.

11. Militia—Military and Naval Service and Defence.

12. Beacons, Buoys, Light Houses, and Sable Island.

13. Navigation and Shipping.

14. Quarantine.

15. Sea Coast and Inland Fisheries.

16. Ferries between any Province and a Foreign Country, or between any two Provinces.

17. Currency and Coinage.

18. Banking—Incorporation of Banks and the issue of paper money.

19. Savings Banks.

20. Weights and Measures.

21. Bills of Exchange and Promissory Notes.

22. Interest.

23. Legal Tender.

24. Bankruptcy and Insolvency.

25. Patents of Invention and Discovery.

26. Copy Rights.

27. Indians and Lands reserved for the Indians.

28. Naturalisation and Aliens.

29. Marriage and Divorce.

30. The Criminal Law, excepting the Constitution of Courts of Criminal Jurisdiction but including the procedure on Criminal matters.

31. The establishment, maintenance, and management of Penitentiaries.

32. Rendering uniform all or any of the laws relative to property and civil rights in Upper Canada, Nova Scotia, and New Brunswick, and rendering uniform the procedure of all or any of the Courts in these Provinces : but any Statute for this purpose shall have no force or authority in any Province until sanctioned by the Legislature, and when so sanctioned the power of amending, altering, or repealing such laws shall thenceforward be vested in the Parliament only.

33. Immigration.

34. Agriculture.

35. To establish a General Court of Appeal, and in order to the due execution of the Laws of Parliament additional Courts, when necessary.

36. To fix and provide for the salaries and allowances of the Governors of the several Provinces, and of the Judges and all other officers of the Union and of the Superior, District, County and Recorder's Courts, and of the Admiralty Courts, in cases where the Judges thereof are paid by salaries.

37. And also for the peace, welfare and good government of the Union respecting all matters of a general character, not specially and exclusively herein reserved for the Legislatures, and such laws shall control and supersede any laws in any wise repugnant thereto or inconsistent therewith which may have been made prior thereto : and any law made by any Legislature in pursuance of the authority hereby conferred upon it in regard to matters and subjects in which concurrent jurisdiction is hereby given to the Parliament shall, so far as the same is repugnant to or inconsistent with any Act passed by the Parliament, be null and void.

53. The Senate, or the Members thereof, and the House of Commons, or the Members thereof, are respectively to be entitled to, and shall and may exercise, as branches of the Parliament of the Kingdom of Canada, all the powers and privileges, and be subject to all the responsibilities and duties which the

House of Lords or the House of Commons of the United Kingdom of Great Britain and Ireland, or the Members thereof enjoy (as the case may be), or are subject to, except as herein provided, and except also as to the Judicial functions of the House of Lords.

54. The first Elections for Members of the House of Commons of Canada, and for Members of the Legislative Assemblies respectively of Ontario, Quebec, Nova Scotia, and New Brunswick, shall be held upon the same day, and be taken by the same Returning Officer.

Revenues, Civil List, &c.

55. From and after the Union, all Duties and Revenues over which the respective Legislatures of the said Provinces before and at the time of the passing of this Act had, and have power of Appropriation, except such portions thereof as are by this Act reserved to the Local Governments, or raised by them in accordance with the Special powers conferred upon them by this Act, shall form one Consolidated Revenue Fund, to be appropriated for the Public Service of Canada, in the manner, and subject to the charges hereinafter mentioned.

56. The said Consolidated Revenue Fund of Canada shall be permanently charged with all the costs, charges, and expenses incident to the collection, management, and receipt thereof, such costs, charges and expenses being subject, nevertheless, to be reviewed and audited in such manner as shall be directed by any Act of the Parliament thereof.

57. Out of the Consolidated Revenue Fund of Canada, there shall be payable every year to Her Majesty, her heirs and successors, the sum of
for defraying the expenses of the several services and purposes named in the Schedule marked A to this Act annexed : and during the life of The Queen, and for five years after the demise of The Queen, there shall be payable to the Queen, out of the said Consolidated Revenue Fund, a further sum of
for defraying the expense of the several services and purposes named in the Schedule marked C to this Act annexed : the said sums of   to be issued by the
in discharge of such warrant or warrants as shall be from time to time directed to him under the Hand and Seal of the Governor-General : and the said

shall account to the Queen for the same through the Lord High Treasurer or Lords Commissioners, of The Queen's Treasury, in such manner and form as The Queen shall be graciously pleased to direct.

58. Until altered by any Act of the Parliament of Canada, the salary of the Governor-General shall be that set against his office in the said Schedule B ; and accounts in detail of the expenditure of the said sum of
hereinbefore granted, and of every part thereof shall be laid before the Senate and House of Commons of Canada, within thirty days next after the beginning of the Session after such expenditure shall have been made.

59. During the time for which the said sum of
is payable, the same shall be accepted and taken by the Queen, by way of Civil List, instead of all territorial and other revenues now at the disposal of the Crown, arising in Canada, and three-fifths of the net produce of the said territorial and other revenues now at the disposal of the Crown within Canada shall be paid over to the account of the said Consolidated Revenue Fund ; and also during the life of The Queen, and for five years after the demise of The Queen, the remaining two-fifths of the net produce of the said territorial and other revenues now at the disposal of the Crown within Canada, shall be also paid over in like manner to the account of the said Consolidated Revenue Fund.

60. The consolidation of the duties and revenues of the said Province shall not be taken to affect the payment out of the said Consolidated Revenue Fund of any sum or sums heretofore charged upon the rates and duties already raised, levied and collected, or to be raised, levied and collected, to and for the use of Canada, for such time as shall have been appointed by the several Acts of the Legislatures of the Provinces of Canada, Nova Scotia, and New Brunswick, by which such charges were severally authorised.

61. That the expenses of the collection, management, and receipt of the said Consolidated Revenue Fund shall form the first charge thereon ; and that the annual interest of the public debt of the Provinces of New Brunswick or either of them at the time of the Union, shall form the second charge thereon ; and the said sum of
shall form the third charge thereon ; and the other charges upon

the rates and duties levied within Canada, hereinbefore reserved, shall form the sixth charge thereon, so long as such charges shall continue to be payable.

62. Subject to the several payments hereby charged on the said Consolidated Revenue Fund, the same shall be appropriated by the Parliament of Canada for the public service, in such manner as they shall think proper.

LOCAL CONSTITUTIONS.

63. For each Province of Upper Canada, Lower Canada, Nova Scotia and New Brunswick, there shall be an officer, styled the Lieutenant-Governor, to be appointed by the Governor-General in Council, under the great seal of Canada.

64. A Lieutenant-Governor shall hold office during the pleasure of the Governor-General in Council, but any Lieutenant-Governor appointed after the commencement of the first Session of the Parliament of Canada, shall not be removable within five years from his appointment, except for cause assigned, which shall be communicated to him in writing within one month after the order for his removal is made, and shall be communicated by message to each of the Houses of Parliament within one week thereafter, if the Parliament is then sitting, and if not, then within one week after the commencement of the next sitting of the Parliament.

65. The salaries of Lieutenant-Governors shall be fixed and provided by an Act of the Parliament of Canada.

66. In each Province, the Lieutenant-Governor may, by and with the advice and consent of the Legislature, make laws in relation to matters coming within the classes of subjects next hereinafter enumerated :—

(1) The amendment from time to time of their Constitutions except as relates to the office of Lieutenant-Governor:

(2) Direct Taxation within the Province in order to the raising of a revenue for Provincial Purposes, including, in the case of New Brunswick, the levying, by the mode and to the extent (if any) established by Law at the Union, Dues on Timber, not being the produce of any of the Provinces other than New Brunswick:

(3) The borrowing of money on the sole credit of the Province for Provincial Purposes:

(4) The establishment and tenure of Provincial offices, and the appointment and payment of Provincial officers:

(5) The management and sale of the public lands belonging to the Province:

(6) The establishment, maintenance and management of public and reformatory prisons in and for the Province :

(7) The establishment, maintenance and management of hospitals, asylums, charities, and eleemosynary institutions in and for the Province (other than marine hospitals) :

(8) Municipal institutions in the Province:

(9) Shop, saloon, tavern, auctioneer, and other licenses, in order to the raising of a revenue for provincial, local, or municipal purposes:

(10) All works and undertakings:

(11) The incorporation of Companies with exclusively Provincial objects :

(12) The solemnisation of marriage in the Province.

(13) Property and Civil Rights.

(14) The administration of justice in the Province, including the constitution, maintenance, and organisation of Provincial Courts, both of Civil and Criminal Jurisdiction, and including procedure in Civil matters in those Courts.

(15) The imposition of punishment by fine, penalty, or imprisonment for enforcing any Provincial Law made in relation to any matter coming within any of the classes of subjects enumerated in this section.

67. In each Province the Lieutenant-Governor may, by and with the consent of the Legislative Assembly, make laws in relation to Education in the Province, subject and according to the following provisions :—

(1) Nothing in any such law shall prejudicially affect any right or privilege with respect to Denominational Schools which any class of persons have by Law in the Province at the Union.

(2) All the powers, privileges, and duties at the Union by Law conferred and imposed in Upper Canada on the separate Schools and School Trustees of The Queen's Roman Catholic subjects, shall be extended to the Dissentient Schools of The Queen's Protestant and Roman Catholic subjects in Lower Canada.

(3) Where in any Province a system of separate or Dissentient Schools by Law obtains or is hereafter established by the Legislature thereof, an appeal shall lie to the Governor-General in Council from any Act or decision of any Provincial authority affecting any right or privilege of the Protestant or Catholic minority in relation to Education.

(4) In case any such Provincial Law as from time to time seems to the Governor-General in Council requisite for the due execution of the provisions of this section is not made, or in case any decision of the Governor-General in Council on any appeal under this section is not duly executed by the proper Provincial Authority in that behalf, then and in every such case, and as far only as the circumstances of each case require, the Parliament of Canada shall have power to make remedial Laws for the due execution of the provisions of this section and of any such decision of the Governor-General in Council.

68. From and after the Union, such portions of the duties and revenues, over which the respective Legislatures of the said Provinces, before the time of the proving of this Act, had powers of appropriation, which are by this Act reserved to the Local Governments or Legislatures ; and all duties and revenues by them hereafter raised in accordance with the special powers conferred upon them by this Act, shall form in each Province one Consolidated Revenue Fund to be appropriated for the public service of the said Province.

Nova Scotia.

69. There shall be two chambers as at present styled respectively, the Legislative Council and the House of Assembly.

70. The Legislative Council shall consist of

71. The Legislative Assembly shall consist of

NEW BRUNSWICK.

72. There shall be two chambers as at present styled respectively, the Legislative Council and the House of Assembly.

73. The Legislative Council shall consist of

74. The Legislative Assembly shall consist of

LEGISLATURE OF ONTARIO.

75. There shall be one Chamber, to be styled

QUEBEC.

76. There shall be two chambers as at present styled respectively, the Legislative Council and the House of Assembly.

77. The Legislative Council shall consist of

78. The Legislative Assembly shall consist of

MISCELLANEOUS.

79. Any Act of the Parliament of Canada may, notwithstanding anything in this Act, from time to time, provide for the constitution, maintenance, and organisation of a General Court of Appeal, and of such Courts as may be deemed necessary by the Parliament of Canada.

80. Notwithstanding anything in this Act, any Act of the Parliament of Canada may from time to time make provision in relation to :—

(1) Agriculture in all or any of the Provinces.

(2) Immigration into all or any of the Provinces.

(3) All works and undertakings.

And in each Province provincial laws may make provision in relation to :—

(1) Agriculture in the Provinces.

(2) Immigration into the Provinces.

(3) All works and undertakings in the Province :

But any such Provincial Law shall have the force of law in and for the Province as long and so far only as it is not repugnant to any Act of the Parliament of Canada.

81. Either the English or the French language may be used by any person in the debates of the Houses of Parliament of Canada, and of the Houses of Parliament of Lower Canada, and both of these languages shall be used in the respective records

and journals of those Houses, and either of those languages may be used by any person or in any pleading or process in or issuing from any Court of Canada, and in or from all or any of the Provincial Courts of Lower Canada.

82. It shall be lawful for the Queen at any time hereafter to admit into the Union all or any of the Colonies of Newfoundland, Prince Edward Island, or the North-Western Territory or British Columbia, on such terms and conditions as the Parliament of Canada shall deem equitable, and as shall receive the assent of Her Majesty ; and in the case of Newfoundland, Prince Edward Island and British Columbia as shall be agreed upon by their respective Legislatures : and in the event of the admission of Newfoundland and Prince Edward Island, or either of them, each shall be entitled to a representation in the Senate of Canada of four Members, but after the admission of Prince Edward Island into the Confederation, the representation of Nova Scotia and New Brunswick in the Senate of Canada shall upon any reduction by death or otherwise to the number of Ten Members from each or either of those Provinces not be replaced beyond that number, except as hereinbefore provided ; and it shall be lawful for The Queen at any time hereafter to declare by proclamation, that any or either of the Colonies of Newfoundland, Prince Edward Island, the North-Western Territory or British Columbia, upon, from, and after a certain day in such proclamation to be appointed shall so form a portion of the Kingdom of Canada, and henceforth such Colony as the case may be, shall be and become a portion of the Kingdom, upon, from, and after the day so appointed as aforesaid, and upon such terms and conditions as may be therein expressed.

INTERCOLONIAL RAILWAY.

83. And whereas the construction of a railway from the river St. Lawrence to the city of Halifax, in the Province of Nova Scotia, is necessary ;

And whereas it has been agreed between the Provinces that such railway shall be constructed with all convenient speed.

Be it enacted, that the General Government shall within months after the Union commence such railway, and within months thereafter complete the same.

FOURTH DRAFT (OF CONFERENCE).

A

BILL

To provide for the Union and Government of British North America.

WHEREAS the Provinces of CANADA, NOVA SCOTIA and NEW BRUNSWICK have expressed their desire to form a Federal Union under the British Crown, for the purposes of Government and Legislation, based upon the principles of the British Constitution.

BE IT THEREFORE ENACTED BY THE QUEEN'S MOST EXCELLENT MAJESTY, by and with the advice and consent of the Lords Spiritual and Temporal, and Commons in this present Parliament assembled, and by the authority of the same as follows :—

PRELIMINARY.

1. This Act may be cited as " The British North American Act, 1867."

INTERPRETATION.

2. In the construction of this Act the following rules shall be observed with respect to the following terms, unless otherwise expressly provided for, or such construction would be inconsistent with the manifest intention of the Act, or repugnant to the context—that is to say :—

The words " The Queen," shall mean Her Majesty, her Heirs, and Successors, Sovereigns of the United Kingdom of Great Britain and Ireland.

The words " from and after the Union," shall mean from and after the day on which the proclamation, declaring the Union of the Provinces, shall take effect.

The word " Parliament " shall mean the Legislature or Parliament of the Kingdom of Canada.

The word "Legislature" shall mean the Local Legislature of any of the Provinces of the Union.

The word "Union," shall mean the Union of the Provinces of Canada, Nova Scotia, and New Brunswick.

The words "Governor-General," shall mean the Chief Executive Officer or Administrator for the time being of the Government appointed by the Queen, by whatever name designated.

The words "Governor-General in Council," shall mean the Chief Executive Officer or Administrator, Governor or person administering for the time being the Government of Canada, acting by and with the advice of the Privy Council thereof.

The words "Lieutenant-Governor," shall mean the Chief Executive Officer or Administrator for the time being of the Government of any Province in the Union.

The words "Lieutenant-Governor in Council," shall mean the Lieutenant-Governor or Administrator for the time being of the Government of either of the Provinces of Ontario, Quebec, Nova Scotia, or New Brunswick, acting by and with the advice of the Executive Council thereof.

The word "Kingdom" shall mean and comprehend the United Provinces of Ontario, Quebec, Nova Scotia, and New Brunswick.

The words "Privy Council" shall mean such persons as may from time to time be appointed, by the Governor-General, and sworn to aid and advise in the Government of the Kingdom.

The word "Canada" (when not applied to the Province of Canada) shall mean the Kingdom of Canada hereby constituted.

The words "Upper Canada" shall mean all that part of the Province of Canada which formerly constituted the Province of Upper Canada.

The words "Lower Canada" shall mean all that part of the Province of Canada which formerly constituted the Province of Lower Canada.

The word "Ontario" shall mean the Province of Ontario hereby constituted, and the said Province shall be held to have the same boundaries as that part of the late Province of Canada known as Upper Canada prior to and at the time of the passing of this Act.

The word "Quebec" shall mean the Province of Quebec hereby constituted, and the said Province shall be held to have the same boundaries as that part of the late Province of Canada known as Lower Canada prior to and at the time of the passing of this Act.

The words "Nova Scotia" shall mean the Province of Nova Scotia, and the said Province shall be held to have the same boundaries as existing prior to and at the time of the passing of this Act.

The words "New Brunswick" shall mean the Province of New Brunswick, and the said Province shall be held to have the same boundaries as existing prior to and at the time of the passing of this Act.

The word "month" shall mean a calendar month.

Words importing the singular number or the masculine gender only, shall include more persons, parties, or things of the same kind than one, and females as well as males, and the converse.

The word "oath" shall be construed as meaning a solemn affirmation whenever the context applies to any person and case by whom and in which a solemn affirmation may be made instead of an oath ; and in every case where an oath or affirmation is directed to be made before any person or officer, such person or officer shall have full power and authority to administer the same and to certify its having been made ; and the wilful making of any false statement in any such oath or affirmation shall be wilful and corrupt perjury ; and the wilful making of any false statement in any declaration required or authorized by any such act as aforesaid, shall be a misdemeanour punishable as wilful and corrupt perjury.

REPEALING CLAUSE.

3. From and after the Union, all Acts and parts of Acts passed by the Parliament of Great Britain, the Parliament of the United Kingdom of Great Britain and Ireland, the Legislature of Upper Canada, the Legislature of Lower Canada, the Legislature of Canada, the Legislature of Nova Scotia, or the Legislature of New Brunswick, which are repugnant to or inconsistent with the provisions of this Act shall be and the same are hereby repealed : Provided always that the repeal of the said several Acts of Parliament and parts of Acts of Parliament shall not be

held to revive or give any force or effect to any enactment which has, by the said Acts or any of them, been repealed or determined, nor shall the repeal of the said Acts and parts of Acts affect—

1. Any penalty, forfeiture, or liability, civil or criminal, incurred before the time of such repeal, or any proceedings for enforcing the same, had, done, completed or pending at the time of such repeal.

2. Nor any indictment, information, conviction, sentence, or prosecution had, done, completed, or pending at the time of such repeal.

3. Nor any action, suit, judgment, decree, certificate, execution, process, order, rule, or any proceeding, matter or thing whatever respecting the same, had, done, made, entered, granted, completed, pending, existing, or in force at the time of such repeal.

4. Nor any act, deed, right, title, interest, grant, assurance, descent, will, registry, contract, lien, charge, matter, or thing, had, done, made, acquired, established or existing at the time of such repeal.

5. Nor any office, appointment, commission, salary, allowance, security, duty, or any matter or thing appertaining thereto, at the time of such repeal.

6. Nor any marriage certificate or registry thereof, lawfully had, made, granted, or existing before or at the time of such repeal.

7. Nor shall such repeal defeat, disturb, invalidate, or prejudicially affect any other matter or thing whatsoever had, done, completed, existing or pending at the time of such repeal.

8. But every

Such penalty, forfeiture, and liability, and every such

Indictment, information, conviction, sentence, and prosecution, and every such

Action, suit, judgment, decree, certificate, execution, process, order, rule, proceeding, matter, or thing, and every such

Act, deed, right, title, interest, grant, assurance, descent, will, registry, contract, lien, charge, matter or thing, and every such

Office, appointment, commission, salary, allowance, security, and duty, and every such

Marriage certificate and registry, and every such other matter and thing, and the force and effect thereof respectively, may and shall, both at law and in equity, remain and continue as if no such repeal had taken place, and, so far as necessary, may and shall be continued, prosecuted, enforced, and proceeded with under the said Laws, so far as applicable thereto.

UNION.

4. It shall be lawful for The Queen to declare by Proclamation that the said Provinces of Canada, Nova Scotia, and New Brunswick, upon, from, and after a certain day in such proclamation to be appointed, which day shall be within six months next after the passing of this Act, shall form and be one united dominion under the name of the Kingdom of Canada, and thenceforth the said Provinces shall constitute and be One Kingdom under the Name aforesaid, upon, from, and after the day so appointed as aforesaid.

5. The seat of Government of Canada shall be the City of Ottawa, subject to the Royal Prerogative.

6. From and after the Union, Upper Canada and Lower Canada shall be severed, and each shall form a separate Province.

7. From and after the Union, Upper Canada shall be named and known as the Province of Ontario, and Lower Canada shall be named and known as the Province of Quebec.

8. Subject to any future action of the Governments of the Provinces respectively, the seats of Government shall be as follows :—

In Ontario, the City of Toronto ; in Quebec, the City of Quebec ; in Nova Scotia, the City of Halifax ; and in New Brunswick, the City of Fredericton.

THE EXECUTIVE POWER.

9. The Executive Government and authority is and shall be vested in the Queen.

10. The Queen has and shall have the Command-in-Chief of the Land and Naval Militia, and of all Naval and Military Forces whatsoever.

11. The Governor-General may, by instrument under the Great Seal of Canada, constitute a Privy Council, and he may from time to time appoint and remove Members thereof.

12. All powers, authorities and functions which by any Act of the Parliament of Great Britain, or of the Parliament of the United Kingdom of Great Britain and Ireland, or by any Act of the Legislature of Upper Canada, Lower Canada, Canada, Nova Scotia, or New Brunswick respectively, are vested in, or are authorised or required to be exercised by the respective Governors or Lieutenant-Governors of the said Provinces, with the advice, or with the advice and consent, of the Executive Council of such Provinces respectively, or in conjunction with such Executive Council, or with any number of the Members thereof, or by the said Governors or Lieutenant-Governors individually and alone, shall, in so far as the same are not repugnant to or inconsistent with the provisions of this Act, be vested in and may be exercised by the Governor-General of the Kingdom of Canada, with the advice, or with the advice and consent of, or in conjunction, as the case may require, with the Privy Council, or any Members thereof, as may be appointed by the Queen for the affairs of the Kingdom of Canada, or by the Governor-General of the Kingdom of Canada individually and alone, where the advice, consent, or concurrence of the Privy Council is not required.

13. The Governor-General may assign, depute, substitute, and appoint any person or persons jointly or severally, to be his deputy or deputies within any part or parts of Canada, and in that capacity to exercise, perform and execute during the pleasure of the said Governor-General such of the powers, functions and authorities as may under this Act be vested in or exercised by the Governor-General as the Governor-General shall deem to be necessary or expedient, but the appointment of a Deputy or Deputies as aforesaid shall not abridge, alter, or in any way affect the power or authority of the Governor-General.

THE LEGISLATIVE POWER.

14. From and after the Union, there shall be in and for the Kingdom of Canada one Parliament, which shall be composed of the Queen, an Upper House to be called the Senate, and a House of Commons.

SENATE.

15. For the purpose of forming the Senate the Kingdom of Canada shall be considered as consisting of three Divisions :—

  (1) Ontario.

  (2) Quebec.

(3) The Maritime Provinces of Nova Scotia and New Brunswick :

And each Division shall have an equal representation in the
Senate.

16. Ontario shall be represented in the Senate by twenty-four
Members, Quebec by twenty-four Members, and the Maritime Provinces by twenty-four Members, of which Nova Scotia shall have
twelve Members, and New Brunswick twelve Members.

17. For the purpose of composing the Senate, it shall be lawful for the Governor-General, before the time to be appointed for
the first meeting of Parliament, by an instrument or instruments
under the Great Seal of Canada, to summon to the Senate such
persons as The Queen may think fit, subject to the provisions of
this Act : and it shall also be lawful for the Governor-General
in like manner to summon to the Senate such other person or persons as The Queen shall think fit, subject to the provisions of
this Act, and every person who shall be so summoned shall thereby become a Senator.

18. The Senators shall each be of the full age of thirty years,
shall each be a natural born subject of the Queen, or her subject
naturalised by Act of the Parliament of the United Kingdom
of Great Britain and Ireland, or by an Act of any or either or one
of the Legislatures of the Provinces of Canada, Upper Canada,
Lower Canada, Nova Scotia, or New Brunswick, or by an Act of
the Parliament of Canada hereby created, and shall each be legally or equitably seised or entitled as of freehold for his own use
and benefit of lands or tenements held in free and common socage, or seised and possessed for his own use and benefit of lands
or tenements held in franc-alleu or roture, in the Province for
which he shall be appointed, of the value of four thousand dollars
over and above all debts, charges, dues, and incumbrances thereon, and shall each be and continue to be worth the sum last aforesaid over and above his debts and liabilities ; and shall each also
possess a continuous residence in the Province for which he is
appointed, except during the time that he shall hold an office
under the Government, the duties of which shall require his
continuous attendance at the seat of Government of Canada.

19. In the case of Quebec, each of the twenty-four Senators
representing such Province shall be appointed to represent one
of the twenty-four Electoral Divisions of Lower Canada mention-

ed in Schedule A of Chapter First of the Consolidated Statutes of Canada, and such Senator shall reside or possess his qualification in the Electoral Division he is appointed to represent.

20. On the application of the Government of Canada, Her Majesty in Council may from time to time sanction an appointment of additional Senators, so as that the whole number shall in no case exceed seventy-eight, the proportion allotted to each of the three divisions being preserved. In case of vacancies after any such increase above seventy-two ; no appointment shall be made without the sanction of the British Government till the whole number is reduced below seventy-two.

21. Whenever after the first appointment a vacancy in the Senate shall take place, it shall be lawful for the Governor-General, in the Queen's Name, by an instrument under the Great Seal of Canada, to summon to the said Senate a person duly qualified according to the provisions of this Act to fill such vacancy.

22. Every Senator shall hold his seat in the Senate for the term of his life, subject to the provisions of this Act.

23. If any Senator shall, for two successive Sessions of Parliament, fail to give his attendance in the Senate, or if he shall take any oath or make any declaration or acknowledgment of allegiance, obedience, or otherwise, to any Foreign Prince or Power, or shall do, concur in, or adopt any act whereby he may become a subject or a citizen of any foreign state or power, or whereby he may become entitled to the rights, privileges, or immunities of a subject or citizen of any Foreign State or Power, or shall cease to have any of the qualifications required by this Act, or shall become bankrupt or take the benefit of any Act relating to insolvent debtors, or become a defaulter, or be attainted of treason, or be convicted of felony or of any infamous crime, his seat in the Senate shall thereby become vacant.

24. Every Senator shall, before taking his seat, make and subscribe before the Governor-General or some person or persons authorized by him to administer the same, the oath of Allegiance to the Queen and the declaration respectively set forth in Schedule A.

25. Any person who at the time of the Union is a Member of the Legislative Council of Nova Scotia, or of New Brunswick, and who may accept the office of Senator, shall, by his acceptance, be held to have vacated his seat in such Legislative Council ; and

any person who at the time of the Union is a Member of the Legislative Council of Canada, Nova Scotia or New Brunswick, and to whom the office of Senator is offered, who shall not within thirty days thereafter signify his acceptance thereof, the same shall be held to have declined such office.

26. Any Senator may, by writing under his hand, addressed to the Governor-General, resign his seat in the Senate, and thereupon such seat shall become vacant.

27. If any question respecting the qualification of a Senator or respecting a vacancy in the Senate shall arise, the same shall be heard and determined by the Senate.

28. The Governor-General shall have power, by an instrument under the Great Seal of Canada, to appoint one Member of the Senate to be Speaker thereof, and to remove him and appoint another in his stead.

29. Subject to alteration by Parliament, the presence of at least fifteen Members of the Senate, including the Speaker, shall be necessary to constitute a Meeting for the exercise of its powers.

30. The Speaker shall vote as other Members, and in case of an equality of votes, it shall be held that the decision is in the negative.

House of Commons.

31. The House of Commons shall consist of one hundred and eighty-one Members, of whom eighty-two shall be elected for Ontario, sixty-five for Quebec, nineteen for Nova Scotia, and fifteen for New Brunswick.

32. Until otherwise provided by Parliament, Ontario, Quebec, Nova Scotia, and New Brunswick, shall for the purposes of the Election of Members in the House of Commons, be and the same are hereby respectively divided into Electoral Districts as follows :—

1. Ontario.

For the purpose of representation in Parliament, Ontario shall be territorially divided into the Counties, Ridings of Counties, Cities, and Towns hereinafter mentioned, which shall form

Electoral Districts, and each such Electoral District, as hereinafter numbered, shall be represented by one Member in the House
of Commons.*

2. QUEBEC.

Quebec shall be divided into sixty-five Electoral Districts, to
be composed of the sixty-five Electoral Divisions into which
Lower Canada is now divided, under Chapter 2 of the Consolidated Statutes of Canada, chapter 75 of the Consolidated
Statutes for Lower Canada, and the Act of the Province of
Canada 23 Victoria, Chapter 1, or of any other Act amending the
same in force at the time of the Union : and each such Electoral
Division is hereby constituted an Electoral District for the purposes of this Act, and shall be entitled to return one Member to
the House of Commons.

3. NOVA SCOTIA.

Each of the eighteen counties of Nova Scotia shall constitute
an Electoral District. The County of Halifax shall be entitled
to return two Members to the House of Commons, and each of
the other Counties one Member.

4. NEW BRUNSWICK.

New Brunswick shall be divided into fifteen Electoral Districts (of which the City of Saint John shall be one, and entitled
to return one Member), and each of the fourteen Counties into
which New Brunswick is divided, shall constitute an Electoral
District, and shall be entitled to return one Member to the House
of Commons.

33. There shall be a General Census of the people taken in
the year One thousand eight hundred and seventy-one, and decennially afterwards ; and immediately after the said Census, and
immediately after every decennial census thereafter, the representation from each Province in the House of Commons shall be
re-adjusted by such authority, and in such manner, as any Act of
Parliament from time to time directs, according to the following
rules :—

    (1) Quebec shall have the fixed Number of Sixty-five Mem-
        bers :

* Here follows the first Schedule of the B. N. A. Act.

(2) There shall be assigned to each of the other Provinces such a Number of Members as shall bear the same Proportion to the Number of its Population (ascertained at such Census) as the Number Sixty-five bears to the Number of the Population of Quebec (so ascertained).

(3) In the computation of the Number of Members for a Province a fractional part less than one-half of the whole number requisite for entitling the Province to a Member shall be disregarded ; but a fractional part exceeding one-half of that number shall be equivalent to the whole number.

(4) On any such Re-adjustment the Number of Members for a Province shall not be reduced unless the Proportion which the number of the Population of the Province bore to the Number of the aggregate Population of Canada at the then last preceding Re-adjustment of the Number of Members for the Province is ascertained at the then latest Census to be diminished by One Twentieth Part or upwards.

(5) Such Re-adjustment shall not take effect until after the termination of the then existing Parliament.

34. The Number of Members may be from time to time increased by Parliament provided the proportionate representation of the several Provinces prescribed by this Act is not thereby disturbed.

35. Every House of Commons shall continue for Five Years from the Day of the Return of the Writs for choosing the same and no longer, (subject to be sooner prorogued or dissolved by the Governor-General).

36. Until other provisions are made by Parliament, all the laws which at the time of the Union are in force in the Provinces respectively relating to the qualification and disqualification of persons to be elected, or to sit or vote as Members of the House of Assembly or Legislative Assembly in the respective Provinces, relating to the qualification or disqualification of voters, or to the oaths to be taken by voters, or to Returning Officers, and their powers and duties, or relating to the proceedings at elections, or to the period during which such elections may be continued, or relating to the trial of controverted elections, and the proceed-

ings incident thereto, or relating to the vacating of seats of Members, or to the execution of new writs in case of any seat being vacated otherwise than by a dissolution, shall respectively apply to Elections of Members to serve in the House of Commons.

37. Every Member of the House of Commons shall, before taking his seat, make and subscribe before the Governor-General, or some person authorized by him to administer the same, the oath of Allegiance to the Queen set forth in Schedule A.

38. The Governor-General shall, within six months from and after the Union, cause writs to be issued in such form and by such person, and to such Returning Officers as he may prescribe for the first election of Members to serve in the House of Commons, and such person shall have all such and the same powers as are possessed by the Officers, at the time of the passing of this Act, charged with the issue of writs for the election of Members to serve in the House of Assembly, or Legislative Assembly of each of the Provinces of Canada, Nova Scotia, or New Brunswick, or of Returning Officers (as the case may be), and in case any vacancy in the representation of an Electoral District shall occur in the House of Commons before the meeting of Parliament, or after the meeting of Parliament, and before provision is made by Parliament in such respect, a writ in respect of such vacant Electoral District may be issued in like manner, and the Governor shall, within six months after the Union, and thereafter from time to time, as occasion shall require, in The Queen's name, and by an instrument or instruments under the Great Seal, summon and call together a House of Commons.

39. The House of Commons shall, upon its first assembling, after every general election, proceed forthwith to elect one of its number to be Speaker, and in case of his death, resignation, or removal by a vote, the said House of Commons shall forthwith proceed to elect another of their Members to be Speaker ; and the Speaker so elected shall preside at all Meetings of the Commons. And until otherwise provided by Act of Parliament, in case of the absence from the Chair of the House from any cause of the Speaker of the House of Commons for a period of forty-eight consecutive hours, the House of Commons may elect one of its number to act as Speaker, and such one so appointed shall, during the continued absence of the Speaker, preside at all Meetings of the Commons, and for the time being execute all the powers and privileges of the Speaker.

40. Except for the purposes of the previous section, the presence of at least twenty Members of the House of Commons, including the Speaker, shall be necessary to constitute a Meeting of the House of Commons for the exercise of its powers, and all questions which shall arise in the Commons shall be decided by the majority of voices of such Members as shall be present, other than the Speaker ; and when the voices shall be equal the Speaker shall have the casting vote.

41. No Senator shall be capable of being elected, or of sitting or voting as a Member of the House of Commons.

Money.

42. Bills for appropriating any part of the Public Revenue of Canada or for imposing any Tax or Impost shall originate in the House of Commons.

43. It shall not be lawful for the House of Commons to originate or pass any vote, resolution, address, or bill for the appropriation of any part of the Public Revenue, or of any Tax or Impost, to any purpose that has not been first recommended to that House by message of the Governor-General in the Session in which such vote, resolution, address, or bill is proposed.

Royal Assent, &c.

44. Where a bill passed by the Houses of Parliament is presented to the Governor-General for The Queen's assent, he shall declare according to his discretion, but subject to the provisions of this Act and to Her Majesty's instructions, either that he assents thereto in The Queen's name, or that he withholds The Queen's assent, or that he reserves the Bill for the signification of The Queen's pleasure.

45. Where the Governor-General assents to a Bill in the Queen's name, he shall by the first convenient opportunity send an authentic copy of the Act to one of The Queen's principal Secretaries of State, and if the Queen in Council within two years after receipt thereof by the Secretary of State thinks fit to disallow the Act, such disallowance (with a certificate of the Secretary of State on the day on which the Act was received by him) being signified by the Governor-General, by speech or message to the Houses of Parliament, or by proclamation, shall annul the Act from and after the day of such signification.

46. A bill reserved for the signification of The Queen's pleasure shall not have any force unless and until within two years from the day on which it was presented to the Governor-General for the Queen's assent, the Governor-General signifies, by speech or message to each of the Houses of Parliament or by proclamation, that it has received the assent of The Queen in Council ; an entry of every such speech, message, or proclamation shall be made in the Journal of each House, and a duplicate thereof duly attested shall be delivered to the proper officer to be kept among the records of Canada.

ANNUAL SESSION.

47. There shall be a Session of Parliament once at least in every year, so that a period of twelve months shall not intervene between the last sitting of the Parliament in one Session, and the first sitting thereof in the next Session.

POWERS OF PARLIAMENT.

48. It shall be lawful for the Queen, by and with the advice and consent of the Senate and House of Commons to make laws for the peace, order, and good government of the Kingdom of Canada, in relation to all matters not coming within the classes of subjects by this Act assigned exclusively to the Legislatures ; and for greater certainty, but not so as to restrict the generality of the foregoing terms of this Section, it is hereby declared that the Legislative Authority of Parliament extends to all matters coming within the classes of subjects next hereinafter enumerated, that is to say :—

1. The Public Debt and Property.
2. The regulation of Trade and Commerce.
3. The raising of money by all or any mode or system of Taxation.
4. The borrowing of money on the Public Credit.
5. Postal Service.
6. Lines of Steamships or other Ships, Railways, Canals, and other works connecting any two or more of the Provinces together, or extending beyond the limits of any Province.
7. Lines of Steamships or other Ships between Canada and other countries.

8. Telegraphic Communication and the incorporation of Telegraph Companies.

9. All such works as shall, although lying wholly within any Province, be specially declared by the Acts authorizing them to be for the general advantage.

10. The Census and Statistics.

11. Militia—Military and Naval Service and Defence.

12. Beacons, Buoys, Light Houses, and Sable Island.

13. Navigation and Shipping.

14. Quarantine and the Establishment and Maintenance of Marine Hospitals.

15. Sea Coast and Inland Fisheries.

16. Ferries between any Province and a Foreign Country, or between any two Provinces.

17. Currency and Coinage.

18. Banking—Incorporation of Banks and the issue of paper money.

19. Savings Banks.

20. Weights and Measures.

21. Bills of Exchange and Promissory Notes.

22. Interest.

23. Legal Tender.

24. Bankruptcy and Insolvency.

25. Patents of Invention and Discovery.

26. Copy Rights.

27. Indians and Lands reserved for the Indians.

28. Naturalization and Aliens.

29. Marriage and Divorce.

30. Immigration.

31. Agriculture.

32. The Criminal Law, excepting the Constitution of Courts of Criminal Jurisdiction but including the procedure in Criminal matters.

33. The establishment, maintenance, and management of Penitentiaries.

34. Rendering uniform all or any of the laws relative to property and civil rights in Ontario, Nova Scotia, and New Brunswick, and rendering uniform the procedure of all or any of the Courts in these Provinces ; but any Statute for this purpose shall have no force or authority in any Province until sanctioned by the

Legislature. and when so sanctioned the power of amending. altering, or repealing such laws shall thenceforward be vested in the Parliament only.

35. The establishment of a General Court of Appeal, and in order to the due execution of the Laws of Parliament, the establishment of additional Courts.

36. Fixing and providing for the salaries and allowances of the Lieutenant Governors of the several Provinces, and of all other Officers of Canada, and the salaries, allowances and pensions of the Judges of the Superior, District and County Courts, and of the Admiralty Courts, in cases where the Judges thereof are or shall be paid by salaries.

37. And such laws shall control and supersede any laws in any wise repugnant thereto which may have been made prior thereto ; and any law made by any Legislature in pursuance of the authority hereby conferred upon it in regard to matters and subjects in which concurrent jurisdiction is hereby given to Parliament shall, so far as the same is repugnant to or inconsistent with any Act passed by Parliament, be null and void.

REVENUES, CIVIL LIST, &c.

49. From and after the Union. all Duties and Revenues over which the respective Legislatures of the said Provinces before and at the time of the passing of this Act had, and have power of Appropriation, except such portions thereof as are by this Act reserved to the Local Governments, or raised by them in accordance with the Special powers conferred upon them by this Act. shall form one Consolidated Revenue Fund, to be appropriated for the Public Service of the Kingdom of Canada, in the manner, and subject to the charges hereinafter mentioned.

50. The said Consolidated Revenue Fund of Canada shall be permanently charged with all the costs, charges, and expenses incident to the collection, management, and receipt thereof, such costs, charges, and expenses being subject, nevertheless, to be reviewed and audited in such manner as shall be ordered by the Governor-General in Council until otherwise provided by any Act of Parliament.

51. Unless altered by any Act of Parliament, the salary of the Governor-General shall be ten thousand pounds sterling money of Great Britain.

52. The expenses of the collection, management, and receipt of the said Consolidated Revenue Fund shall form the first charge thereon : and the annual interest of the public debt of the Provinces of Canada, Nova Scotia, and New Brunswick, or either of them at the time of the Union, shall form the second charge thereon.

53. Subject to the several payments hereby charged on the said Consolidated Revenue Fund the same shall be appropriated by Parliament for the public service.

54. All stocks, cash, bankers' balances, and securities for money belonging to each Province at the time of the Union, except as hereinafter mentioned, shall be the property of Canada, and shall so far be considered as reducing the amount of their respective debts at the time of the Union.

55. The following Public Works and Property of each Province shall be the Property of Canada, to wit :—

1. Canals, with lands and water power connected therewith.
2. Public harbours.
3. Light-houses and piers, and Sable Island.
4. Steamboats, dredges, and public vessels.
5. Rivers and lake improvements.
6. Railways and railway stocks, mortgages and other debts due by railway companies.
7. Military roads.
8. Custom-houses, post offices, and all other public buildings, except as may be set aside by the Government of Canada, for the use of the Local Legislatures and Governments.
9. Property transferred by the Imperial Government, and known as Ordnance property.
10. Armouries, drill sheds, military clothing, and munitions of war, and lands set apart for general public purposes.

56. All lands, mines, minerals, and royalties belonging to the Provinces of Canada, Nova Scotia, and New Brunswick, at the time of the Union, shall belong to the Provinces of Ontario, Que-

bec, Nova Scotia, and New Brunswick, in which the same are so situate, subject to any trusts that may exist in respect to any of such lands or to any interest of other persons in respect of the same.

57. All sums due for such lands, mines, or minerals at the time of the Union, shall also belong to the several Provinces.

58. All assets connected with such portions of the Public Debt of any Province as are assumed by such Provinces, shall also belong to such Provinces.

59. Canada shall, from and after the Union, assume the debts and liabilities of each Province existing at the time of the Union.

60. The Provinces of Ontario and Quebec, conjointly, shall assume any excess by which the debt of the present Province of Canada may exceed, at the time of the Union, $62,500,000, and shall be charged with interest at the rate of five per centum thereon.

61. The assets enumerated in Schedule B of this Act hereunto annexed, belonging at the time of the Union to the Province of Canada, shall be the Property of the Provinces of Ontario and Quebec conjointly.

62. Nova Scotia shall in like manner assume any portion of its present Public Debt in excess of $8,000,000, and—

63. New Brunswick shall in like manner assume any portion of its Public Debt in excess of $7,000,000.

64. The several Provinces shall retain all other public property therein subject to the right of Canada to assume any lands or public property required for fortifications or for the defence of the country.

65. In case Nova Scotia or New Brunswick have not contracted debts at the time of Union equal to the amount with which they are respectively entitled to enter the Union as hereinafter provided, they shall receive by half-yearly payments in advance from the Government of Canada, the interest at five per cent. on the difference between the actual amount of their respective debts and such stipulated amounts.

66. The following sums shall be paid yearly by Canada, to each Province for the support of their Local Governments and Legislatures :—

Ontario	$80,000
Quebec ..	70,000
Nova Scotia ..	60,000
New Brunswick ..	50,000
	$260,000

and an annual grant in aid of each Province shall be made, equal to eighty cents per head of the population, as established by the Census of One thousand eight hundred and sixty-one, and in the case of Nova Scotia and New Brunswick, by each subsequent decennial Census until the population of each of these Provinces shall amount to Four hundred thousand souls, at which rate it shall thereafter remain. Such aid shall be in full settlement of all future demands upon Canada for local purposes, and shall be paid half-yearly in advance to each Province ; but the Government of Canada shall deduct from such subsidy all sums paid as interest on the Public Debt of any Province in excess of the amount provided under the   clauses.

67. New Brunswick shall receive by half-yearly payments in advance from Canada for the period of Ten years from the time of the Union, an additional allowance of Sixty-three thousand dollars per annum. But so long as the Public Debt of that Province remains under Seven millions of dollars, a deduction equal to the interest at five per centum on such deficiency shall be made from the said sum of Sixty-three thousand dollars.

68. All payments to be made under this Act or in discharge of liabilities created under any Act of the Provinces of Canada, Nova Scotia, and New Brunswick respectively, and assumed by Canada from and after the time of the Union, and until otherwise directed by Parliament, shall be made in such form and manner as may from time to time be ordered by the Governor-General in Council.

69. From and after the Union, the Customs and Excise Laws of each Province shall continue to be in force until altered by Parliament ; and in any case where the duties enacted to be collected are the same, it shall be lawful for the Governor-General in Council, by proclamation to be issued from time to time, to declare that such goods, wares, and merchandises may be

imported free into any port in the Kingdom of Canada from any of the Provinces of Ontario, Quebec, Nova Scotia, and New Brunswick, upon proof of having already paid duty, and in cases where any larger duties are enacted in any Province, it shall be lawful for the Governor-General in Council in like manner to authorise the importation of such goods, wares and merchandise on payment of the difference of duty between the said Provinces.

70. All articles, the growth or produce, or manufacture of the Provinces of Ontario, Quebec, Nova Scotia and New Brunswick, shall be admitted free into all Ports in Canada, from and after the Union.

71. No lands or property belonging to Canada or any Province thereof shall be liable to taxation.

LOCAL CONSTITUTIONS.

THE EXECUTIVE.

72. For each of the Provinces of Ontario, Quebec, Nova Scotia, and New Brunswick, there shall be an officer, styled the Lieutenant-Governor, to be appointed by the Governor-General in Council, under the Great Seal of Canada.

73. A Lieutenant-Governor shall hold office during the pleasure of the Governor-General, but any Lieutenant-Governor appointed after the commencement of the first Session of the Parliament of Canada, shall not be removable within five years from his appointment, except for cause assigned, which shall be communicated to him in writing within one month after the order for his removal is made, and shall be communicated by message to each of the Houses of Parliament within one week thereafter, if Parliament is then sitting, and if not, then within one week after the commencement of the next session of Parliament; and in the event of the absence, or illness, or inability from any other cause of the Lieutenant-Governor to discharge the duties of his office, the Governor-General in Council may appoint an Administrator to execute the office and functions of Lieutenant-Governor during such absence, illness or other inability.

74. The Lieutenant-Governor of Quebec may, by a proclamation to be issued by him for that purpose under the Great Seal of the Province, and to take effect from a day to be named

therein, constitute Townships in those parts of the Province of Quebec in which Townships are not already constituted, and may fix the metes and bounds thereof.

THE LEGISLATURES.

1. ONTARIO.

75. There shall be a Legislature for Ontario which shall consist of the Lieutenant-Governor and of one Chamber to be called the Legislative Assembly of Ontario.

76. The Legislative Assembly of Ontario shall be composed of eighty-two Members, to be elected to represent the eighty-two Electoral Districts in Ontario, set forth in section   of this Act.

2. QUEBEC.

77. There shall be a Legislature for Quebec which shall consist of the Lieutenant-Governor and two Houses, to be called the Legislative Council of Quebec and the Legislative Assembly of Quebec.

78. The Legislative Council of Quebec shall be composed of twenty-four Members, to be appointed by the Lieutenant-Governor, under the Great Seal of Quebec, each of whom shall hold office for the term of his life ; but if any Legislative Councillor shall, for two consecutive Sessions of the Legislature, fail to give his attendance in the said Council, or if he shall take any oath or make any declaration or acknowledgment of allegiance, obedience or otherwise, to any foreign Prince or Power, or shall do, concur in, or adopt any act whereby he may become a subject or a citizen of any foreign state or power, or whereby he may become entitled to the rights, privileges, or immunities of a subject or citizen of any foreign State or Power, or shall cease to have any of the qualifications required by this Act, or shall become bankrupt or take the benefit of any Act relating to insolvent debtors, or become a defaulter, or be attainted of treason, or be convicted of felony, or of any infamous crime, his seat in the said Council shall thereby become vacant.

79. The Members of the Legislative Council shall each be of the full age of thirty years, shall each be a natural born subject of the Queen, or her subject naturalised by Act of the Parliament of the United Kingdom of Great Britain and Ireland, or by an Act of any or either or one of the Legislatures of the Provinces of Canada, Upper Canada, Lower Canada, Nova Scotia or New

Brunswick, or by an Act of the Parliament of Canada hereby created, and shall each be legally or equitably seised or entitled as of freehold for his own use and benefit of lands or tenements held in free and common socage, or seised and possessed for his own use and benefit of lands or tenements held in franc-alleu or roture, in Quebec, of the value of four thousand dollars over and above all debts, charges, dues, and incumbrances thereon, and shall each be and continue to be worth the sum last aforesaid over and above his debts and liabilities.

80. Each of the twenty-four Legislative Councillors shall be appointed to represent one of the twenty-four Electoral Divisions of Lower Canada mentioned in Schedule A of Chapter First of the Consolidated Statutes of Canada, and such Legislative Councillor shall reside or possess his qualification in the Electoral Division he is appointed to represent.

81. Whenever after the first appointment a vacancy in the Legislative Council shall take place, it shall be lawful for the Lieutenant-Governor, in the Queen's Name, by an instrument under the Great Seal of Quebec, to summon to the said Legislative Council a person duly qualified according to the provisions of this Act to fill such vacancy.

82. Every Legislative Councillor shall, before taking his seat, make and subscribe, before the Lieutenant-Governor or some person or persons authorised by him to administer the same, the Oath of Allegiance to the Queen, and make the declaration of qualification in Schedule A mentioned.

83. Any Legislative Councillor may, by writing under his hand, addressed to the Lieutenant-Governor, resign his seat in the Legislative Council, and thereupon such seat shall become vacant.

84. If any question respecting the qualification of a Legislative Councillor, or respecting a vacancy in the Legislative Council shall arise, the same shall be heard and determined by the Legislative Council.

85. The Lieutenant-Governor shall have power, by an instrument under the Great Seal of Quebec, to appoint one Member of the Legislative Council to be Speaker thereof, and to remove him and appoint another in his stead.

86. Subject to alteration by the Legislature of Quebec, the presence of at least ten Members of the Legislative Council, in-

cluding the Speaker, shall be necessary to constitute a Meeting for the exercise of its powers.

87. The Speaker shall vote as other Members, and in case of an equality of votes, it shall be held that the decision is in the negative.

88. The Legislative Assembly of Quebec shall be composed of sixty-five Members to be elected to represent the sixty-five Electoral Divisions into which Lower Canada is now divided, under Chapter 2 of the Consolidated Statutes of Canada, Chapter 75 of the Consolidated Statutes for Lower Canada, and the Act of the Province of Canada 23 Victoria, Chapter 1, or of any other Act amending the same in force at the time of the Union : Provided that it shall not be lawful to present to the Lieutenant-Governor for assent any Bill of the Legislative Council and Assembly of Quebec, by which the limits of the Electoral Divisions mentioned in the Schedule hereto annexed, marked E, may be altered, unless the second and third readings of such Bill in the Legislative Assembly shall have been passed with the concurrence of the majority of the Members for the time being of the said Legislative Assembly, representing the Electoral Divisions mentioned in said Schedule marked C, and the assent shall not be given to such Bill unless an Address has been presented by the Legislative Assembly to the Lieutenant-Governor that such Bill has been so passed.

NOVA SCOTIA AND NEW BRUNSWICK.

89. The constitution of each of the Provinces of Nova Scotia and New Brunswick shall, subject to the Provisions of this Act, continue as now established at the time of the Union, until altered or amended under the authority of this Act, and the House of Assembly of New Brunswick shall, unless sooner dissolved, continue for the period for which it was elected.

POWERS OF THE LEGISLATURE.

90. In each Province, the Legislature may make Laws in relation to matters coming within the classes of subjects next hereinafter enumerated :—

   (1) The amendment from time to time of their Constitutions except as relates to the office of Lieutenant-Governor:

(2) Direct taxation within the Province in order to the raising of a revenue for Provincial Purposes, and reserving to New Brunswick the right to collect the Lumber Dues provided in Chapter 15, Title III. of the Revised Statutes of that Province, and any amendment thereof made before or after this Act comes into operation, which does not increase the amount, but excepting therefrom the Lumber of any other Province:

(3) The borrowing of money on the credit of the Province:

(4) The establishment and tenure of Provincial offices, and the appointment and payment of Provincial officers:

(5) The management and sale of the public lands belonging to the Province, and all Timber and Wood grown thereon:

(6) The establishment, maintenance, and management of public and reformatory prisons in and for the Province:

(7) The establishment, maintenance, and management of hospitals, asylums, charities and eleemosynary institutions in and for the Province (other than marine hospitals):

(8) Municipal institutions in the Province:

(9) Shop, saloon, tavern, auctioneer, and other licenses, in order to the raising of a revenue for provincial, local, or municipal purposes:

(10) Works and Undertakings:

(11) The incorporation of Companies.

(12) The solemnisation of marriage.

(13) Property and Civil Rights but excepting such portions thereof hereby assigned to Parliament.

(14) The administration of justice in the Province, including the constitution, maintenance, and organisation of Courts, both of Civil and Criminal Jurisdiction, and including procedure in Civil Matters in those Courts.

(15) The imposition of punishment by fine, penalty, or imprisonment for enforcing any Provincial Law made in relation to any matter coming within any of the classes of subjects enumerated in this section.

(16) And generally all matters of a private or local nature not assigned to Parliament.

91. In each Province the Legislature may make Laws in relation to Education in the Province subject and according to the following provisions:—

(1) Nothing in any such law shall prejudicially affect any right or privilege with respect to Denominational Schools which any class of persons have by Law in the Province at the Union.

(2) All the powers, privileges, and duties by Law conferred and imposed in Upper Canada, at the time of the Union, on the separate Schools and School Trustees of The Queen's Roman Catholic subjects, shall be extended to the Dissentient Schools of The Queen's Protestant and Roman Catholic subjects in Lower Canada.

(3) Where in any Province a system of separate or Dissentient Schools by Law obtains or is hereafter established by the Legislature thereof, an appeal shall lie to the Governor-General in Council from any Act or decision of any Provincial authority affecting any right or privilege of the Protestant or Catholic minority in relation to Education.

(4) In case any such Provincial Law as from time to time seems to the Governor-General in Council requisite for the due execution of the provisions of this section is not made, or in case any decision of the Governor-General in Council on any appeal under this section is not duly executed by the proper Provincial Authority in that behalf, then and in every such case, and as far only as the circumstances of each case require, the Parliament of Canada shall have power to make remedial Laws for the due execution of the provisions of this section and of any such decision of the Governor-General in Council.

REVENUES, &c.

92. From and after the Union, such portions of the duties and revenues, over which the respective Legislatures of the said Provinces, before the period thereof, had power of appropriation,

which are by this Act reserved to the Local Governments or Legislatures; and all duties and revenues by them hereafter raised in accordance with the special powers conferred upon them by this Act, shall form in each Province one Consolidated Revenue Fund to be appropriated for the public service of the said Province.

MISCELLANEOUS SECTIONS RESPECTING ONTARIO AND QUEBEC.

The following sections are applicable to Ontario and Quebec only :—

93. The Lieutenant-Governors of Ontario and Quebec shall respectively, within six months after the Union, and thereafter from time to time, as occasion may require, in the Queen's Name, and by an instrument or instruments under the Great Seal of the Province summon and call together a Legislative Assembly in and for each Province.

94. Every Member of the Legislative Assembly shall, before taking his seat, make and subscribe before the Lieutenant-Governor, or some person authorised by him to administer the same, the oath of allegiance to the Queen set forth in Schedule A.

95. The Legislative Assembly shall, upon its first assembling, after every general election, proceed forthwith to elect one of its number to be Speaker, and in case of his death, resignation, or removal by a vote, the said Legislative Assembly shall forthwith proceed to elect another of their Members to be Speaker: and the Speaker so elected shall preside at all Meetings of the Commons. And until otherwise provided by Act of the Legislature, in case of the absence from the Chair of the House from any cause of the Speaker of the Legislative Assembly for a period of forty-eight consecutive hours, the Legislative Assembly may elect one of its number to act as Speaker, and such one so appointed shall, during the continued absence of the Speaker, preside at all Meetings of the Legislative Assembly, and for the time being execute all the powers and privileges of the Speaker.

96. All powers, authorities, and functions which by any Act passed by the Imperial Parliament, or by any Act passed by the Legislature of the Provinces of Lower and Upper Canada respectively, or by the Legislature of the Province of Canada, were or are vested in or authorised or required to be exercised by the respective Governors or Lieutenant-Governors of Canada, or

of Lower Canada or Upper Canada, with the advice or with the advice and consent of the Executive Council of such Provinces respectively, or in conjunction with such Executive Council, or with any number of the Members thereof, or by the said Governors or Lieutenant-Governors individually and alone shall, in so far as the same are not repugnant to or inconsistent with the provisions of this Act, be vested in and may be exercised by the Lieutenant-Governors of Ontario and Quebec respectively, with the advice or with the advice and consent of or in conjunction, as the case may require, with such Executive Council, or any Members thereof as may be appointed for the affairs of Ontario and Quebec, or by the Lieutenant-Governor of Ontario or Quebec respectively, individually and alone, in cases where the advice, consent, or concurrence of the Executive Council is not required.

97. The Lieutenant-Governors of Ontario and Quebec may each appoint, under the Great Seal of the Province, and to hold office during pleasure, the following officers, that is to say :— The Attorney-General, the Secretary, and Registrar of the Province, the Treasurer of the Province, the Commissioner of Crown Lands, and the Commissioner of Agriculture and and Public Works (and for Quebec the Solicitor-General), and may, by and under Order in Council from time to time, prescribe the duties of such officers and of the several departments over which they shall preside, or to which they shall belong, and of the officers and clerks thereof ; and may also appoint other and additional officers to hold office during pleasure, and may from time to time prescribe the duties of such officers, and of the several departments over which they shall preside, or to which they shall belong, and of the officers and clerks thereof ; and all rights, powers, duties, functions, responsibilities, or authorities now vested or imposed in or upon any Attorney-General, Secretary, and Registrar of the Province of Canada, Minister of Finance, Commissioner of Crown Lands, Commissioner of Public Works, and Minister of Agriculture, by any Law, Statute, or Ordinance of the former Provinces of Lower Canada and Upper Canada, or of the Province of Canada, and not repugnant to this Act shall be vested in or imposed upon any officer to be appointed by the Lieutenant-Governor for the discharge of the same or any of them, unless and until, and in such case in so far only as such rights, powers, duties, or authorities be varied, altered, amended, or repealed by the Legislature of

the Province, and the Commissioner of Agriculture and Public Works shall, until it is otherwise ordered by the Legislature, combine and perform the duties and functions of the office of Minister of Agriculture as now imposed by the law of the Province of Canada, as well as those of the Commissioner of Public Works.

98. The Executive Councils of Ontario and Quebec may each be composed of the Attorney-General, the Secretary and Registrar of the Province, the Treasurer of the Province, the Commissioner of Crown Lands and the Commissioner of Agriculture and Public Works, and in Quebec, of the Speaker of the Legislative Council and of the Solicitor-General, and of any other persons who may at any time, or from time to time be appointed to the office of Executive Councillor by instrument under the Great Seal, and to hold office during pleasure.

99. Until altered by the Lieutenant-Governor in Council the Great Seal of Ontario and Quebec respectively shall be the same, or of the same design, in each of the said Provinces, as that used in the Provinces of Upper Canada and Lower Canada, prior to their Union as the Province of Canada.

100. No person accepting or holding any office, commission, or employment, permanent or temporary, at the nomination of the Crown, in either of the Provinces of Ontario or Quebec to which an annual salary, or any fee, allowance, emolument or profit of any kind or amount whatever from the Crown is attached, shall be eligible as a Member of the Legislative Assembly of either Province, nor shall he sit or vote as such : but nothing in this section shall render ineligible as aforesaid any person being a Member of the Executive Council of either of the said Provinces, or holding any of the following offices, that is to say, of Attorney-General, Secretary and Registrar of the Province, Treasurer of the Province, Commissioner of Crown Lands, and the Commissioner of Agriculture and Public Works, and for Quebec, the Solicitor-General, or shall disqualify him to sit or vote in the House for which he is elected, provided he be elected while holding such office and not otherwise disqualified.

101. All laws, statutes, and ordinances of the former Provinces of Lower and Upper Canada, or of the Province of Canada, now in force in the Province of Canada in respect to public lands, or to timber or public lands, and the sale and management thereof respectively, and to public works,

and to the Bureau of Agriculture and Agricultural Societies, shall so far as they are not repugnant to this Act, be and continue in force, and applicable to the Provinces of Ontario and Quebec respectively, unless and until and in such case in so far only as such laws, statutes, and ordinances be varied, altered, amended, or repealed by the Legislature of the Province.

102. Until other provisions are made by the Legislature of Ontario and Quebec respectively, changing the same in either of the said Provinces, all the laws which at the time of the Union shall be in force in each of the said Provinces respectively, relating to the qualification and disqualification of any person to be elected or to sit or vote as a Member of the Assembly of the Province of Canada, and relating to the qualification or disqualification of voters and to the oaths to be taken by voters and to Returning Officers and their powers and duties, and relating to the proceedings at elections and to the period during which such elections may be continued, and relating to the trial of controverted elections and the proceedings incident thereto, and relating to the vacating of the seats of Members and to the issuing and execution of new writs in case of any seat being vacated otherwise than by a dissolution, shall respectively apply to elections of Members to serve in the said Legislative Assembly of Ontario, and in the said the Legislative Assembly of Quebec : Provided that at the first Election for a Member of the Legislative Assembly for the District of Algoma, all persons otherwise qualified except in respect to real property, who are householders, shall have the right to vote at the said Election.

103. The Legislative Assembly of Ontario and the Legislative Assembly of Quebec respectively, shall continue for four years from the day of the return of the writs for choosing the same and no longer, subject nevertheless to either the Legislative Assembly of Ontario, or the Legislative Assembly of Quebec, being sooner prorogued or dissolved by the Lieutenant-Governor of either of the said Provinces respectively ; and except for the purpose of Election of a Speaker the presence of at least twenty Members of the Legislative Assembly, including the Speaker, shall be necessary to constitute a Meeting of the said Legislative Assembly for the exercise of its powers ; and all questions which shall arise in the said Assembly shall be decided by the majority

of voices of such Members as shall be present, other than the Speaker, and when the voices shall be equal, the speaker shall have the casting voice.

104. There shall be a session of the Legislature of each of the said Provinces once at least every year, so that a period of twelve months shall not intervene between the last sitting of the Legislature in each Province in one session, and the first sitting thereof in the next session.

105. And whereas the Legislature of the Province of Canada have from time to time passed enactments, which enactments were to continue in force for a certain number of years after the passing thereof, and from thence to the end of the then next ensuing Session of the Legislatures of the Province in which the same were passed, therefore be it enacted, etc., that whenever the words "and from thence to the end of the then next ensuing Session of the Legislature," or words to the same effect, have been used in any temporary Act of the Province of Canada, which shall not have expired before the Union, the said words shall be construed to extend and apply to the next Session of the Parliament of Canada, if the subject thereof be within the powers of the same, as herein defined, or to the next Sessions of the Legislatures of Ontario and Quebec respectively, if the subject thereof be within the powers of the same, as herein defined.

106. All Laws, Statutes, and Ordinances, which at the time of the Union shall be in force within the said Province of Canada, or the Provinces of Lower Canada or Upper Canada, or either of them, or any part of the same Provinces respectively, shall remain and continue to be of the same force, authority, and effect within the Provinces of Ontario and Quebec respectively, as if this Act had not been made, except in so far as the same are repealed or varied by this Act, or in so far as the same shall or may hereafter, by virtue and under the authority of this Act, be repealed or varied by any Act or Acts of Parliament or of the Legislatures of Ontario or Quebec respectively, as the case may be.

107. All the Courts of Civil and Criminal Jurisdiction within the Province of Canada, or within Lower Canada, or Upper Canada, and all legal Commissions, Powers, and Authorities, and all Officers judicial, administrative, or ministerial within the said Province of Canada, or within Lower Canada, or Upper Canada, except in so far as the same may be abolished, altered, or varied

by, or may be inconsistent with the Provisions of this Act, or shall be abolished, altered, or varied by any Act or Acts of Parliament of the Legislatures of the Provinces of Ontario and Quebec respectively, as the case may be, shall continue to subsist within Ontario and Quebec in the same form and with the same effect as if this Act had not been passed.

108. From and after the Union the use of the words " Upper Canada " instead of " Ontario," or " Lower Canada " instead of " Quebec," in any deed, document, writ, process, pleading, matter or thing whatsoever, shall not invalidate the same.

109. Any proclamation under the Great Seal of the Province of Canada which shall, at the time of the Union have been issued to take effect on a day or at a time which may be subsequent to the said Union and whether relating to the said Province or to Lower Canada, or to Upper Canada, and the several matters and things therein proclaimed shall be, remain, and continue of full force and effect from and after the day or time mentioned in such Proclamation.

110. Any proclamation authorised by any Act of the Legislature of the Province of Canada to be issued under the Great Seal of the Province of Canada, and whether relating to the said Province, or to Lower Canada, or to Upper Canada, and which shall not, at the time of the Union, have been issued, may be issued by the Lieutenant-Governor of Ontario or Quebec, as the subject matter of such proclamation may require under the Great Seal thereof, and from and after the issue of such proclamation the same and the several matters and things therein proclaimed shall be, remain and continue of full force and effect in such Province.

111. The Provincial Penitentiary of Canada shall, until otherwise provided by Parliament, be and continue the Penitentiary of and for Ontario and Quebec respectively.

112. The division and adjustment of the debts, credits, liabilities, properties and assets of the Provinces of Upper and Lower Canada, shall be referred to the arbitrament of three arbitrators, one to be chosen by the Government of Ontario, the other by the Government of Quebec and the third by the Government of Canada ; and the selection of the arbitrators shall not take place until after Parliament and the Legislatures for Ontario and Quebec have been elected, and the third arbitrator shall not be a resident in either Ontario or Quebec.

113. The Governor-General in Council may from time to time order that such and so many of the records, books and documents as belong to the Province of Canada shall be appropriated and delivered either to Quebec or Ontario, and the same shall thenceforth become the property of such Province ; and any copy or extract therefrom, duly certified by the officer having charge of the original thereof, shall be deemed and taken as evidence in the Courts of either Province.

114. The Lieutenant-Governors of Ontario, Quebec, and Nova Scotia respectively shall cause writs to be issued for the first Election of Members of the Legislative Assembly in such form and by such persons as he may prescribe, and at such time and to such Returning Officer as the Governor-General shall direct : and so that the first Election of Member of Assembly for any Electoral District shall be held at one and the same time with the Election for Member of the House of Assembly for such Electoral Division.

MISCELLANEOUS SECTIONS RESPECTING ONTARIO, QUEBEC, NOVA SCOTIA AND NEW BRUNSWICK.

115. The following sections are applicable to Ontario, Quebec, Nova Scotia, and New Brunswick :—

116. Bills for appropriating any part of the Public Revenue, or for imposing any Tax or Impost shall originate in the Legislative Assembly of each Province.

117. It shall not be lawful for the Legislative Assembly of any Province to originate, or pass any vote, resolution, address, or bill for the appropriation of any part of the Public Revenue, or of any tax or impost, to any purpose that has not been first recommended to that House by message of the Lieutenant-Governor in the Session in which such vote, resolution, address, or bill is proposed.

118. Where a bill passed is presented to the Lieutenant-Governor for his assent, he shall declare according to his discretion, but subject to the provisions of this Act, either that he assents thereto or that he withholds his consent, or that he reserves the Bill for the signification of the pleasure of the Governor-General.

119. Where the Lieutenant-Governor assents to a Bill he shall by the first convenient opportunity send an authentic copy

of the Act to the Governor-General, and if the Governor-General in Council within one year after the passing thereof, thinks fit to disallow the Act, such disallowance being signified by the Governor-General to the Lieutenant-Governor, or by proclamation, shall annul the Act from and after the day of such signification or proclamation.

120. A Bill reserved for the signification of the Governor-General's pleasure shall not have any force unless and until within one year from the day on which it was reserved, the Governor-General signifies to the Lieutenant-Governor, or by proclamation that it has received the assent of the Governor-General in Council ; an entry of every such signification or proclamation when transmitted by message from the Lieutenant-Governor, shall be made in the Journals of each House, as the case may be.

MISCELLANEOUS.

121. It shall be lawful for Parliament by any Act or Acts to define the privileges, immunities and powers to be held, enjoyed, and exercised by the Senate and the House of Commons, and by the Members thereof respectively : Provided that no such privileges, immunities, or powers, shall exceed those now held, enjoyed and exercised by the Commons House of the Imperial Parliament, or the Members thereof.

122. The Parliament and Government of Canada shall have all powers necessary or proper for performing the obligations of Canada or of any Province thereof, as part of the British Empire to Foreign Countries, arising under treaties between the Empire and such Foreign Countries.

123. The Governor-General shall appoint the Judges of the Superior, District and County Courts in each Province, and until the consolidation of the Laws of Ontario, Nova Scotia, and New Brunswick, such Judges shall be selected from their respective Bars.

124. The Judges of the Courts of Quebec shall be selected from the Bar of Quebec.

125. The Judges of the Superior Courts shall hold their offices during good behaviour, and shall be removable on the address of both Houses of Parliament.

126. Notwithstanding anything in this Act, any Act of Parliament may from time to time make provision in relation to :—

(1) Agriculture in all or any of the Provinces.

(2) Immigration into all or any of the Provinces.

(3) All works and undertakings.

And in each Province the Legislature may make provision in relation to :—

(1) Agriculture in the Province.

(2) Immigration into the Province.

(3) All works and undertakings in the Province :

But any Law passed by such Legislature shall have the force of law in and for the Province as long and so far only as it is not repugnant to any Act of Parliament.

127. Either the English or the French language may be used by any person in the Debates of the Houses of Parliament, and of the Houses of the Legislature of Quebec, and both of these languages shall be used in the respective records and journals of Parliament and of the Legislature of Quebec, and the Laws and Statutes of Parliament, and of the Legislature of Quebec, shall be printed and published in separate volumes of the English and French languages respectively, and either of those languages may be used by any person or in any pleading or process in or issuing from any Court of Canada, created under this Act, and in or from all or any of the Courts of Quebec.

128. It shall be lawful for the Queen at any time hereafter to admit into the Union all or any of the Colonies or Provinces of Newfoundland, Prince Edward Island, or Rupert's Land, or the North-Western Territory, or British Columbia, on such terms and conditions as the Parliament of Canada shall deem equitable, and as shall receive the assent of The Queen ; and in the case of Newfoundland , Prince Edward Island and British Columbia, as shall be agreed upon by their respective Legislatures ; and in the event of the admission of Newfoundland and Prince Edward Island, or either of them, each shall be entitled to a representation in the Senate of Canada of four Members, but after the admission of Prince Edward Island into the Union, the representation of Nova Scotia and New Brunswick in the Senate of Canada upon any reduction by death or otherwise to the number of Ten Members from each or either of those Provinces shall not

be replaced beyond that number, except as provided by the sections of this Act ; and it shall be lawful for The Queen, upon any such admission into the Union at any time hereafter, to declare by proclamation, that any or either of the Colonies or Provinces of Newfoundland, Prince Edward Island, Rupert's Land, the North Western Territory, or British Columbia, upon, from, and after a certain day in such proclamation to be appointed shall so form a portion of the Kingdom of Canada, and henceforth the same as the case may be, shall be and become a portion of the Kingdom, upon, from, and after the day so appointed as aforesaid, and upon such terms and conditions as may be expressed in such Proclamation.

INTERCOLONIAL RAILWAY.

129. And whereas the construction of a railway from the River St. Lawrence to the city of Halifax, in the Province of Nova Scotia is necessary :

And whereas it has been agreed between the Provinces that such railway shall be constructed with all convenient speed.

Be it enacted, that the General Government shall within six months after the union commence such railway, and within three years thereafter complete the same.

SCHEDULE A.

Substantially the same as the fifth schedule of the B. N. A. Act.

SCHEDULE B.

Substantially the same as the fourth schedule of the B. N. A. Act.

SCHEDULE C.

Same as the second schedule of the B. N. A. Act.

British North America.

DRAFT

OF A

BILL

FOR

The Union of Canada, Nova Scotia, and New Brunswick, and the Government thereof as united; and for Purposes connected therewith.

WHEREAS the Provinces of Canada, Nova Scotia, and New Brunswick have expressed their Desire to be federally united into one Dominion under the Crown of the United Kingdom of Great Britain and Ireland, with a Constitution similar in Principle to that of the United Kingdom :

And whereas such a Union would conduce to the Welfare of the Provinces and promote the Interests of the British Empire :

And whereas on the Establishment of the Union by Authority of Parliament it is expedient, not only that the Constitution of the Legislative Authority in the Dominion be provided for, but also that the Nature of the Executive Government therein be declared :

And whereas it is expedient that provision be made for the eventual Admission into the Union of other Parts of British North America :

Be it therefore enacted and declared by the Queen's Most Excellent Majesty, by and with the Advice and Consent of the Lords Spiritual and Temporal, and Commons, in this present Parliament assembled, and by the Authority of the same, as follows :

I.—PRELIMINARY.

1. This Act may be cited as the British North America Act, 1867. *Short title.*

2. The Provisions of this Act referring to Her Majesty the Queen extend also to the Heirs and Successors of Her Majesty, Kings and Queens of the United Kingdom of Great Britain and Ireland. *Application of Provisions referring to the Queen.*

II.—UNION.

3. It shall be lawful for the Queen, by and with the Advice of Her Majesty's Most Honourable Privy Council, to declare by Proclamation that, on and after a Day therein appointed, not being more than Six Months after the passing of this Act, the Provinces of Canada, Nova Scotia and New Brunswick shall form and be One Dominion under the Name of Canada ; and on and after that Day those three Provinces shall form and be One Dominion under that Name accordingly. *Declaration of Union.*

4. The subsequent Provisions of this Act shall, unless it is otherwise expressed or implied, commence on and after the Union ; that is to say, on and after the Day appointed for the Union taking effect in the Queen's Proclamation ; and in the same Provisions, unless it is otherwise expressed or implied, the Name Canada shall be taken to mean Canada as constituted under this Act. *Construction of subsequent Provisions of Act.*

Provinces.

5. Canada shall be divided into Four Provinces, named Ontario, Quebec, Nova Scotia, and New Brunswick. *Four Provinces.*

6. The Parts of the Province of Canada (as it exists at the passing of this Act) which formerly constituted respectively the Provinces of Upper Canada and Lower Canada shall be deemed to be severed, and shall form Two Separate Provinces. The Part which formerly constituted the Province of Upper Canada shall constitute the Province of Ontario, and the Part which formerly constituted the Province of Lower Canada shall constitute the Province of Quebec. *Provinces of Ontario and Quebec.*

Provinces of Nova Scotia and New Brunswick 7. The Provinces of Nova Scotia and New Bruns-wick shall have the same Limits as at the passing of this Act.

Decennial Census. 8. In the general Census of the Population of Can-ada which is hereby required to be taken in the Year One thousand eight hundred and seventy-one, and in every Tenth Year thereafter, the respective Populations of the Four Provinces shall be distinguished.

III.—EXECUTIVE POWER.

Declaration of Executive Power in the Queen. 9. The Executive Government and Authority of and over the Dominion of Canada is hereby declared to con-tinue and be vested in the Queen.

Application of Provisions referring to Governor General. 10. The Provisions of this Act referring to the Governor-General shall extend and apply to the Gover-nor-General for the Time being of the Dominion of Can-ada, or other the Chief Executive Officer or Administra-tor for the Time being carrying on the Government of Canada on behalf and in the Name of the Queen, by whatever Title he is designated.

Constitution of Privy Council. 11. There shall be a Council to aid and advise in the Government of Canada, to be styled the Queen's Privy Council for Canada ; and the Members of that Council shall be from Time to Time chosen and summoned by the Governor-General and sworn in as Privy Councillors, and may be from Time to Time removed by the Governor-General.

Powers to be exercised by Governor General with Advice or alone. 12. All Powers, Authorities, and Functions which by any Act of the Parliament of Great Britain, or of the Par-liament of the United Kingdom of Great Britain and Ire-land, or of the Legislature of Upper Canada, Lower Can-ada, Canada, Nova Scotia, or New Brunswick, are at the Union vested in or authorized or required to be exercised by the respective Governors or Lieutenant-Governors of those Provinces, with the Advice, or with the Advice and Consent, of the respective Executive Councils thereof, or in conjunction with those Councils, or with any Num-ber of Members thereof, or by those Governors or Lieu-tenant-Governors individually, as far as the same relate to the Government of Canada and continue in existence

and capable of being exercised after the Union, shall be
vested in and shall or may be exercised by the Governor-
General, with the Advice or with the Advice and Consent of or in conjunction with the Queen's Privy Council
for Canada, or any Members thereof, or by the Governor-
General individually, as the case requires.

13. The Provisions of this Act referring to the Governor-General in Council shall be construed as referring
to the Governor-General acting by and with the Advice
of the Queen's Privy Council for Canada.

Application of Provisions referring to Governor General in Council.

14. The Governor-General may appoint any Person
or any Persons jointly or severally to be his Deputy or
Deputies within any Part or Parts of Canada, and in that
Capacity to exercise during the Pleasure of the Governor-
General such of the Powers, Authorities, and Functions
of the Governor-General as the Governor-General deems
it necessary or expedient to assign to him or them ; but
the Appointment of such a Deputy or Deputies shall not
affect the Exercise by the Governor-General himself of
any Power, Authority, or Function.

Appointment of Deputies by Governor-General.

15. The Commander-in-Chief of the Land and Naval
Militia, and of all Naval and Military Forces, of and in
the Dominion of Canada, is hereby declared to continue
and be vested in the Queen.

Command of Armed Forces.

16. Until the Queen otherwise directs the Seat of
Government of Canada shall be Ottawa.

Seat of Government of Canada.

IV.—LEGISLATIVE POWER.

17. There shall be One Parliament for Canada, consisting of the Queen, an Upper House styled the Senate,
and the House of Commons.

Constitution of Parliament of Canada.

18. The Privileges, Immunities, and Powers to be
held, enjoyed, and exercised by the Senate and House of
Commons and the Members thereof respectively shall be
such as are from Time to Time defined by Act of the Parliament of Canada, but so that the same shall never exceed
those at the passing of this Act held, enjoyed, and exercised by the Commons House of Parliament of the
United Kingdom of Great Britain and Ireland or the
Members thereof.

Privileges, &c. of Houses.

First Session of the Parliament.

19. The Parliament of Canada shall be called together not later than Six Months after the Union.

Annual Session.

Yearly Session of Parliament.

20. There shall be a Session of the Parliament of Canada once at least in every Year, so that a Period of Twelve Months shall not intervene between the last Sitting of the Parliament in one Session and the first Sitting thereof in the next Session.

The Senate.

Number of Senators.

21. The Senate shall, subject to the Provisions of this Act, consist of Seventy-two Members, who shall be styled Senators.

Representation of Provinces in Senate.

22. In relation to the Constitution of the Senate Canada shall be deemed to consist of Three Divisions :—

1. Ontario ;
2. Quebec ;
3. The Maritime Provinces, Nova Scotia and New Brunswick ;

which Three Divisions shall (subject to the Provisions of this Act) be equally represented in the Senate as follows: Ontario by Twenty-four Senators ; Quebec by Twenty-four Senators ; and the Maritime Provinces by Twenty-four Senators. Twelve thereof representing Nova Scotia, and Twelve thereof representing New Brunswick.

In the case of Quebec each of the Twenty-four Senators representing that Province shall be appointed for One of the Twenty-four Electoral Divisions of Lower Canada specified in Schedule A. to Chapter One of the Consolidated Statutes of Canada.

Qualifications of Senators.

23. The Qualifications of a Senator shall be as follows :—

(1) He shall be of the full Age of Thirty Years :

(2) He shall be either a Natural-born Subject of the Queen, or a Subject of the Queen naturalized by an Act of the Parliament of Great Britain, or of the Parliament of the United Kingdom of Great Britain and Ireland, or of the Legislature of One of the Provinces of

Upper Canada, Lower Canada, Canada, Nova Scotia, or New Brunswick, before the Union, or of the Parliament of Canada after the Union :

(3) He shall be legally or equitably seised as of Freehold for his own Use and Benefit of Lands or Tenements held in Free and Common Socage, or seised or possessed for his own Use and Benefit of Lands or Tenements held in Franc-alleu or Roture, within the Province for which he is appointed, of the Value of Four thousand Dollars, over and above all rents, Dues, Debts, Charges, Mortgages, and Incumbrances due or payable out of or charged on or affecting the same :

(4) His Property shall be worth Four Thousand Dollars over and above his Debts and Liabilities :

(5) He shall be resident in the Province for which he is appointed :

(6) In the Case of Quebec he shall have his real Property Qualification in the Electoral Division for which he is appointed, or shall be resident in that Division.

24. The Governor-General shall from Time to Time, by Instrument under the Great Seal of Canada, summon qualified Persons to the Senate ; and, subject to the Provisions of this Act, every Person so summoned shall become and be a Member of the Senate and a Senator. *Summons of Senator.*

25. Such Persons shall be first summoned to the Senate after the Union as the Queen by Warrant under Her Majesty's Royal Sign Manual thinks fit to approve. *Summons of First Body of Senators.*

26. If at any Time on the Recommendation of the Governor-General the Queen thinks fit to direct that Three or Six Members be added to the Senate, the Governor-General may summon to the Senate such Three or Six Persons (as the Case may be) representing equally the Three Divisions of Canada. *Addition of Senators in certain Cases.*

Reduction of Senate to normal Numbers.

27. In case of the Appointment at any Time of such additional Three or Six Senators the Governor-General shall not Summon any Person to the Senate, except on a further like Direction by the Queen on the like Recommendation, until each of the Three Divisions of Canada is represented by Twenty-four Senators and no more.

Maximum Number of Senators.

28. The Number of Senators shall not at any Time, notwithstanding anything in this Act, exceed Seventy-eight.

Legislative Councillors of Provinces becoming Senators.

29. Any Person who, being a Member of the Legislative Council of Nova Scotia or New Brunswick, accepts a Place in the Senate shall thereby vacate his Seat in such Legislative Council, and if any Person, being a Member of the Legislative Council of Canada, Nova Scotia, or New Brunswick, to whom a Place in the Senate is offered, does not within Thirty Days thereafter by Writing under his Hand, addressed to the Governor-General accept the same, he shall be deemed to have declined the same.

Tenure of place in Senate.

30. A Senator shall, subject to the Provisions of this Act, hold his Place in the Senate for Life.

Resignation of Place.

31. A Senator may by Writing under his Hand addressed to the Governor-General resign his place in the Senate, and thereupon the same shall be vacant.

Disqualification of Senators.

32. The Place of a Senator shall become vacant in any of the following Cases :—

(1) If for Two consecutive Sessions of the Parliament he fails to give his Attendance in the Senate :

(2) If he takes an Oath or makes a Declaration or Acknowledgment of Allegiance, Obedience, or Adherence to a Foreign Power, or does an Act whereby he becomes a Subject or Citizen, or entitled to the Rights or Privileges of a Subject or Citizen, of a Foreign Power :

(3) If he is adjudged Bankrupt or Insolvent, or applies for the Benefit of any Law relating to Insolvent Debtors, or becomes a public Defaulter :

(4) If he is attainted of Treason or convicted of Felony or of any infamous Crime :

(5) If he ceases to be qualified in respect of Property or of Residence : provided, that a Senator shall not be deemed to have ceased to be qualified in respect of Residence by reason only of his residing at the Seat of the Government of Canada while holding an Office under that Government requiring his Presence there.

33. When a Vacancy happens in the Senate by Resignation, Death, or otherwise, the Governor-General shall by Summons to a fit and qualified Person fill the Vacancy. *Summons on Vacancy.*

34. If any Question arises respecting the Qualification of a Senator or a Vacancy in the Senate the same shall be heard and determined by the Senate. *Questions as to Vacancies, &c.*

35. The Governor-General may from Time to Time, by Instrument under the Great Seal of Canada, appoint a Senator to be Speaker of the Senate, and may remove him and appoint another in his Stead. *Speaker of Senate.*

36. Until the Parliament of Canada otherwise provides, the Presence of at least Fifteen Senators, including the Speaker, shall be necessary to constitute a Meeting of the Senate for the Exercise of its Powers. *Quorum of Senate.*

37. Questions arising in the Senate shall be decided by a Majority of Voices, and the Speaker shall in all Cases have a Vote, and when the Voices are equal the Decision shall be deemed to be in the Negative. *Voting in Senate.*

House of Commons.

38. The House of Commons shall, subject to the Provisions of this Act, consist of One hundred and eighty-one Members, of whom eighty-two shall be elected for Ontario, Sixty-five for Quebec, Nineteen for Nova Scotia, and Fifteen for New Brunswick. *Constitution of House of Commons.*

39. The Governor-General shall from Time to Time, in the Queen's Name, by Instrument under the Great Seal of Canada, summon and call together the House of Commons. *Summoning of House of Commons.*

Exclusion of senators.

40. A Senator shall not be capable of being elected or of sitting or voting as a Member of the House of Commons.

Electoral Districts.

Electoral Divisions of the Four Provinces.

41. Until the Parliament of Canada otherwise provides Ontario, Quebec, Nova Scotia, and New Brunswick shall, for the Purposes of the Election of Members to serve in the House of Commons, be divided into Electoral Districts as follows :—

1.—ONTARIO.

Ontario shall be divided into the Counties, Ridings of Counties, Cities, Parts of Cities, and Towns enumerated in the   Schedule to this Act, each whereof shall be an Electoral District, and each such District as numbered in that Schedule entitled to return One Member.

2.—QUEBEC.

Quebec shall be divided into Sixty-five Electoral Districts, composed of the Sixty-five Electoral Divisions into which Lower Canada is at the passing of this Act divided under Chapter Two of the Consolidated Statutes of Canada, Chapter Seventy-five of the Consolidated Statutes for Lower Canada, and the Act of the Province of Canada of the Twenty-third Year of the Queen, Chapter One, or any other Act amending the same in force at the Union, so that each such Electoral Division shall be for the Purposes of this Act, an Electoral District entitled to return one Member.

3.—NOVA SCOTIA.

Each of the Eighteen Counties of Nova Scotia shall be an Electoral District.

The County of Halifax shall be entitled to return Two Members, and each of the other Counties One Member.

4.—NEW BRUNSWICK.

Each of the Fourteen Counties into which New Brunswick is divided, including the City and County of St. John, shall be an Electoral District. The City of St.

John shall also be a separate Electoral District. Each of those Fifteen Electoral Districts shall be entitled to return One Member.

42. Until the Parliament of Canada otherwise provides, all Laws in force in the several Provinces at the Union relative to the following Matters or any of them, namely,—the Qualifications and Disqualifications of Persons to be elected or to sit or vote as Members of the House of Assembly or Legislative Assembly in the respective Provinces, the Voters at Elections of such Members, the Oaths to be taken by Voters, the Returning Officers, their Powers and Duties, the Proceedings at Elections, the Periods during which Elections may be continued, the Trial of Controverted Elections, and Proceedings incident thereto, the vacating of Seats of Members, and the Execution of new Writs in case of Seats vacated otherwise than by Dissolution,—shall respectively apply to Elections of Members to serve in the House of Commons. *Continuance of Existing Election Laws.*

Until the Parliament of Canada otherwise provides, at any Election for a Member of the House of Commons for the District of Algoma every Householder otherwise qualified except in respect of Real Property shall, notwithstanding anything in this Act, have a Vote.

43. For the First Election of Members to serve in the House of Commons the Governor-General shall cause Writs to be issued by such Person, in such Form, and addressed to such Returning Officers as he thinks fit. *Writs for First Election.*

The Person issuing Writs under this Section shall have the like Powers as are possessed at the Union by the Officers charged with the issuing of Writs for the Election of Members to serve in the respective House of Assembly or Legislative Assembly of the Province of Canada, Nova Scotia, or New Brunswick : and the Returning Officers to whom Writs are directed under this Section shall have the like Powers as are possessed at the Union by the Officers charged with the Returning of Writs for the Election of Members to serve in the same respective House of Assembly or Legislative Assembly.

Casual
Vacancies.

44. In case a Vacancy in the Representation in the House of Commons or any Electoral District happens before the Meeting of the Parliament, or after the Meetnig of the Parliament before Provision is made by the Parliament in this Behalf, a Writ in respect of such vacant District may be issued in like Manner.

Speaker of
House of
Commons.

45. The House of Commons on its first assembling after a General Election shall proceed with all practicable Speed to elect One of its Members to be Speaker.

Vacancy
in office of
Speaker.

46. In case of a Vacancy happening in the Office of Speaker by Death, Resignation, or otherwise, the House of Commons shall with all practicable Speed proceed to elect another of its Members to be Speaker.

Speaker to
preside.

47. The Speaker shall preside at all Meetings of the House of Commons.

Provision
for absence
of Speaker.

48. Until the Parliament of Canada otherwise provides, in case of the Absence for any Reason of the Speaker from the Chair of the House of Commons for a Period of Forty-eight consecutive Hours, the House may elect another of its Members to act as Speaker, and the Member so elected shall during the Continuance of such Absence of the Speaker have and execute all the Powers, Privileges, and Duties of Speaker.

Quorum of
House of
Commons.

49. The presence of at least Twenty Members of the House of Commons shall be necessary to constitute a Meeting of the House for the Exercise of its Powers ; and for that Purpose the Speaker shall be reckoned as a Member.

Voting in
House of
Commons.

50. Questions arising in the House of Commons shall be decided by a Majority of Voices other than that of the Speaker, and when the Voices are equal but not otherwise, the Speaker shall have a Vote.

Decennial
Re-adjust-
ment of
Represen-
tation.

51. On the Completion of the Census in the Year One thousand eight hundred and seventy-one, and of each subsequent decennial Census, the Representation of the Four Provinces shall be re-adjusted by such Authority, in such Manner, and from such Time, as any Act of the Parliament of Canada from Time to Time directs, according to the following Rules :—

(1) Quebec shall have the fixed Number of Sixty-five Members :

(2) There shall be assigned to each of the other Provinces such a Number of Members as will bear the same Proportion to the Number of its Population (ascertained at such Census) as the Number Sixty-five bears to the Number of the Population of Quebec (so ascertained) :

(3) In the Computation of the Number of Members for a Province a fractional Part less than One Half of the whole Number requisite for entitling the Province to a Member shall be disregarded ; but a fractional Part exceeding One Half of that Number shall be equivalent to the whole Number :

(4) On any such Re-adjustment the Number of Members for a Province shall not be reduced unless the Proportion which the Number of the Population of the Province bore to the Number of the aggregate Population of the United Colony at the then last preceding Readjustment of the Number of Members for the Province is ascertained at the then latest Census to be diminished by One Twentieth Part or upwards :

(5) Such Re-adjustment shall not take effect until the termination of the then existing Parliament :

52. The Number of Members of the House of Commons may be from Time to Time increased by Act of the Parliament of Canada, provided the proportionate Representation of the Provinces prescribed by this Act is not thereby disturbed.

Increase of Number of House of Commons.

53. Every House of Commons shall continue for Five Years from the Day of the Return of the Writs for choosing the House (subject to be sooner dissolved by the Governor-General), and no longer.

Duration of House of Commons.

V.—MONEY VOTES; ROYAL ASSENT, &c.

Appropriation and Tax Bills. 54. Bills for appropriating any Part of the Public Revenue of Canada, or for imposing any Tax or Impost, shall originate in the House of Commons.

Recommendation of Money votes. 55. It shall not be lawful for the House of Commons to adopt or pass any Vote, Resolution, Address, or Bill for the Appropriation of any Part of the Public Revenue, or of any Tax or Impost, to any Purpose that has not been first recommended to that House by Message of the Governor-General in the Session in which such Vote, Resolution, Address, or Bill is proposed to be adopted or passed.

Royal Assent to Bills, &c. 56. Where a Bill passed by the Houses of the Parliament is presented to the Governor General for the Queen's Assent, he shall declare, according to his Discretion, but subject to the Provisions of this Act and to Her Majesty's Instructions, either that he assents thereto in the Queen's Name, or that he withholds the Queen's Assent, or that he reserves the Bill for the Signification of the Queen's pleasure.

Disallowance by Order in Council of Act assented to by Governor. 57. Where the Governor-General assents to a Bill in the Queen's Name, he shall by the first convenient Opportunity send an authentic Copy of the Act to One of Her Majesty's Principal Secretaries of State, and if the Queen in Council within Two Years after Receipt thereof by the Secretary of State thinks fit to disallow the Act, such Disallowance (with a Certificate of the Secretary of State of the Day on which the Act was received by him) being signified by the Governor General, by Speech or Message to the Houses of the Parliament or by Proclamation, shall annul the Act from and after the Day of such Signification.

Signification of Pleasure on Bill reserved. 58. A Bill reserved for the Signification of the Queen's Pleasure shall not have any Force unless and until within Two Years from the Day on which it was presented to the Governor-General for the Queen's Assent, the Governor-General signifies, by Speech or Message to each of the Houses of the Parliament or by Proclamation, that it has received the Assent of the Queen in Council.

An entry of every such Speech, Message, or Proclamation shall be made in the Journal of each House, and a duplicate thereof duly attested shall be delivered to the proper Officer to be kept among the Records of Canada.

VI.—PROVINCIAL CONSTITUTIONS.

Lieutenant-Governors:

59. For each Province there shall be an Officer, styled the Lieutenant-Governor, appointed by the Governor-General in Council by Instrument under the Great Seal of Canada. ^{Lieutenant Governors of Provinces.}

60. A Lieutenant-Governor shall hold office during the Pleasure of the Governor-General, but any Lieutenant-Governor appointed after the Commencement of the First Session of the Parliament of Canada shall not be removable within Five Years from his Appointment, except for Cause assigned, which shall be communicated to him in Writing within One Month after the Order for his Removal is made, and shall be communicated by Message to the Senate and to the House of Commons within One Week thereafter if the Parliament is then sitting, and if not then within One Week after the Commencement of the next Session of the Parliament. ^{Tenure of Office of Lieutenant Governor.}

61. The Salaries of the Lieutenant-Governors shall be fixed and provided by Act of the Parliament of Canada. ^{Salaries of Lieutenant Governors.}

62. Every Lieutenant Governor shall, before assuming the Duties of his Office, make and subscribe before the Governor-General or some Person authorized by him to administer the same, Oaths of Allegiance and Office similar to those taken by the Governor-General. ^{Oath, &c. of Lieutenant Governor.}

63. The Provisions of this Act referring to the Lieutenant-Governor shall extend and apply to the Lieutenant-Governor for the Time being or other the Chief Executive Officer or Administrator for the Time being carrying on the Government of the Province, by whatever title he is designated. ^{Application of Provisions referring to Lieutenant Governor.}

64. The Lieutenant-Governors of Ontario and Quebec may each appoint under the Great Seal of the Province, and to hold Office during Pleasure, the following Officers, that is to say, the Attorney-General, the Secretary and ^{Appointment of Executive Officers for Ontario and Quebec.}

Registrar of the Province, the Treasurer of the Province, the Commissioner of Crown Lands, and the Commissioner of Agriculture and Public Works, and in the Case of Quebec, the Solicitor-General ; and may, by and under Order in Council, from Time to Time prescribe the Duties of such Officers and of the several Departments over which they shall preside or to which they shall belong, and of the Officers and Clerks thereof : and may also appoint other and additional Officers to hold Office during Pleasure, and may from Time to Time prescribe the Duties of such Officers, and of the several Departments over which they shall preside or to which they shall belong, and of the Officers and Clerks thereof ; and all Rights, Powers, Duties, Functions, Responsibilities, or Authorities at the passing of this Act vested or imposed in or upon any Attorney-General, Secretary and Registrar of the Province of Canada, Minister of Finance, Commissioner of Crown Lands, Commissioner of Public Works, and Minister of Agriculture, by any Law, Statute, or Ordinance of the former Provinces of Upper Canada and Lower Canada, or of the Province of Canada, and not repugnant to this Act, shall be vested in or imposed upon any Officer to be appointed by the Lieutenant-Governor for the Discharge of the same or any of them, unless and until and as far only as such Rights, Powers, Duties, or Authorities be varied, altered, amended, or repealed by the Legislature of the Province.

The Commissioner of Agriculture and Public Works shall, until it is otherwise ordered by the Legislature, combine and perform the Duties and Functions of the Office of Minister of Agriculture as at the passing of this Act imposed by the Law of the Province of Canada, as well as those of the Commissioner of Public Works.

Executive Councils of Ontario and Quebec.

65. The Executive Councils of Ontario and Quebec may each be composed of the Attorney-General, the Secretary and Registrar of the Province, the Treasurer of the Province, the Commissioner of Crown Lands, and the Commissioner of Agriculture and Public Works ; and in Quebec, of the Speaker of the Legislative Council and of the Solicitor-General, and of any other Persons at any

Time or from Time to Time appointed to the Office of
Executive Councillor by Instrument under the Great Seal,
and to hold Office during Pleasure.

66. Until altered by the Lieutenant-Governor in
Council the Great Seal of Ontario and Quebec respectively shall be the same, or of the same Design, in each of the
said Provinces as that used in the Provinces of Upper
Canada and Lower Canada before their Union as the Province of Canada. *Great Seals.*

67. All Powers, Authorities, and Functions which by
any Act of the Parliament of Great Britain, or of the Parliament of the United Kingdom of Great Britain and Ireland, or of the Legislature of Upper Canada, or of Lower
Canada, or of the Province of Canada, were or are before
or at the Union vested in or authorized or required to be
exercised by the respective Governors or Lieutenant-Governors of those Provinces, with the Advice, or with the
Advice and Consent, of the respective Executive Councils
thereof, or in conjunction with those Councils, or with
any Number of Members thereof, or by those Governors
or Lieutenant-Governors individually as far as the same
relate to the Government of Ontario and Quebec respectively, and are capable of being exercised after the Union,
shall be vested in and shall or may be exercised by the
Governor-General, with the Advice or with the Advice
and Consent of or in conjunction with the Executive
Council appointed for the Affairs of Ontario and Quebec
respectively, or any Members thereof, or by the Lieuten-
ant-Governor individually, as the Case requires. *Powers to be exercised by Lieutenant Governor with Advice or alone.*

68. The Provisions of this Act referring to the Lieutenant-Governor in Council shall be construed as referring to the Lieutenant-Governor of the Province acting
by and with the Advice of the Executive Council thereof. *Application of Provisions referring to Lieutenant Governor in Council.*

69. In the event of the Absence or Illness or Inability from any other Cause of the Lieutenant-Governor to
discharge the Duties of his Office, the Governor-General
in Council may appoint an Administrator to execute the
Office and Functions of Lieutenant-Governor during such
Absence, Illness, or other Inability. *Administration in Absence, &c. of Lieutenant Governor.*

Seats of Provincial Governments.

70. Unless and until the Executive Government of any Province otherwise directs with respect to that Province, the Seats of Government of the Provinces shall be as follows ; namely, of Ontario, the City of Toronto : of Quebec, the City of Quebec ; of Nova Scotia, the City of Halifax ; and of New Brunswick, the City of Fredericton.

Legislatures of Provinces.

1.—ONTARIO.

Legislature for Ontario.

71. There shall be a Legislature for Ontario consisting of the Lieutenant-Governor and of One House, styled the Legislative Assembly of Ontario.

Electoral Districts.

72. The Legislative Assembly of Ontario shall be composed of Eighty-two Members, to be elected to represent the Eighty-two Electoral Districts, set forth in the Schedule to this Act.

2.—QUEBEC.

Legislature for Quebec.

73. There shall be a Legislature for Quebec consisting of the Lieutenant-Governor and of Two Houses, styled the Legislative Council of Quebec and the Legislative Assembly of Quebec.

Constitution of Legislative Council.

74. The Legislative Council of Quebec shall be composed of Twenty-four Members, to be appointed by the Lieutenant-Governor, under the Great Seal of Quebec, one being appointed to represent each of the Twenty-four Electoral Divisions of Lower Canada in this Act, referred to, and each holding Office for the Term of his Life.

Qualification of Legislative Councillors for Quebec.

75. The Qualifications of the Legislative Councillors of Quebec shall be the same as those for the Senators for Quebec.

Disqualification of Legislative Councillors for Quebec.

76. The Place of a Legislative Councillor of Quebec shall become vacant in the like Cases, mutatis mutandis in which the Place of Senator becomes vacant under this Act.

Vacancies.

77. When a Vacancy happens in the Legislative Council by Death, Resignation, or otherwise, the Lieutenant-Governor, in the Queen's Name, by Instrument under

the Great Seal of Quebec, shall summon to the said Legislative Council a fit and qualified Person to fill the Vacancy.

78. A Legislative Councillor may, by Writing under his Hand addressed to the Lieutenant-Governor, resign his Seat in the Legislative Council, and thereupon the same shall be vacant. *Resignation of Seat.*

79. If any Question arises respecting the Qualification of a Legislative Councillor, or a Vacancy in the Legislative Council, the same shall be heard and determined by the Legislative Council. *Questions as to Vacancies, &c.*

80. The Lieutenant-Governor may from Time to Time, by Instrument under the Great Seal of Quebec, appoint a Member of the Legislative Council to be Speaker thereof, and may remove him and appoint another in his Stead. *Speaker of Legislative Council.*

81. Until the Legislature of Quebec otherwise provides, the presence of at least Ten Members of the Legislative Council, including the Speaker, shall be necessary to constitute a Meeting for the Exercise of its Powers. *Quorum of Legislative Council.*

82. The Speaker shall vote as other Members, and in case of an Equality of Votes it shall be held that the Decision is in the Negative.

83. The Legislative Assembly of Quebec shall be composed of Sixty-five Members, to be elected to represent the Sixty-five Electoral Divisions or Districts of Lower Canada in this Act referred to, subject to Alteration of those Divisions by Act of the Legislature of Quebec : Provided that it shall not be lawful to present to the Lieutenant-Governor for Assent any Bill of the Legislative Council and Assembly of Quebec by which the Limits of the Electoral Divisions or Districts mentioned in the Schedule to this Act are altered, unless the Second and Third Readings of such Bill in the Legislative Assembly have been passed with the Concurrence of the Majority of the Members for the Time being of the said Legislative Assembly representing those Electoral Divisions or Districts, and the Assent shall not be given to such Bill unless an Address has been presented by the Legislative Assembly to the Lieutenant-Governor stating that such Bill has been so passed.

First Session of Legislatures.

84. The Legislatures of Ontario and Quebec respectively shall be called together not later than Six Months after the Union.

Summoning of Legislative Assembly.

85. The Lieutenant-Governors of Ontario and Quebec respectively shall from Time to Time, in the Queen's Name, by Instrument under the Great Seal of the Province, summon and call together the Legislative Assembly of the Province.

Restriction on Election of Powers of Officers.

86. A Person accepting or holding any Office, Commission, or Employment, permanent or temporary, at the Nomination of the Lieutenant-Governor, in either of the Provinces of Ontario or Quebec to which an annual Salary, or any Fee, Allowance, Emolument, or Profit of any Kind or Amount whatever from the Province is attached, shall not be eligible as a Member of the Legislative Assembly of either Province, nor shall he sit or vote as such : but nothing in this Section shall make ineligible as aforesaid any Person being a Member of the Executive Council of either of the said Provinces, or holding any of the following Offices, that is to say, of Attorney-General, Secretary and Registrar of the Province, Treasurer of the Province, Commissioner of Crown Lands, and the Commissioner of Agriculture and Public Works, and for Quebec the Solicitor-General, or shall disqualify him to sit or vote in the House for which he is elected, provided he be elected while holding such Office and not otherwise disqualified.

87. Until the Legislatures of Ontario and Quebec respectively otherwise provide, all Laws which at the Union are in force in those Provinces respectively, relative to the following Matters, or any of them, namely, the Qualifications and Disqualifications of Persons to be elected or to sit or vote as Members of the Assembly of the Province of Canada, the Qualifications or Disqualifications of Voters, the Oaths to be taken by Voters, the Returning Officers, their Powers and Duties, the Proceedings at Elections, the Periods during which such Elections may be continued, and the Trial of Controverted Elections and the Proceedings incident thereto, the vacating of the

Seats of Members and the issuing and Execution of new Writs in case of Seats vacated otherwise than by Dissolution, shall respectively apply to Elections of Members to serve in the Legislative Assembly of Ontario and in the Legislative Assembly of Quebec : Provided that until the Legislature of Ontario otherwise provides, at any Election for a Member of the Legislative Assembly of Ontario for the District of Algoma all Householders otherwise qualified except in respect of Real Property shall have Votes.

88. Every Legislative Assembly of Ontario and every Legislative Assembly of Quebec shall continue for Four Years from the Day of the Return of the Writs for choosing the same (subject nevertheless to either the Legislative Assembly of Ontario or the Legislative Assembly of Quebec being sooner dissolved by the Lieutenant-Governor of the Province), and no longer.

89. There shall be a Session of the Legislature of each of the said Provinces once at least every Year so that a Period of Twelve Months shall not intervene between the last Sitting of the Legislature in each Province in one Session and the first Sitting thereof in the next Session.

90. The following Provisions of this Act respecting the House of Commons of Canada shall extend and apply to the Legislative Assemblies of Ontario and Quebec respectively ; that is to say, the Provisions relating to the Election of a Speaker originally and on Vacancies, the Proceedings of the Speaker, the Absence of the Speaker, and the Quorum of the House and the Mode of voting therein as if those Provisions were here re-enacted and made applicable in Terms to each such Legislative Assembly.

3.—NOVA SCOTIA AND NEW BRUNSWICK.

91. The Constitution of each of the Provinces of Nova Scotia and New Brunswick shall, subject to the Provisions of this Act, continue as it exists at the Union until altered or amended under the Authority of this Act, and

Constitutions of Nova Scotia and New Brunswick

the House of Assembly of New Brunswick shall, unless sooner dissolved, continue for the Period for which it was elected.

4.—ONTARIO, QUEBEC, AND NOVA SCOTIA.

First
Elections.

92. Each of the Lieutenant-Governors of Ontario, Quebec, and Nova Scotia respectively shall cause Writs to be issued for the First Election of Members of the Legislative Assembly thereof in such Form and by such Person as he prescribes, and at such Time and to such Returning Officer as the Governor-General directs, and so that the First Election of Member of Assembly for any Electoral District shall be held at one and the same Time with the Election for Member of the House of Commons for such Electoral District.

5.—THE FOUR PROVINCES.

Applica-
tion to
Legisla-
tures of
Provinces
respecting
Money
Bills, &c.

93. The Provisions of Part V. of this Act shall extend and apply to the Legislatures of the several Provinces as if those Provisions were here re-enacted and made applicable in Terms to the respective Provinces and the Legislatures thereof.

VII.—JUDICATURE.

Appoint-
ment of
Judges.

94. The Governor-General shall appoint the Judges of the Superior, District, County, and Recorders Courts in each Province, except those of the Courts of Probate in Nova Scotia and New Brunswick.

Selection
of Judges
in Ontario,
&c.

95. Until the Laws relative to Property and Civil Rights in Ontario, Nova Scotia, and New Brunswick, and the Procedure of the Courts in those Provinces, are made uniform, the Judges of the Courts of those Provinces appointed by the Governor-General shall be selected from the respective Bars of those Provinces.

Selection
of Judges
in Quebec.

96. The Judges of the Courts of Quebec shall be selected from the Bar of that Province.

Tenure of
Office of
Judges of
Superior
Courts.

97. The Judges of the Superior Courts shall hold Office during good Behaviour, but shall be removable by the Governor-General on Address of the Senate and House of Commons.

98. The Salaries, Allowances, and Pensions of the Salaries, &c. of Judges of the Superior, District, and County Courts, and Judges. of the Admiralty Courts in Cases where the Judges thereof are for the Time being paid by Salary, shall be fixed and provided by the Parliament of Canada.

VIII.—DISTRIBUTION OF LEGISLATIVE POWERS.

Powers of the Parliament.

99. It shall be lawful for the Queen, by and with the Legislative Authority of Parliament of Canada. Advice and Consent of the Senate and House of Commons, to make Laws for the Peace, Order, and good Government of the Dominion of Canada, in relation to all Matters not coming within the Classes of Subjects by this Act assigned exclusively to the Legislatures of the Provinces ; and for greater Certainty, but not so as to restrict the Generality of the foregoing Terms of this Section, it is hereby declared that the Legislative Authority of the Parliament of Canada extends to all Matters coming within the Classes of Subjects next hereinafter enumerated ; that is to say,—

1. The Public Debt and Property.

2. The Regulation of Trade and Commerce.

3. The raising of Money by any Mode or System of Taxation.

4. The borrowing of Money on the Public Credit.

5. Postal Service.

6. The Census and Statistics.

7. Militia, Military and Naval Service. and Defence.

7a. The fixing of and providing for the Salaries and Allowances of Civil and other Officers of the Government of Canada.

8. Beacons, Buoys, Lighthouses, and Sable Island.

9. Navigation and Shipping.

10. Quarantine and the Establishment and Maintenance of Marine Hospitals.

11. Sea Coast and Inland Fisheries.

11a. Ferries between a Province and any British or Foreign Country or between Two Provinces.

12. Currency and Coinage.

13. Banking, Incorporation of Banks, and the Issue of Paper Money.

14. Savings Banks.

15. Weights and Measures.

16. Bills of Exchange and Promissory Notes.

17. Interest.

18. Legal Tender.

19. Bankruptcy and Insolvency.

20. Patents of Invention and Discovery.

21. Copyrights.

22. Indians, and Lands reserved for the Indians.

23. Naturalization and Aliens.

24. Marriage and Divorce.

25. The Criminal Law, except the Constitution of Courts of Criminal Jurisdiction, but including the Procedure in Criminal Matters.

26. The Establishment, Maintenance, and Management of Penitentiaries.

27. Such Classes of Subjects as are by this Act expressly excepted in the Enumeration of the Classes of Subjects by this Act assigned exclusively to the Legislatures of the Provinces.

And any Matter coming within any of the Classes of Subjects enumerated in this Section shall not be deemed to come within the Subject of Property and Civil Rights comprised in the Enumeration of the Classes of Subjects by this Act assigned exclusively to the Legislatures of the Provinces.

Exclusive Powers of Provincial Legislature.

Subject of exclusive Provincial Legislation.

100. In each Province the Legislature may exclusively make Laws in relation to Matters coming within the Classes of Subjects next herein-after enumerated ; that is to say,—

1. The Amendment from Time to Time of the Constitution of the Province, except as regards the Office of Lieutenant-Governor :

2. Direct Taxation within the Province in order to the raising of a Revenue for Provincial Purposes, with Reservation to New Brunswick of the Right to collect the Lumber Dues provided in Chapter Fifteen, Title Three, of the Revised Statutes of that Province, and any Amendment thereof made before or after the Union that does not increase the Amount of such Dues, but excepting the Lumber of any of the Provinces other than New Brunswick :

3. The borrowing of Money on the sole Credit of the Province for Provincial Purposes :

4. The Establishment and Tenure of Provincial Offices and the Appointment and Payment of Provincial Officers :

5. The Management and Sale of the Public Lands belonging to the Province and of the Timber and Wood thereon :

6. The Establishment, Maintenance, and Management of Public and Reformatory Prisons in and for the Province :

7. The Establishment, Maintenance, and Management of Hospitals, Asylums, Charities, and Eleemosynary Institutions in and for the Province, other than Marine Hospitals :

8. Municipal Institutions in the Province :

9. Shop, Saloon, Tavern, Auctioneer, and other Licenses in order to the raising of a Revenue for Provincial, Local, or Municipal Purposes :

10. Works and Undertakings :

11. The Incorporation of Companies with exclusively Provincial Objects :

12. The Solemnization of Marriage in the Province :

13. Property and Civil Rights in the Province :

14. The Administration of Justice in the Province, including the Constitution, Maintenance, and Organization of Provincial Courts, both of Civil and of Criminal Jurisdiction, and including Procedure in Civil Matters in those Courts :

15. The Imposition of Punishment by Fine, Penalty, or Imprisonment for enforcing any Law of the Province made in relation to any Matter coming within any of the Classes of Subjects enumerated in this Section :

16. Such other Classes of Subjects (if any) as are from Time to Time added to the Enumeration in this Section by any Act of the Parliament of Canada.

Education.

Legislation respecting Education.

101. In and for each Province the Legislature may exclusively make Laws in relation to Education, subject and according to the following Provisions :

(1) Nothing in any such Law shall prejudicially affect any Right or Privilege with respect to Denominational Schools which any Class of Persons have by Law in the Province at the Union :

(2) All the Powers, Privileges, and Duties at the Union by Law conferred and imposed in Upper Canada on the Separate Schools and School Trustees of the Queen's Roman Catholic Subjects shall be extended to the Dissentient Schools of the Queen's Protestant and Roman Catholic Subjects in Lower Canada :

(3) Where in any Province a System of Separate or Dissentient Schools exists by Law at the Union or is thereafter established by the Legislature of the Province, an Appeal shall lie to the Governor-General in Council from any Act or Decision of any Provincial Authority affecting any Right or Privilege in relation to Education of the Queen's Protestant or Roman Catholic Subjects, being the Minority of the Population of the Province :

(4) In case any such Provincial Law as from Time to Time seems to the Governor-General in Council requisite for the due Execution of the Provisions of this Section is not made, or in case any Decision of the Governor-General in Council on any Appeal under this Section is not duly executed by the proper Provincial Authority in that behalf, then and in every such Case, and as far only as the Circumstances of each Case require, the Parliament of Canada may make remedial Laws for the due Execution of the Provisions of this Section and of any Decision of the Governor-General in Council under this Section.

Uniformity of Laws in Ontario, Nova Scotia and New Brunswick.

102. Notwithstanding anything in this Act, any Act of the Parliament of Canada may make Provision for the Uniformity of all or any of the Laws relative to Property and Civil Rights in Ontario, Nova Scotia, and New Brunswick, and of the Procedure of all or any of the Courts in those Three Provinces, and thenceforth the Power of the Parliament of Canada to make Laws in relation to any Matter comprised in any such Act shall, notwithstanding anything in this Act, be unrestricted ; but any Act of the Parliament of Canada making Provision for such Uniformity shall not have effect in any Province unless and until it is adopted and enacted as Law by the Legislature thereof. *Legislation for Uniformity of Laws in Three Provinces.*

Court of Appeal, &c.

103. Any Act of the Parliament of Canada may, notwithstanding anything in this Act, from Time to Time provide for the Constitution, Maintenance, and Organization of a General Court of Appeal for Canada, and for the Establishment of any additional Court in any Province. *General Court of Appeal &c.*

Agriculture, Immigration, Public Works.

Concurrent Powers of Legislation respecting Agriculture, &c.

104. In each Province the Legislature may make Laws in relation to Matters coming within the Classes of Subjects next hereinafter enumerated : that is to say,

1. Agriculture in the Province :

2. Immigration into the Province :

3. Works and Undertakings in the Province :

And it is hereby declared that the Parliament of Canada may from Time to Time make Laws in relation to Matters coming within the Classes of Subjects next hereinafter enumerated ; that is to say,

1. Agriculture in all or any of the Provinces :

3. Immigration into all or any of the Provinces :

3. Works and Undertakings of the following Classes,—

 (a) Lines of Steam or other Ships, Railways, Canals, and other Works, and Undertakings connecting any Province with any other or others of the Provinces, or extending beyond the Limits of any Province :

 (b) Lines of Steam Ships between any Province and any British or Foreign Country :

 (c) Such Works as although wholly situate within One Province are before or after their Execution declared by Act of the Parliament of Canada to be for the general Advantage of Canada or for the Advantage of Two or more of the Provinces :

And any Law of the Legislature of a Province relative to any Matter coming within the Classes of Subjects in this Section enumerated shall have effect in and for the Province as long and as far only as it is not repugnant to any Act of the Parliament of Canada.

IV.—REVENUES, PROPERTIES, &c.

Creation of Consolidated Revenue Fund.

105. All Duties and Revenues over which the respective Legislatures of Canada, Nova Scotia, and New Brunswick before and at the Union had and have Power of Ap-

propriation, except such Portions thereof as are by this Act reserved to the respective Legislatures of the Provinces, or are raised by them in accordance with the special Powers conferred on them by this Act, shall form One Consolidated Revenue Fund, to be appropriated for the Public Service of Canada in the Manner and subject to the Charges in this Act provided.

106. The Consolidated Revenue Fund of Canada shall be permanently charged with all the Costs, Charges, and Expenses incident to the Collection, Management, and Receipt thereof, and the same shall form the First Charge thereon, such Costs, Charges, and Expenses being subject nevertheless to be reviewed and audited in such Manner as shall be ordered by the Governor-General in Council until otherwise provided by any Act of the Parliament.
Expenses of Collection, &c.

107. The annual Interest of the Public Debt of the several Provinces of Canada, Nova Scotia, and New Brunswick at the Union shall form the second Charge on the Consolidated Revenue Fund of Canada.
Interest of Public Debt.

108. Unless altered by any Act of the Parliament of Canada, the Salary of the Governor-General shall be Ten Thousand Pounds Sterling Money of the United Kingdom of Great Britain and Ireland, payable out of the Consolidated Revenue Fund of Canada, and the same shall form the Third Charge thereon.
Salary of Governor General.

109. Subject to the several Payments by this Act charged on the Consolidated Revenue Fund of Canada, the same shall be appropriated by the Parliament of Canada for the Public Service.
Appropriation from Time to Time.

110. All Stocks, Cash, Banker's Balances, and Securities for Money belonging to each Province at the Time of the Union, except as in this Act mentioned, shall be the Property of Canada, and shall be taken in Reduction of the Amount of their respective Debts at the Union.
Transfer of Stocks, &c.

111. The Public Works and Property of each Province, enumerated in the   Schedule to this Act, shall be the Property of Canada.
Transfer of Property in Schedule.

Property in Lands, Mines, &c. 112. All Lands, Mines, Minerals, and Royalties belonging to the several Provinces of Canada, Nova Scotia, and New Brunswick, and all Sums due for such Lands, Mines, or Minerals, at the Union, shall belong to the several Provinces of Ontario, Quebec, Nova Scotia, and New Brunswick in which the same are situate or arise, subject to any Trusts existing in respect thereof, and to any Interest of other Persons in the same.

Assets connected with Provincial Debts. 113. All Assets connected with such Portions of the Public Debt of any Province as are assumed by such Province shall belong to such Province.

Assumption of Provincial Debts. 114. Canada shall assume the Debts and Liabilities of each Province existing at the Union.

Debts of Ontario and Quebec. 115. Ontario and Quebec conjointly shall assume the Excess (if any) by which the Debt of the Province of Canada exceeds at the Union Sixty-two millions five hundred thousand Dollars, and shall be charged with Interest at the Rate of Five per Centum per Annum thereon.

Assets of Ontario and Quebec. 116. The Assets enumerated in the   Schedule to this Act belonging at the Union to the Province of Canada shall be the property of Ontario and Quebec conjointly.

Debt of Nova Scotia. 117. Nova Scotia shall assume the Excess (if any) by which its Public Debt exceeds at the Union Eight million Dollars, and shall be charged with Interest at the Rate of Five per Centum per Annum thereon.

Debt of New Brunswick 118. New Brunswick shall assume the Excess (if any) by which its Public Debt exceeds at the Union Seven million Dollars, and shall be charged with Interest at the Rate of Five per Centum per Annum thereon.

Payment of interest to Nova Scotia and New Brunswick 119. In case the Public Debts of Nova Scotia and New Brunswick do not at the Union amount to Eight million and Seven million Dollars respectively, they shall respectively receive by half-yearly Payments in advance from the Government of Canada the Interest at Five per Centum per Annum on the Difference between the actual Amount of their respective Debts and such stipulated Amounts.

120. The several Provinces shall retain all Public Property not otherwise disposed of in this Act, subject to the Right of Canada to assume any Lands or Public Property required for Fortifications or for the Defence of the Country.

Provincial Public Property.

121. The following Sums shall be paid yearly by Canada to the several Provinces for the Support of their Governments and Legislatures :

Grants to Provinces.

Ontario.	$80,000
Quebec.	70,000
Nova Scotia.	60,000
New Brunswick. . . .	50,000
	$260,000

and an annual Grant in aid of each Province shall be made, equal to Eighty Cents per Head of the Population as ascertained by the Census of One thousand eight hundred and sixty-one : and in the Case of Nova Scotia and New Brunswick, by each subsequent Decennial Census until the Population of each of these Provinces amounts to Four hundred thousand Souls, at which Rate such Grant shall thereafter remain. Such Grant shall be in full Settlement of all future Demands on Canada, and shall be paid half-yearly in advance to each Province : but the Government of Canada shall deduct from such Grant, as against any Province, all sums chargeable as Interest on the Public Debt of that Province in excess of the several Amounts stipulated in this Act.

122. New Brunswick shall receive by half-yearly Payments in advance from Canada for the Period of Ten Years from the Union an additional Allowance of Sixty-three thousand Dollars per Annum ; but as long as the Public Debt of that Province remains under Seven millions of Dollars, a Deduction equal to the Interest at Five per Centum per Annum on such Deficiency shall be made from that Allowance of Sixty-three thousand Dollars.

Further Grant to New Brunswick.

123. All Payments to be made under this Act, or in discharge of Liabilities created under any Act of the Provinces of Canada, Nova Scotia, and New Brunswick re-

Form of Payments.

spectively, and assumed by Canada, shall, until otherwise Parliament directs, be made in such Form and Manner as may from Time to Time be ordered by the Governor-General in Council.

Customs and Excise. 124. The Customs and Excise Laws of each Province shall continue in force until altered by Parliament : and in any Case where the Duties enacted to be collected on any Goods, Wares, or Merchandise are the same, the Governor-General in Council may from Time to Time, by Proclamation, declare that such Goods, Wares and Merchandise may be imported free into any Port in Canada from Ontario, Quebec, Nova Scotia, or New Brunswick, on Proof of Duty having been already paid thereon : and where larger Duties are leviable in any Province on any Goods, Wares, or Merchandise, the Governor-General in Council may from Time to Time, by Proclamation, authorize the Importation into Canada of such Goods, Wares, and Merchandise on Payment of the Difference of Duty.

Canadian Manufactures, &c. 125. All Articles the Growth or Produce or Manufacture of Ontario, Quebec, Nova Scotia, or New Brunswick, shall be admitted free into all Ports in Canada.

Exemption of Public Lands, &c. 126. No Lands or Property belonging to Canada or any Province shall be liable to Taxation.

Provincial Consolidated Revenue Fund. 127. Such Portions of the Duties and Revenues over which the respective Legislatures of Canada, Nova Scotia, and New Brunswick, had before the Union Power of Appropriation as are by this Act reserved to the respective Governments or Legislatures of the Provinces, and all Duties and Revenues raised by them in accordance with the special Powers conferred upon them by this Act, shall in each Province form One Consolidated Revenue Fund to be appropriated for the Public Service of the Province.

X.—MISCELLANEOUS PROVISIONS.

General.

Oath of Allegiance &c. 128. Every Member of the Senate or House of Commons shall before taking his Seat therein take and subscribe before the Governor-General or some person au-

thorized by him, and every Member of a Legislative
Council or Legislative Assembly under this Act shall before taking his Seat therein take and subscribe before the
Lieutenant-Governor of the Province or some Person authorized by him, the Oath of Allegiance and the Declaration given in the　　　　　　　Schedule to this Act.

129. Except as otherwise provided by this Act, all Continu-
Laws in force in Canada, Nova Scotia, or New Brunswick existing
at the Union, and all Courts of Civil and Criminal Juris- Laws,
diction, and all Legal Commissions, Powers, and Authori- Officers,
ties, and all Officers, Judicial, Administrative, and Minis- &c.
terial, existing therein at the Union, shall continue in
Ontario, Quebec, Nova Scotia, and New Brunswick respectively, as if this Act had not been passed : subject
nevertheless (except with respect to such as are enacted
by or exist by Force of Acts of the Parliament of Great
Britain or of the Parliament of the United Kingdom of
Great Britain and Ireland,) to be repealed, abolished, or
altered by Act of the Parliament of Canada, or by Act of
the Legislature of the respective Province, according to
the Authority of that Parliament or Legislature under this
Act.

130. The Parliament and Government of Canada Treaty
shall have all Powers necessary or proper for performing Obliga-
the Obligations of Canada or of any Province thereof, as tions.
Part of the British Empire, towards Foreign Countries,
arising under Treaties between the Empire and such
Foreign Countries.

131. Either the English or the French Language may Use of
be used by any Person in the Debates of the Houses of English
the Parliament of Canada and of the Houses of the Legis- and French
lature of Quebec, and both of those Languages shall be Languages.
used in the respective Records and Journals of those
Houses, and either of those Languages may be used by
any Person or in any Pleading or Process in or issuing
from any Court of Canada established under this Act, and
in or from all or any of the Courts of Quebec.

The Acts of the Parliament of Canada and of the Legislature of Quebec shall be printed and published in separate Volumes in the English and French Languages respectively.

Ontario and Quebec.

Construction of temporary Acts. 132. The Words " and from thence to the End of the " then next ensuing Session of the Legislature," or Words to the same Effect, used in any temporary Act of the Province of Canada not expired before the Union, shall be construed to extend and apply to the next Session of the Parliament of Canada, if the subject Matter of the Act is within the Powers of the same, as defined by this Act, or to the next Sessions of the Legislatures of Ontario and Quebec respectively, if the subject Matter of the Act is within the Powers of the same as defined by this Act.

Errors in Names. 133. From and after the Union the Use of the Words " Upper Canada " instead of " Ontario," or " Lower Canada " instead of " Quebec," in any Deed, Document, Writ, Process, Pleading, Matter, or Thing whatsoever, shall not invalidate the same.

Proclamations commencing after Union. 134. Any proclamation under the Great Seal of the Province of Canada issued before the Union to take effect at a Time which is subsequent to the said Union, whether relating to that Province, or to Upper Canada, or to Lower Canada, and the several Matters and Things therein proclaimed shall be, remain, and continue of full Force and Effect from and after the Time mentioned in such Proclamation.

Issue of Proclamations after Union. 135. Any Proclamation which is authorized by any Act of the Legislature of the Province of Canada, to be issued under the Great Seal of the Province of Canada, whether relating to that Province, or to Upper Canada, or to Lower Canada, and which is not issued before the Union, may be issued by the Lieutenant-Governor of Ontario or Quebec, as the Subject Matter of such Proclamation requires, under the Great Seal thereof, and from and after the Issue of such Proclamation the same and the several

Matters and Things therein proclaimed shall be, remain, and continue of Full Force and Effect in Ontario or Quebec.

136. The Provincial Penitentiary of Canada shall, until Parliament otherwise provides, be and continue the Penitentiary of and for Ontario and Quebec respectively. *Penitentiary.*

137. The Division and Adjustment of the Debts, Credits, Liabilities, Properties, and Assets of the Provinces of Upper and Lower Canada shall be referred to the Arbitrament of Three Arbitrators, one to be chosen by the Government of Ontario, the other by the Government of Quebec, and the third by the Government of Canada ; and the Selection of the Arbitrators shall not take place until after the Parliament of Canada and the Legislatures for Ontario and Quebec have met, and the Third Arbitrator shall not be a resident in either Ontario or Quebec. *Arbitration respecting Debts, &c.*

138. The Governor-General in Council may from Time to Time order that such and so many of the Records, Books, and Documents as belong to the Province of Canada shall be appropriated and delivered either to Ontario or to Quebec, and the same shall thenceforth become the Property of such Province : and any Copy or Extract therefrom, duly certified by the Officer having charge of the Original thereof, shall be admitted as Evidence in the Courts of either Province. *Division of Records, &c.*

139. The Lieutenant-Governor of Quebec may from Time to Time, by Proclamation under the Great Seal of the Province, to take effect from a Day to be appointed therein, constitute Townships in those Parts of the Province of Quebec in which Townships are not then already constituted, and fix the Metes and Bounds thereof. *Constitution of Townships in Quebec.*

140. All Laws, Statutes, and Ordinances of the former Provinces of Upper and Lower Canada, or of the Province of Canada, in force at the Union in the Province *Continuance of Provincial Laws.*

of Canada in respect to Public Lands, or to Timber on
Public Lands, and the Sale and Management thereof respectively, and to Public Works, and to the Bureau of
Agriculture and Agricultural Societies, shall, as far as
they are not repugnant to this Act, continue in force, and
apply to the Provinces of Ontario and Quebec respectively, unless and until and as far only as such Laws,
Statutes, and Ordinances are varied, altered, amended, or
repealed by the Legislature of the Province.

XI.—INTERCOLONIAL RAILWAY.

Duty of Governor of Canada to make Railway.

141. Inasmuch as the Provinces of Canada, Nova
Scotia, and New Brunswick have joined in a Declaration
to the Effect that the Construction of the Intercolonial
Railway being essential to the Consolidation of the Union
of British North America, and to the Assent of the Maritime Provinces of Nova Scotia and New Brunswick thereto, it was agreed by them that Provision should be made
for its immediate Construction by the Government of
Canada : Therefore, in order to give Effect to that Agreement, it is hereby enacted that it shall be the Duty of the
Government and Parliament of Canada to provide for the
Commencement, within Six Months after the First Meeting of the Parliament, of a Railway from the River St.
Lawrence to the City of Halifax in Nova Scotia, and for
the Construction and Completion thereof without Intermission and with all practicable Speed.

XII.—ADMISSION OF OTHER COLONIES.

Power to admit Newfound-land, &c.

142. It shall be lawful for the Queen, by and with the
Advice of Her Majesty's Most Honourable Privy Council,
on Address from the Houses of the Parliament of Canada, and from the Houses of the respective Legislatures
of the Colonies or Provinces of Newfoundland, Prince
Edward Island, Rupert's Land, the North-western Territory, and British Columbia, to admit those Colonies or
Provinces into the Union on the Terms and Conditions
in the Addresses expressed : and the Provisions of any
Order in Council in that Behalf shall have effect as if they
had been enacted in this Act.

143. In case of the Admission of Newfoundland and Prince Edward Island, or either of them, each shall be entitled to a Representation in the Senate of Canada of Four Members ; but after the Admission of Prince Edward Island into the Union, the Representation of Nova Scotia and New Brunswick in the Senate of Canada shall, as Vacancies occur, be reduced from Twelve to Ten Members respectively, and the Representation of those Provinces shall not be increased at any Time beyond Ten, except under the Provisions of this Act for the Appointment of additional Senators under the Authority of a Warrant of the Queen under Her Royal Sign Manual.

Representation of Newfoundland and Prince Edward Island in Senate.

SCHEDULES.

Same as in Act.

VICTORIÆ REGINÆ.

CAP. III.

An Act for the Union of Canada, Nova Scotia, and New Brunswick, and the Government thereof; and for Purposes connected therewith.

[29th March, 1867.]

WHEREAS the Provinces of Canada, Nova Scotia, and New Brunswick have expressed their Desire to be federally united into One Dominion under the Crown of the United Kingdom of Great Britain and Ireland, with a Constitution similar in Principle to that of the United Kingdom :

And whereas such a Union would conduce to the Welfare of the Provinces and Promote the Interests of the British Empire :

And whereas on the Establishment of the Union by Authority of Parliament it is expedient, not only that the Constitution of the Legislative Authority in the Dominion be provided for, but also that the Nature of the Executive Government therein be declared :

And whereas it is expedient that Provision be made for the eventual Admission into the Union of other Parts of British North America :

Be it therefore enacted and declared by the Queen's most Excellent Majesty, by and with the Advice and Consent of the Lords Spiritual and Temporal, and Commons, in this present Parliament assembled, and by the Authority of the same, as follows :

I.—Preliminary.

1. This Act may be cited as the British North America Act, 1867.

Short Title.

2. The Provisions of this Act referring to Her Majesty the Queen extend also to the Heirs and Successors of Her Majesty, Kings and Queens of the United Kingdom of Great Britain and Ireland.

Application of Provisions referring to the Queen.

II.—Union.

3. It shall be lawful for the Queen, by and with the Advice of Her Majesty's Most Honourable Privy Council, to declare by Proclamation that, on and after a Day therein appointed, not being more than Six Months after the passing of this Act, the Provinces of Canada, Nova Scotia, and New Brunswick shall form and be One Dominion under the Name of Canada; and on and after that Day those Three Provinces shall form and be One Dominion under that Name accordingly.

Declaration of Union.

4. The subsequent Provisions of this Act shall, unless it is otherwise expressed or implied, commence and have effect on and after the Union, that is to say, on and after the Day appointed for the Union taking effect in the Queen's Proclamation; and in the same Provisions unless it is otherwise expressed or implied, the Name Canada shall be taken to mean Canada as constituted under this Act.

Construction of subsequent Provisions of Act.

5. Canada shall be divided into Four Provinces, named Ontario, Quebec, Nova Scotia, and New Brunswick.

Four Provinces.

6. The Parts of the Province of Canada (as it exists at the passing of this Act) which formerly constituted respectively the Provinces of Upper Canada and Lower Canada shall be deemed to be severed, and shall form Two Separate Provinces. The Part which formerly constituted the Province of Upper Canada shall constitute the Province of Ontario; and the Part which formerly constituted the Province of Lower Canada shall constitute the Province of Quebec.

Provinces of Ontario and Quebec.

Provinces of Nova Scotia and New Brunswick.

7. The Provinces of Nova Scotia and New Brunswick shall have the same Limits as at the passing of this Act.

Decennial Census.

8. In the general Census of the Population of Canada which is hereby required to be taken in the Year One thousand eight hundred and seventy-one, and in every Tenth Year thereafter, the respective Populations of the Four Provinces shall be distinguished.

III.—EXECUTIVE POWER.

Declaration of Executive Power in the Queen.

9. The Executive Government and Authority of and over Canada is hereby declared to continue and be vested in the Queen.

Application of Provisions referring to Governor-General.

10. The Provisions of this Act referring to the Governor-General extend and apply to the Governor-General for the Time being of Canada, or other the Chief Executive Officer or Administrator for the Time being carrying on the Government of Canada on behalf and in the Name of the Queen, by whatever Title he is designated.

Constitution of Privy Council for Canada.

11. There shall be a Council to aid and advise in the Government of Canada, to be styled the Queen's Privy Council for Canada ; and the Persons who are to be Members of that Council shall be from Time to Time chosen and summoned by the Governor-General and sworn in as Privy Councillors, and Members thereof may be from Time to Time removed by the Governor-General.

All Powers under Acts to be exercised by Governor-General with advice of Privy Council or alone.

12. All Powers, Authorities, and Functions which under any Act of the Parliament of Great Britain, or of the Parliament of the United Kingdom of Great Britain and Ireland, or of the Legislature of Upper Canada, Lower Canada, Canada, Nova Scotia, or New Brunswick, are at the Union vested in or exerciseable by the respective Governors or Lieutenant-Governors of those Provinces, with the Advice, or with the Advice and Consent, of the respective Executive Councils thereof, or in conjunction with those Councils, or with any Number of Members thereof, or by those Governors or Lieutenant-Governors individually, shall, as far as the same continue in existence and capable of being exercised after the Union in relation to the Government of Canada, be

vested in and exerciseable by the Governor-General, with the Advice or with the Advice and Consent of or in conjunction with the Queen's Privy Council for Canada, or any Members thereof, or by the Governor-General individually, as the Case requires, subject nevertheless (except with respect to such as exist under Acts of the Parliament of Great Britain or of the Parliament of the United Kingdom of Great Britain and Ireland) to be abolished or altered by the Parliament of Canada.

13. The Provisions of this Act referring to the Governor-General in Council shall be construed as referring to the Governor-General acting by and with the Advice of the Queen's Privy Council for Canada.

Application of Provisions referring to Governor-General in Council.

14. It shall be lawful for the Queen, if Her Majesty thinks fit, to authorize the Governor-General from Time to Time to appoint any Person or any Persons jointly or severally to be his Deputy or Deputies within any Part or Parts of Canada, and in that Capacity to exercise during the Pleasure of the Governor-General such of the Powers, Authorities, and Functions of the Governor-General as the Governor-General deems it necessary or expedient to assign to him or them, subject to any Limitations or Directions expressed or given by the Queen ; but the Appointment of such a Deputy or Deputies shall not affect the Exercise by the Governor-General himself of any Power, Authority, or Function.

Power to Her Majesty to authorize Governor-General to appoint Deputies.

15. The Command-in-Chief of the Land and Naval Militia, and of all Naval and Military Forces, of and in Canada, is hereby declared to continue and be vested in the Queen.

Command of Armed Forces to continue to be vested in the Queen.

16. Until the Queen otherwise directs the Seat of Government of Canada shall be Ottawa.

Seat of Government of Canada.

IV.—LEGISLATIVE POWER.

17. There shall be One Parliament for Canada, consisting of the Queen, an Upper House styled the Senate, and the House of Commons.

Constitution of Parliament of Canada.

Privileges, &c., of Houses.

18. The Privileges, Immunities, and Powers to be held enjoyed, and exercised by the Senate and by the House of Commons and by the Members thereof respectively shall be such as are from Time to Time defined by Act of the Parliament of Canada, but so that the same shall never exceed those at the passing of this Act held, enjoyed, and exercised by the Commons House of Parliament of the United Kingdom of Great Britain and Ireland and by the Members thereof.

First Session of the Parliament of Canada.

19. The Parliament of Canada shall be called together not later than Six Months after the Union.

Yearly Session of the Parliament of Canada.

20. There shall be a Session of the Parliament of Canada once at least in every Year, so that Twelve Months shall not intervene between the last Sitting of the Parliament in one Session and its first Sitting in the next Session.

The Senate.

Number of Senators.

21. The Senate shall, subject to the Provisions of this Act, consist of Seventy-two Members, who shall be styled Senators.

Representation of Provinces in Senate.

22. In relation to the Constitution of the Senate, Canada shall be deemed to consist of Three Divisions—

1. Ontario ;

2. Quebec ;

3. The Maritime Provinces, Nova Scotia and New Brunswick ; which Three Divisions shall (subject to the Provisions of this Act) be equally represented in the Senate as follows : Ontario by Twenty-four Senators ; Quebec by Twenty-four Senators ; and the Maritime Provinces by Twenty-four Senators, Twelve thereof representing Nova Scotia, and Twelve thereof representing New Brunswick.

In the case of Quebec each of the Twenty-four Senators representing that Province shall be appointed for One of the Twenty-four Electoral Divisions of Lower Canada specified in Schedule A. to Chapter One of the Consolidated Statutes of Canada.

23. The Qualification of a Senator shall be as follows :—

    (1) He shall be of the full Age of Thirty Years :

    (2) He shall be either a Natural-born Subject of the
        Queen, or a Subject of the Queen naturalized
        by an Act of the Parliament of Great Britain,
        or of the Parliament of the United Kingdom
        of Great Britain and Ireland, or of the Legis-
        lature of One of the Provinces of Upper Ca-
        nada, Lower Canada, Canada, Nova Scotia, or
        New Brunswick, before the Union, or of the
        Parliament of Canada after the Union :

    (3) He shall be legally or equitably seised as of
        Freehold for his own Use and Benefit of
        Lands or Tenements held in free and common
        Socage, or seised or possessed for his own Use
        and Benefit of Lands or Tenements held in
        Franc-alleu or in Roture, within the Province
        for which he is appointed, of the value of Four
        thousand Dollars, over and above all Rents,
        Dues, Debts, Charges, Mortgages, and Incum-
        brances due or payable out of or charged on
        or affecting the same :

    (4) His Real and Personal Property shall be to-
        gether worth Four thousand Dollars over and
        above his Debts and Liabilities :

    (5) He shall be resident in the Province for which
        he is appointed :

    (6) In the Case of Quebec he shall have his Real Pro-
        perty Qualification in the Electoral Division
        for which he is appointed, or shall be resident
        in that Division :

24. The Governor-General shall from Time to Time,
in the Queen's Name, by Instrument under the Great
Seal of Canada, summon Qualified Persons to the Senate ;
and, subject to the Provisions of this Act, every Person
so summoned shall become and be a Member of the Senate and a Senator.

Summons of First Body of Senators.

25. Such Persons shall be first summoned to the Senate as the Queen by Warrant under Her Majesty's Royal Sign Manual thinks fit to approve, and their Names shall be inserted in the Queen's Proclamation of Union.

Addition of Senators in certain cases.

26. If at any Time on the Recommendation of the Governor-General the Queen thinks fit to direct that Three or Six Members be added to the Senate, the Governor-General may by Summons to Three or Six qualified Persons (as the Case may be), representing equally the Three Divisions of Canada, add to the Senate accordingly.

Reduction of Senate to normal number.

27. In case of such Addition being at any Time made the Governor-General shall not summon any Person to the Senate, except on a further like Direction by the Queen on the like Recommendation, until each of the Three Divisions of Canada is represented by Twenty-four Senators and no more.

Maximum number of Senators.

28. The Number of Senators shall not at any Time exceed Seventy-eight.

Tenure of place in Senate.

29. A Senator shall, subject to the Provisions of this Act, hold his Place in the Senate for Life.

Resignation of Place in Senate.

30. A Senator may by Writing under his Hand addressed to the Governor-General resign his Place in the Senate, and thereupon the same shall be vacant.

Disqualification of Senators.

31. The Place of a Senator shall become vacant in any of the following Cases :—

(1) If for Two consecutive Sessions of the Parliament he fails to give his Attendance in the Senate :

(2) If he takes an Oath or makes a Declaration or Acknowledgment of Allegiance, Obedience, or Adherence to a Foreign Power, or does an Act whereby he becomes a Subject or Citizen, or entitled to the Rights or Privileges of a Subject or Citizen, of a Foreign Power :

(3) If he is adjudged Bankrupt or Insolvent, or applies for the Benefit of any Law relating to Insolvent Debtors, or becomes a public Defaulter :

(4) If he is attainted of Treason or convicted of Felony or of any infamous Crime :

(5) If he ceases to be qualified in respect of Property or of Residence : provided, that a Senator shall not be deemed to have ceased to be qualified in respect of Residence by reason only of his residing at the Seat of the Government of Canada while holding an Office under that Government requiring his Presence there.

32. When a Vacancy happens in the Senate by Resignation, Death, or otherwise, the Governor-General shall by Summons to a fit and qualified Person fill the Vacancy. *Summons on Vacancy in Senate.*

33. If any Question arises respecting the Qualification of a Senator or a Vacancy in the Senate the same shall be heard and determined by the Senate. *Questions as to Qualifications and Vacancies in Senate.*

34. The Governor-General may from Time to Time, by Instrument under the Great Seal of Canada, appoint a Senator to be Speaker of the Senate, and may remove him and appoint another in his Stead. *Appointment of Speaker of Senate.*

35. Until the Parliament of Canada otherwise provides, the Presence of at least Fifteen Senators, including the Speaker, shall be necesssary to constitute a Meeting of the Senate for the Exercise of its Powers. *Quorum of Senate.*

36. Questions arising in the Senate shall be decided by a Majority of Voices, and the Speaker shall in all Cases have a Vote, and when the Voices are equal the Decision shall be deemed to be in the Negative. *Voting in Senate.*

The House of Commons.

37. The House of Commons shall, subject to the Provisions of this Act, consist of One hundred and eighty-one Members, of whom Eighty-two shall be elected for Ontario, Sixty-five for Quebec, Nineteen for Nova Scotia, and Fifteen for New Brunswick. *Constitution of House of Commons in Canada.*

38. The Governor-General shall from Time to Time, in the Queen's Name, by Instrument under the Great Seal of Canada, summon and call together the House of Commons. *Summoning of House of Commons.*

Senators
not to sit in
House of
Commons.

39. A Senator shall not be capable of being elected or of sitting or voting as a Member of the House of Commons.

Electoral
districts of
the four
Provinces.

40. Until the Parliament of Canada otherwise provides, Ontario, Quebec, Nova Scotia, and New Brunswick shall, for the Purposes of the Election of Members to serve in the House of Commons, be divided into Electoral Districts as follows :—

1.—ONTARIO.

Ontario shall be divided into the Counties, Ridings of Counties, Cities, Parts of Cities, and Towns enumerated in the First Schedule to this Act, each whereof shall be an Electoral District, each such District as numbered in that Schedule being entitled to return One Member.

2.—QUEBEC.

Quebec shall be divided into Sixty-five Electoral Districts, composed of the Sixty-five Electoral Divisions into which Lower Canada is at the passing of this Act divided under Chapter Two of the Consolidated Statutes of Canada, Chapter Seventy-five of the Consolidated Statutes for Lower Canada, and the Act of the Province of Canada of the Twenty-third Year of the Queen, Chapter One, or any other Act amending the same in force at the Union, so that each such Electoral Division shall be for the Purposes of this Act an Electoral District entitled to return One Member.

3.—NOVA SCOTIA.

Each of the Eighteen Counties of Nova Scotia shall be an Electoral District. The County of Halifax shall be entitled to return Two Members, and each of the other Counties One Member.

4—NEW BRUNSWICK.

Each of the Fourteen Counties into which New Brunswick is divided, including the City and County of St. John, shall be an Electoral District. The City of St. John shall also be a separate Electoral District. Each of those Fifteen Electoral Districts shall be entitled to return One Member.

41. Until the Parliament of Canada otherwise provides, all Laws in force in the several Provinces at the Union relative to the following Matters or any of them, namely,—the Qualifications and Disqualifications of Persons to be elected or to sit or vote as Members of the House of Assembly or Legislative Assembly in the several Provinces, the Voters at Elections of such Members, the Oaths to be taken by Voters, the Returning Officers, their Powers and Duties, the Proceedings at Elections, the Periods during which Elections may be continued, the Trial of controverted Elections, and Proceedings incident thereto, the vacating of Seats of Members, and the Execution of new Writs in case of Seats vacated otherwise than by Dissolution,—shall respectively apply to Elections of Members to serve in the House of Commons for the same several Provinces.

Continuance of existing Election Laws until Parliament of Canada otherwise provides.

Provided that, until the Parliament of Canada otherwise provides, at any Election for a Member of the House of Commons for the District of Algoma, in addition to Persons qualified by the Law of the Province of Canada to vote, every male British Subject, aged Twenty-one Years or Upwards, being a Householder, shall have a Vote.

42. For the First Election of Members to serve in the House of Commons the Governor-General shall cause Writs to be issued by such Person, in such Form, and addressed to such Returning Officers as he thinks fit.

Writs for first Election.

The person issuing Writs under this Section shall have the like Powers as are possessed at the Union by the Officers charged with the issuing of Writs for the Election of Members to serve in the respective House of Assembly or Legislative Assembly of the Province of Canada, Nova Scotia, or New Brunswick ; and the Returning Officers to whom Writs are directed under this Section shall have the like Powers as are possessed at the Union by the Officers charged with the returning of Writs for the Election of Members to serve in the same respective House of Assembly or Legislative Assembly.

43. In case a Vacancy in the Representation in the House of Commons of any Electoral District happens be-

As to Casual Vacancies.

fore the Meeting of the Parliament, or after the Meeting of the Parliament before Provision is made by the Parliament in this Behalf, the Provisions of the last foregoing Section of this Act shall extend and apply to the issuing and returning of a Writ in respect of such vacant District.

As to Election of Speaker of House of Commons. **44.** The House of Commons on its first assembling after a General Election shall proceed with all practicable Speed to elect One of its Members to be Speaker.

As to filling up Vacancy in Office of Speaker. **45.** In case of a Vacancy happening in the Office of Speaker by Death, Resignation, or otherwise, the House of Commons shall with all practicable Speed proceed to elect another of its Members to be Speaker.

Speaker to preside. **46.** The Speaker shall preside at all Meetings of the House of Commons.

Provision in case of absence of Speaker. **47.** Until the Parliament of Canada otherwise provides, in case of the Absence for any Reason of the Speaker from the Chair of the House of Commons for a Period of Forty-eight consecutive Hours, the House may elect another of its Members to act as Speaker, and the Member so elected shall during the continuance of such Absence of the Speaker have and execute all the Powers, Privileges, and Duties of Speaker.

Quorum of House of Commons. **48.** The Presence of at least Twenty Members of the House of Commons shall be necessary to constitute a Meeting of the House for the Exercise of its Powers ; and for that Purpose the Speaker shall be reckoned as a Member.

Voting in House of Commons. **49.** Questions arising in the House of Commons shall be decided by a Majority of Voices other than that of the Speaker, and when the Voices are equal, but not otherwise, the Speaker shall have a Vote.

Duration of House of Commons. **50.** Every House of Commons shall continue for Five Years from the Day of the Return of the Writs for choosing the House (subject to be sooner dissolved by the Governor-General), and no longer.

Decennial Readjustment of Representation. **51.** On the Completion of the Census in the Year One thousand eight hundred and seventy-one, and of each subsequent decennial Census, the Representation of the

Four Provinces shall be re-adjusted by such Authority, in such Manner, and from such Time, as the Parliament of Canada from Time to Time provides, subject and according to the following Rules :—

(1) Quebec shall have the fixed Number of Sixty-five Members :

(2) There shall be assigned to each of the other Provinces such a Number of Members as will bear the same Proportion to the Number of its Population (ascertained at such Census) as the Number Sixty-five bears to the Number of the Population of Quebec (so ascertained) :

(3) In the Computation of the Number of Members for a Province a fractional Part not exceeding One Half of the whole Number requisite for entitling the Province to a Member shall be disregarded ; but a fractional Part exceeding One Half of that Number shall be equivalent to the whole Number :

(4) On any such Re-adjustment the Number of Members for a Province shall not be reduced unless the Proportion which the Number of the Population of the Province bore to the Number of the aggregate Population of Canada at the then last preceding Re-adjustment of the Number of Members for the Province is ascertained at the then latest Census to be diminished by One Twentieth Part or upwards :

(5) Such Re-adjustment shall not take effect until the Termination of the then existing Parliament.

52. The Number of Members of the House of Commons may be from Time to Time increased by the Parliament of Canada, provided the proportionate Representation of the Provinces prescribed by this Act is not thereby disturbed. *Increase of number of House of Commons.*

Money Votes; Royal Assent.

53. Bills for appropriating any Part of the Public Revenue, or for imposing any Tax or Impost, shall originate in the House of Commons. *Appropriation and tax Bills.*

Recommendation of money votes.

54. It shall not be lawful for the House of Commons to adopt or pass any Vote, Resolution, Address, or Bill for the Appropriation of any Part of the Public Revenue, or of any Tax or Impost, to any Purpose that has not been first recommended to that House by Message of the Governor-General in the Session in which such Vote, Resolution, Address, or Bill is proposed.

Royal Assent to Bills, &c.

55. Where a Bill passed by the Houses of the Parliament is presented to the Governor-General for the Queen's Assent, he shall declare, according to his Discretion, but subject to the Provisions of this Act and to Her Majesty's Instructions, either that he assents thereto in the Queen's Name, or that he withholds the Queen's Assent, or that he reserves the Bill for the Signification of the Queen's Pleasure.

Disallowance by order in Council of Act assented to by Governor-General.

56. Where the Governor-General assents to a Bill in the Queen's Name, he shall by the first convenient Opportunity send an authentic Copy of the Act to One of Her Majesty's Principal Secretaries of State, and if the Queen in Council within Two Years after Receipt thereof by the Secretary of State thinks fit to disallow the Act, such Disallowance (with a certificate of the Secretary of State of the Day on which the Act was received by him) being signified by the Governor-General, by Speech or Message to each of the Houses of the Parliament or by Proclamation, shall annul the Act from and after the Day of such Signification.

Signification of Queen's pleasure on Bill reserved.

57. A Bill reserved for the Signification of the Queen's Pleasure shall not have any Force unless and until within Two Years from the Day on which it was presented to the Governor-General for the Queen's Assent, the Governor-General signifies, by Speech or Message to each of the Houses of the Parliament or by Proclamation, that it has received the Assent of the Queen in Council.

An entry of every such Speech, Message, or Proclamation shall be made in the Journal of each House, and a Duplicate thereof duly attested shall be delivered to the proper Officer to be kept among the Records of Canada.

V.—Provincial Constitutions.

Executive Power.

58. For each Province there shall be an Officer, styled the Lieutenant-Governor, appointed by the Governor-General in Council by Instrument under the Great Seal of Canada.

Appointment of Lieutenant-Governors of Provinces.

59. A Lieutenant-Governor shall hold Office during the Pleasure of the Governor-General ; but any Lieutenant-Governor appointed after the Commencement of the First Session of the Parliament of Canada shall not be removable within Five Years from his Appointment, except for Cause assigned, which shall be communicated to him in Writing within One Month after the Order for his removal is made, and shall be communicated by Message to the Senate and to the House of Commons within One Week thereafter if the Parliament is then sitting, and if not then within One Week after the Commencement of the next Session of the Parliament.

Tenure of office of Lieutenant-Governor.

60. The Salaries of the Lieutenant-Governors shall be fixed and provided by the Parliament of Canada.

Salaries of Lieutenant-Governors.

61. Every Lieutenant-Governor shall, before assuming the Duties of his Office, make and subscribe before the Governor-General or some Person authorized by him, Oaths of Allegiance and Office similar to those taken by the Governor-General.

Oaths, &c., of Lieutenant-Governor.

62. The Provisions of this Act referring to the Lieutenant-Governor extend and apply to the Lieutenant-Governor for the Time being of each Province or other the Chief Executive Officer or Administrator for the Time being carrying on the Government of the Province, by whatever Title he is designated.

Application of provisions referring to Lieutenant-Governor.

63. The Executive Council of Ontario and of Quebec shall be composed of such Persons as the Lieutenant-Governor from Time to Time thinks fit, and in the first instance of the following Officers, namely,—the Attorney-General, the Secretary and Registrar of the Province, the Treasurer of the Province, the Commissioner of Crown Lands, and the Commissioner of Agriculture and Public

Appointment of Executive Officers for Ontario and Quebec.

Works, with, in Quebec, the Speaker of the Legislative Council and the Solicitor-General.

Executive Government of Nova Scotia and New Brunswick.

64. The Constitution of the Executive Authority in each of the Provinces of Nova Scotia and New Brunswick shall, subject to the Provisions of this Act, continue as it exists at the Union until altered under the Authority of this Act.

Powers to be exercised by Lieutenant-Governor of Ontario or Quebec with advice or alone.

65. All Powers, Authorities, and Functions which under any Act of the Parliament of Great Britain, or of the Parliament of the United Kingdom of Great Britain and Ireland, or of the Legislature of Upper Canada, Lower Canada, or Canada, were or are before or at the Union vested in or exerciseable by the respective Governors or Lieutenant-Governors of those Provinces, with the Advice, or with the Advice and Consent, of the respective Executive Councils thereof, or in conjunction with those Councils, or with any Number of Members thereof, or by those Governors or Lieutenant-Governors individually, shall, as far as the same are capable of being exercised after the Union in relation to the Government of Ontario and Quebec respectively, be vested in and shall or may be exercised by the Lieutenant-Governor of Ontario and Quebec respectively, with the Advice, or with the Advice and Consent of or in conjunction with the respective Executive Councils, or any Members thereof, or by the Lieutenant-Governor individually, as the Case requires, subject nevertheless (except with respect to such as exist under Acts of the Parliament of Great Britain, or of the Parliament of the United Kingdom of Great Britain and Ireland), to be abolished or altered by the respective Legislatures of Ontario and Quebec.

Application of provisions referring to Lieutenant-Governor in Council.

66. The Provisions of this Act referring to the Lieutenant-Governor in Council shall be construed as referring to the Lieutenant-Governor of the Province acting by and with the Advice of the Executive Council thereof.

Administration in absence, &c., of Lieutenant-Governor.

67. The Governor-General in Council may from Time to Time appoint an Administrator to execute the Office and Functions of Lieutenant-Governor during his Absence, Illness, or other Inability.

68. Unless and until the Executive Government of any Province otherwise directs with respect to that Province, the seats of Government of the Provinces shall be as follows, namely,—of Ontario, the City of Toronto ; of Quebec, the City of Quebec ; of Nova Scotia, the City of Halifax ; and of New Brunswick, the City of Fredericton.

Seats of Provincial Governments.

Legislative Power.

1.—ONTARIO.

69. There shall be a Legislature for Ontario consisting of the Lieutenant-Governor and of One House, styled the Legislative Assembly of Ontario.

Legislature for Ontario.

70. The Legislative Assembly of Ontario shall be composed of Eighty-two Members, to be elected to represent the Eighty-two Electoral Districts set forth in the First Schedule to this Act.

Electoral districts.

2.—QUEBEC.

71. There shall be a Legislature for Quebec consisting of the Lieutenant-Governor and of Two Houses, styled the Legislative Council of Quebec and the Legislative Assembly of Quebec.

Legislature for Quebec.

72. The Legislative Council of Quebec shall be composed of Twenty-four Members, to be appointed by the Lieutenant-Governor in the Queen's Name, by Instrument under the Great Seal of Quebec, one being appointed to represent each of the Twenty-four Electoral Divisions of Lower Canada in this Act referred to, and each holding Office for the Term of his Life, unless the Legislature of Quebec otherwise provides under the Provisions of this Act.

Constitution of Legislative Council.

73. The Qualifications of the Legislative Councillors of Quebec shall be the same as those of the Senators for Quebec.

Qualification of Legislative Councillors.

74. The Place of a Legislative Councillor of Quebec shall become vacant in the Cases, *mutatis mutandis*, in which the Place of Senator becomes vacant.

Resignation, Disqualification, &c.

Vacancies.

75. When a Vacancy happens in the Legislative Council of Quebec by Resignation, Death, or otherwise, the Lieutenant-Governor, in the Queen's Name, by Instrument under the Great Seal of Quebec, shall appoint a fit and qualified Person to fill the Vacancy.

Questions as to Vacancies, &c.

76. If any Question arises respecting the Qualification of a Legislative Councillor of Quebec, or a Vacancy in the Legislative Council of Quebec, the same shall be heard and determined by the Legislative Council.

Speaker of Legislative Council.

77. The Lieutenant-Governor may from Time to Time, by Instrument under the Great Seal of Quebec, appoint a Member of the Legislative Council of Quebec to be Speaker thereof, and may remove him and appoint another in his Stead.

Quorum of Legislative Council.

78. Until the Legislature of Quebec otherwise provides, the Presence of at least Ten Members of the Legislative Council, including the Speaker, shall be necessary to constitute a Meeting for the Exercise of its Powers.

Voting in Legislative Council.

79. Questions arising in the Legislative Council of Quebec shall be decided by a Majority of Voices, and the Speaker shall in all Cases have a Vote, and when the Voices are equal the Decision shall be deemed to be in the negative.

Constitution of Legislative Assembly of Quebec.

80. The Legislative Assembly of Quebec shall be composed of Sixty-five Members, to be elected to represent the Sixty-five Electoral Divisions or Districts of Lower Canada in this Act referred to, subject to Alteration thereof by the Legislature of Quebec: Provided that it shall not be lawful to present to the Lieutenant-Governor of Quebec for Assent any Bill for altering the Limits of any of the Electoral Divisions, or Districts mentioned in the Second Schedule to this Act, unless the Second and Third Readings of such Bill have been passed in the Legislative Assembly with the Concurrence of the Majority of the Members representing all those Electoral Divisions or Districts, and the Assent shall not be given to such Bill unless an Address has been presented by the Legislative Assembly to the Lieutenant-Governor stating that it has been so passed.

3.—ONTARIO AND QUEBEC.

81. The Legislatures of Ontario and Quebec respectively shall be called together not later than Six Months after the Union.

First Session of Legislatures.

82. The Lieutenant-Governor of Ontario and of Quebec shall from Time to Time, in the Queen's Name, by Instrument under the Great Seal of the Province, summon and call together the Legislative Assembly of the Province.

Summoning of Legislative Assemblies

83. Until the Legislature of Ontario or of Quebec otherwise provides, a Person accepting or holding in Ontario or in Quebec any Office, Commission, or Employment permanent or temporary, at the Nomination of the Lieutenant-Governor, to which an annual Salary, or any Fee, Allowance, Emolument, or profit of any Kind or Amount whatever from the Province is attached, shall not be eligible as a Member of the Legislative Assembly of the respective Province, nor shall he sit or vote as such ; but nothing in this Section shall make ineligible any Person being a Member of the Executive Council of the respective Province, or holding any of the following Offices, that is to say, the Offices of Attorney-General, Secretary and Registrar of the Province, Treasurer of the Province, Commissioner of Crown Lands, and Commissioner of Agriculture and Public Works, and in Quebec Solicitor-General, or shall disqualify him to sit or vote in the House for which he is elected, provided he is elected while holding such Office.

Restriction on election of holders of offices.

84. Until the Legislatures of Ontario and Quebec respectively otherwise provide, all Laws which at the Union are in force in those Provinces respectively, relative to the following Matters, or any of them, namely,—the Qualifications and Disqualifications of Persons to be elected or to sit or vote as Members of the Assembly of Canada, the Qualifications or Disqualifications of Voters, the Oaths to be taken by Voters, the Returning Officers, their Powers and Duties, the Proceedings at Elections, the Periods during which such Elections may be continued, and the Trial of controverted Elections and the Proceedings incident thereto, the vacating of the Seats of

Continuance of existing election Laws.

Members and the issuing and Execution of new Writs in case of Seats vacated otherwise than by Dissolution, shall respectively apply to Elections of Members to serve in the respective Legislative Assemblies of Ontario and Quebec.

Provided that until the Legislature of Ontario otherwise provides, at any Election for a Member of the Legislative Assembly of Ontario for the District of Algoma, in addition to Persons qualified by the Law of the Province of Canada to vote, every male British Subject, aged Twenty-one Years or Upwards, being a Householder, shall have a Vote.

Duration of Legislative Assemblies. 85. Every Legislative Assembly of Ontario and every Legislative Assembly of Quebec shall continue for Four Years from the Day of the Return of the Writs for choosing the same (subject nevertheless to either the Legislative Assembly of Ontario or the Legislative Assembly of Quebec being sooner dissolved by the Lieutenant-Governor of the Province), and no longer.

Yearly Session of Legislature. 86. There shall be a Session of the Legislature of Ontario and of that of Quebec once at least in every Year, so that Twelve Months shall not intervene between the last Sitting of the Legislature in each Province in one Session and its first Sitting in the next Session.

Speaker, Quorum, &c. 87. The following Provisions of this Act respecting the House of Commons of Canada shall extend and apply to the Legislative Assemblies of Ontario and Quebec, that is to say,—the Provisions relating to the Election of a Speaker originally and on Vacancies, the Duties of the Speaker, the Absence of the Speaker, the Quorum, and the Mode of voting, as if those Provisions were here re-enacted and made applicable in Terms to each such Legistive Assembly.

4.—NOVA SCOTIA AND NEW BRUNSWICK.

Constitutions of Legislatures of Nova Scotia and New Brunswick. 88. The Constitution of the Legislature of each of the Provinces of Nova Scotia and New Brunswick shall, subject to the Provisions of this Act, continue as it exists at the Union until altered under the Authority of this Act ; and the House of Assembly of New Brunswick existing at the passing of this Act shall, unless sooner dissolved, continue for the Period for which it was elected.

5.—ONTARIO, QUEBEC AND NOVA SCOTIA.

89. Each of the Lieutenant-Governors of Ontario, Quebec, and Nova Scotia shall cause Writs to be issued for the First Election of Members of the Legislative Assembly thereof, in such Form and by such Person as he thinks fit, and at such Time and addressed to such Returning Officer as the Governor-General directs, and so that the First Election of Member of Assembly for any Electoral District or any Subdivision thereof shall be held at the same Time and at the same Places as the Election for a Member to serve in the House of Commons of Canada for that Electoral District.

First Elections.

6.—THE FOUR PROVINCES.

90. The following Provisions of this Act respecting the Parliament of Canada, namely,—the Provisions relating to Appropriation and Tax Bills, the Recommendation of Money Votes, the Assent of Bills, the Disallowance of Acts and the Signification of Pleasure on Bills reserved,—shall extend and apply to the Legislatures of the several Provinces as if those Provisions were here re-enacted and made applicable in Terms to the respective Provinces and the Legislatures thereof, with the Substitution of the Lieutenant-Governor of the Province for the Governor-General, of the Governor-General for the Queen and for a Secretary of State, of One Year for Two Years, and of the Province for Canada.

Application to Legislatures of provisions respecting money votes, &c.

VI.—DISTRIBUTION OF LEGISLATIVE POWERS.

Powers of the Parliament.

91. It shall be lawful for the Queen, by and with the Advice and Consent of the Senate and House of Commons, to make Laws for the Peace, Order, and good Government of Canada, in relation to all Matters not coming within the Classes of Subjects by this Act assigned exclusively to the Legislatures of the Provinces ; and for greater Certainty, but not so as to restrict the Generality of the foregoing Terms of this Section, it is hereby declared that (notwithstanding anything in this Act) the exclusive Legislative Authority of the Parliament of Ca-

Legislative Authority of Parliament of Canada.

nada extends to all Matters coming within the Classes of Subjects next hereinafter enumerated ; that is to say :—

1. The Public Debt and Property.
2. The Regulation of Trade and Commerce.
3. The raising of Money by any Mode or System of Taxation.
4. The borrowing of Money on the Public Credit.
5. Postal Service.
6. The Census and Statistics.
7. Militia, Military and Naval Service, and Defence.
8. The fixing of and providing for the Salaries and Allowances of Civil and other Officers of the Government of Canada.
9. Beacons, Buoys, Lighthouses, and Sable Island.
10. Navigation and Shipping.
11. Quarantine and the Establishment and Maintenance of Marine Hospitals.
12. Sea Coast and Inland Fisheries.
13. Ferries between a Province and any British or Foreign Country or between Two Provinces.
14. Currency and Coinage.
15. Banking, Incorporation of Banks, and the Issue of Paper Money.
16. Savings Banks.
17. Weights and Measures.
18. Bills of Exchange and Promissory Notes.
19. Interest.
20. Legal Tender.
21. Bankruptcy and Insolvency.
22. Patents of Invention and Discovery.
23. Copyrights.
24. Indians, and Lands reserved for the Indians.
25. Naturalization and Aliens.
26. Marriage and Divorce.
27. The Criminal Law, except the Constitution of Courts of Criminal Jurisdiction, but including the Procedure in Criminal Matters.

28. The Establishment, Maintenance, and Management of Penitentiaries.

29. Such Classes of Subjects as are expressly excepted in the Enumeration of the Classes of Subjects by this Act assigned exclusively to the Legislatures of the Provinces.

And any Matter coming within any of the Classes of Subjects enumerated in this Section shall not be deemed to come within the Class of Matters of a local or private Nature comprised in the Enumeration of the Classes of Subjects by this Act assigned exclusively to the Legislatures of the Provinces.

Exclusive Powers of Provincial Legislatures.

92. In each Province the Legislature may exclusively make Laws in relation to Matters coming within the Classes of Subjects next hereinafter enumerated, that is to say,— *Subjects of exclusive Provincial Legislation.*

1. The Amendment from Time to Time, notwithstanding anything in this Act, of the Constitution of the Province, except as regards the Office of Lieutenant-Governor.

2. Direct Taxation within the Province in order to the raising of a Revenue for Provincial Purposes.

3. The borrowing of Money on the sole Credit of the Province.

4. The Establishment and Tenure of Provincial Offices and the Appointment and Payment of Provincial Officers.

5. The Management and Sale of the Public Lands belonging to the Province and of the Timber and Wood thereon.

6. The Establishment, Maintenance, and Management of Public and Reformatory Prisons in and for the Province.

7. The Establishment, Maintenance, and Management of Hospitals, Asylums, Charities, and Eleemosynary Institutions in and for the Province, other than Marine Hospitals.

8. Municipal Institutions in the Province.

9. Shop, Saloon, Tavern, Auctioneer, and other Licenses in order to the raising of a Revenue for Provincial, Local, or Municipal Purposes.

10. Local Works and Undertakings other than such as are of the following Classes,—

    (a) Lines of Steam or other Ships, Railways, Canals, Telegraphs, and other Works and Undertakings connecting the Province with any other or others of the Provinces, or extending beyond the Limits of the Province :

    (b) Lines of Steam Ships between the Province and any British or Foreign Country :

    (c) Such Works as, although wholly situate within the Province, are before or after their Execution declared by the Parliament of Canada to be for the General Advantage of Canada or for the Advantage of Two or more of the Provinces.

11. The Incorporataion of Companies with Provincial Objects.

12. The Solemnization of Marriage in the Province.

13. Property and Civil Rights in the Province.

14. The Administration of Justice in the Province, including the Constitution, Maintenance, and Organization of Provincial Courts, both of Civil and of Criminal Jurisdiction, and including Procedure in Civil Matters in those Courts.

15. The Imposition of Punishment by Fine, Penalty, or Imprisonment for enforcing any Law of the Province made in relation to any Matter coming within any of the Classes of Subjects enumerated in this Section.

16. Generally all Matters of a merely local or private Nature in the Province.

Education.

93. In and for each Province the Legislature may exclusively make Laws in relation to Education, subject and according to the following Provisions :—

(1) Nothing in any such Law shall prejudicially affect any Right or Privilege with respect to Denominational Schools which any Class of Persons have by Law in the Province at the Union :

(2) All the Powers, Privileges, and Duties at the Union by Law conferred and imposed in Upper Canada on the Separate Schools and School Trustees of the Queen's Roman Catholic Subjects shall be and the same are hereby extended to the Dissentient Schools of the Queen's Protestant and Roman Catholic Subjects in Quebec :

(3) Where in any Province a System of Separate or Dissentient Schools exists by Law at the Union or is thereafter established by the Legislature of the Province, an Appeal shall lie to the Governor-General in Council from any Act or Decision of any Provincial Authority affecting any Right or Privilege of the Protestant or Roman Catholic Minority of the Queen's Subjects in relation to Education :

(4) In case any such Provincial Law as from Time to Time seems to the Governor-General in Council requisite for the due Execution of the Provisions of this Section is not made, or in case any decision of the Governor-General in Council on any Appeal under this Section is not duly executed by the proper Provincial Authority in that Behalf, then and in every such case, and as far only as the Circumstances of each Case require, the Parliament of Canada may make remedial Laws for the due Execution of the Provisions of this Section and of any Decision of the Governor-General in Council under this Section.

Uniformity of Laws in Ontario, Nova Scotia, and New Brunswick.

Legislation for uniformity of Laws in three Provinces.

94. Notwithstanding anything in this Act, the Parliament of Canada may make Provision for the Uniformity of all or any of the Laws relative to Property and Civil Rights in Ontario, Nova Scotia, and New Brunswick, and of the Procedure of all or any of the Courts in those Three Provinces, and from and after the passing of any Act in that Behalf the Power of the Parliament of Canada to make Laws in relation to any Matter comprised in any such Act shall, notwithstanding anything in this Act, be unrestricted; but any Act of the Parliament of Canada making Provision for such Uniformity shall not have effect in any Province unless and until it is adopted and enacted as Law by the Legislature thereof.

Agriculture and Immigration.

Concurrent powers of Legislation respecting Agriculture, &c.

95. In each Province the Legislature may make Laws in relation to Agriculture in the Province, and to Immigration into the Province; and it is hereby declared that the Parliament of Canada may from Time to Time make Laws in relation to Agriculture in all or any of the Provinces, and to Immigration into all or any of the Provinces; and any Law of the Legislature of a Province relative to Agriculture or to Immigration shall have effect in and for the Province as long and as far only as it is not repugnant to any Act of the Parliament of Canada.

VII.—JUDICATURE.

Appointment of Judges.

96. The Governor-General shall appoint the Judges of the Superior, District, and County Courts in each Province, except those of the Courts of Probate in Nova Scotia and New Brunswick.

Selection of Judges in Ontario, &c.

97. Until the Laws relative to Property and Civil Rights in Ontario, Nova Scotia, and New Brunswick, and the Procedure of the Courts in those Provinces are made uniform, the Judges of the Courts of those Provinces appointed by the Governor-General shall be selected from the respective Bars of those Provinces.

98. The Judges of the Courts of Quebec, shall be selected from the Bar of that Province.

Selection of Judges in Quebec.

99. The Judges of the Superior Courts shall hold office during good Behaviour, but shall be removable by the Governor-General on Address of the Senate and House of Commons.

Tenure of office of Judges of Superior Courts.

100. The Salaries, Allowances, and Pensions of the Judges of the Superior, District, and County Courts (except the Courts of Probate in Nova Scotia and New Brunswick), and of the Admiralty Courts in Cases where the Judges thereof are for the Time being paid by Salary, shall be fixed and provided by the Parliament of Canada.

Salaries, &c., of Judges.

101. The Parliament of Canada may, notwithstanding anything in this Act, from Time to Time, provide for the Constitution, Maintenance, and Organization of a General Court of Appeal for Canada, and for the Establishment of any additional Courts for the better Administration of the Laws of Canada.

General Court of Appeal, &c.

VIII.—REVENUES; DEBTS; ASSETS; TAXATION.

102. All Duties and Revenues over which the respective Legislatures of Canada, Nova Scotia, and New Brunswick before and at the Union had and have Power of Appropriation, except such Portions thereof as are by this Act reserved to the respective Legislatures of the Provinces, or are raised by them in accordance with the Special Powers conferred on them by this Act, shall form One Consolidated Revenue Fund, to be appropriated for the Public Service of Canada in the Manner and subject to the Charges in this Act provided.

Creation of a Consolidated revenue fund.

103. The Consolidated Revenue Fund of Canada shall be permanently charged with the Costs, Charges, and Expenses incident to the Collection, Management, and Receipt thereof, and the same shall form the First Charge thereon, subject to be reviewed and audited in such Manner as shall be ordered by the Governor-General in Council until the Parliament otherwise provides.

Expenses of collection, &c.

Interest of
Provincial
public
debts.

104. The annual Interest of the Public Debts of the several Provinces of Canada, Nova Scotia, and New Brunswick at the Union shall form the Second Charge on the Consolidated Revenue Fund of Canada.

Salary of
Governor
General.

105. Unless altered by the Parliament of Canada, the Salary of the Governor-General shall be Ten thousand Pounds Sterling Money of the United Kingdom of Great Britain and Ireland, payable out of the Consolidated Revenue Fund of Canada, and the same shall form the Third Charge thereon.

Appropri-
ation from
time to
time.

106. Subject to the several Payments by this Act charged on the Consolidated Revenue Fund of Canada, the same shall be appropriated by the Parliament of Canada for the Public Service.

Transfer
of stocks,
&c.

107. All Stocks, Cash, Banker's Balances, and Securities for Money belonging to each Province at the Time of the Union, except as in this Act mentioned, shall be the Property of Canada, and shall be taken in Reduction of the amount of the respective Debts of the Provinces at the Union.

Transfer
of pro-
perty in
schedule.

108. The Public Works and Property of each Province, enumerated in the Third Schedule to this Act, shall be the Property of Canada.

Property
in Lands,
Mines, &c.

109. All Lands, Mines, Minerals, and Royalties belonging to the several Provinces of Canada, Nova Scotia, and New Brunswick at the Union, and all Sums then due or payable for such Lands, Mines, Minerals, or Royalties, shall belong to the several Provinces of Ontario, Quebec, Nova Scotia, and New Brunswick, in which the same are situate or arise, subject to any Trusts existing in respect thereof, and to any Interest other than that of the Province in the same.

Assets
connected
with Pro-
vincial
debts.

110. All Assets connected with such Portions of the Public Debt of each Province as are assumed by that Province shall belong to that Province.

Canada to
be liable
for Provin-
cial debts.

111. Canada shall be liable for the Debts and Liabilities of each Province existing at the Union.

112. Ontario and Quebec conjointly shall be liable to Canada for the Amount (if any) by which the Debt of the Province of Canada exceeds at the Union Sixty-two million five hundred thousand Dollars, and shall be charged with Interest at the Rate of Five per Centum per Annum thereon.

113. The Assets enumerated in the Fourth Schedule to this Act belonging at the Union to the Province of Canada shall be the Property of Ontario and Quebec conjointly.

114. Nova Scotia shall be liable to Canada for the Amount (if any) by which its Public Debt exceeds at the Union Eight million Dollars, and shall be charged with Interest at the Rate of Five per Centum per Annum thereon.

115. New Brunswick shall be liable to Canada for the Amount (if any) by which its Public Debt exceeds at the Union Seven million Dollars, and shall be charged with interest at the Rate of Five per Centum per Annum thereon.

116. In case the Public Debts of Nova Scotia and New Brunswick do not at the Union amount to Eight million and Seven million Dollars respectively, they shall respectively receive by half-yearly Payments in advance from the Government of Canada Interest at Five per Centum per Annum on the Difference between the actual Amounts of their respective Debts and such stipulated Amounts.

117. The several Provinces shall retain all their respective Public Property not otherwise disposed of in this Act, subject to the Right of Canada to assume any Lands or Public Property required for Fortifications or for the Defence of the Country.

118. The following Sums shall be paid yearly by Canada

nada to the several Provinces for the Support of their Governments and Legislatures :

	Dollars.
Ontario	Eighty thousand.
Quebec	Seventy thousand.
Nova Scotia	Sixty thousand.
New Brunswick	Fifty thousand.

Two hundred and sixty thousand :

and an annual Grant in aid of each Province shall be made, equal to Eighty Cents per Head of the Population as ascertained by the Census of One thousand eight hundred and sixty-one, and in the Case of Nova Scotia and New Brunswick, by each subsequent Decennial Census until the Population of each of those two Provinces amounts to Four hundred thousand Souls, at which Rate such Grant shall thereafter remain. Such Grants shall be in full Settlement of all future Demands on Canada, and shall be paid half-yearly in advance to each Province ; but the Government of Canada shall deduct from such Grants, as against any Province, all Sums chargeable as Interest on the Public Debt of that Province in excess of the several Amounts stipulated in this Act.

Further grant to New Brunswick. 119. New Brunswick shall receive by half-yearly Payments in advance from Canada for the Period of Ten Years from the Union an additional Allowance of Sixty-three thousand Dollars per annum ; but as long as the Public Debt of that Province remains under Seven million Dollars, a Deduction equal to the Interest at Five per Centum per Annum on such Deficiency shall be made from that Allowance of Sixty-three thousand Dollars.

Form of payments. 120. All Payments to be made under this Act, or in discharge of Liabilities created under any Act of the Provinces of Canada, Nova Scotia, and New Brunswick respectively, and assumed by Canada, shall, until the Parliament of Canada otherwise directs, be made in such Form and Manner as may from Time to Time be ordered by the Governor-General in Council.

Canadian manufactures, &c. 121. All Articles of the Growth, Produce, or Manufacture of any one of the Provinces shall, from and after the Union, be admitted free into each of the other Provinces.

122. The Customs and Excise Laws of each Province shall, subject to the Provisions of this Act, continue in force until altered by the Parliament of Canada.

Continuance of customs and excise Laws.

123. Where Customs Duties are, at the Union, leviable on any Goods, Wares, or Merchandises in any Two Provinces, those Goods, Wares, and Merchandises may, from and after the Union, be imported from one of those Provinces into the other of them on Proof of Payment of the Customs Duty leviable thereon in the Province of Exportation, and on Payment of such further Amount (if any) of Customs Duty as is leviable thereon in the Province of Importation.

Exportation and importation as between two Provinces.

124. Nothing in this Act shall affect the Right of New Brunswick to levy the Lumber Dues provided in Chapter Fifteen of Title Three of the Revised Statutes of New Brunswick, or in any Act amending that Act before or after the Union, and not increasing the Amount of such Dues ; but the Lumber of any of the Provinces other than New Brunswick shall not be subject to such dues.

Lumber Dues in New Brunswick.

125. No Lands or Property belonging to Canada or any Province shall be liable to Taxation.

Exemption of Public Lands, &c.

126. Such Portions of the Duties and Revenues over which the respective Legislatures of Canada, Nova Scotia, and New Brunswick had before the Union Power of Appropriation as are by this Act reserved to the respective Governments or Legislatures of the Provinces, and all Duties and Revenues raised by them in accordance with the special Powers conferred upon them by this Act, shall in each Province form One Consolidated Revenue Fund to be appropriated for the Public Service of the Province.

Provincial Consolidated revenue fund.

IX.—MISCELLANEOUS PROVISIONS.

General.

127. If any Person being at the passing of this Act a Member of the Legislative Council of Canada, Nova Scotia, or New Brunswick, to whom a Place in the Senate is offered, does not within Thirty Days thereafter, by Writing under his Hand addressed to the Governor-

As to Legislative Councillors of Provinces becoming senators.

General of the Province of Canada or to the Lieutenant-Governor of Nova Scotia or New Brunswick (as the Case may be) accept the same, he shall be deemed to have declined the same ; and any Person who, being at the passing of this Act a Member of the Legislative Council of Nova Scotia or New Brunswick, accepts a Place in the Senate, shall thereby vacate his Seat in such Legislative Council.

Oath of Allegiance, &c.

128. Every Member of the Senate or House of Commons of Canada shall before taking his Seat therein take and subscribe before the Governor-General or some Person authorized by him, and every Member of a Legislative Council or Legislative Assembly of any Province shall before taking his Seat therein take and subscribe before the Lieutenant-Governor of the Province or some Person authorized by him, the Oath of Allegiance contained in the Fifth Schedule to this Act ; and every Member of the Senate of Canada and every Member of the Legislative Council of Quebec shall also, before taking his Seat therein, take and subscribe before the Governor-General, or some Person authorized by him, the Declaration of Qualification contained in the same Schedule.

Continuance of existing Laws, Courts, Officers, &c.

129. Except as otherwise provided by this Act, all Laws in force in Canada, Nova Scotia, or New Brunswick at the Union, and all Courts of Civil and Criminal Jurisdiction, and all Legal Commissions, Powers, and Authorities, and all Officers, Judicial, Administrative, and Ministerial, existing therein at the Union, shall continue in Ontario, Quebec, Nova Scotia, and New Brunswick respectively, as if the Union had not been made ; subject nevertheless (except with respect to such as are enacted by or exist under Acts of the Parliament of Great Britain or of the Parliament of the United Kingdom of Great Britain and Ireland), to be repealed, abolished, or altered by the Parliament of Canada, or by the Legislature of the respective Province, according to the Authority of the Parliament or of that Legislature under this Act.

Transfer of officers to Canada.

130. Until the Parliament of Canada otherwise provides, all Officers of the several Provinces having Duties to discharge in relation to Matters other than those

coming within the Classes of Subjects by this Act, assigned exclusively to the Legislatures of the Provinces shall be Officers of Canada, and shall continue to discharge the Duties of their respective Offices under the same Liabilities, Responsibilities, and Penalties as if the Union had not been made.

131. Until the Parliament of Canada otherwise provides, the Governor-General in Council may from Time to Time appoint such Officers as the Governor-General in Council deems necessary or proper for the effectual Execution of this Act. *Appointment of new officers.*

132. The Parliament and Government of Canada shall have all Powers necessary or proper for performing the Obligations of Canada or of any Province thereof, as Part of the British Empire, towards Foreign Countries, arising under Treaties between the Empire and such Foreign Countries. *Treaty obligations.*

133. Either the English or the French Language may be used by any Person in the Debates of the Houses of the Parliament of Canada and of the Houses of the Legislature of Quebec; and both those Languages shall be used in the respective Records and Journals of those Houses; and either of those Languages may be used by any Person or in any Pleading or Process in or issuing from any Court of Canada established under this Act, and in or from all or any of the Courts of Quebec. *Use of English and French Languages.*

The Acts of the Parliament of Canada and of the Legislature of Quebec shall be printed and published in both those Languages.

Ontario and Quebec.

134. Until the Legislature of Ontario or of Quebec otherwise provides, the Lieutenant-Governors of Ontario and Quebec may each appoint under the Great Seal of the Province the following Officers, to hold Office during Pleasure, that is to say,—the Attorney-General, the Secretary and Registrar of the Province, the Treasurer of the Province, the Commissioner of Crown Lands, and the Commissioner of Agriculture and Public Works, and in the case of Quebec the Solicitor-General; and may, by *Appointment of executive officers for Ontario and Quebec.*

order of the Lieutenant-Governor in Council, from Time to Time prescribe the Duties of those Officers and of the several Departments over which they shall preside or to which they shall belong, and of the Officers and Clerks thereof ; and may also appoint other and additional Officers to hold Office during Pleasure, and may from Time to Time prescribe the Duties of those Officers, and of the several Departments over which they shall preside or to which they shall belong, and of the Officers and Clerks thereof.

Powers, duties, &c., of Executive officers.

135. Until the Legislature of Ontario or Quebec otherwise provides, all Rights, Powers, Duties, Functions, Responsibilities, or Authorities at the passing of this Act vested in or imposed on the Attorney-General, Solicitor-General, Secretary and Registrar of the Province of Canada, Minister of Finance, Commissioner of Crown Lands, Commissioner of Public Works, and Minister of Agriculture and Receiver-General, by any Law, Statute or Ordinance of Upper Canada, Lower Canada, or Canada, and not repugnant to this Act, shall be vested in or imposed on any Officer to be appointed by the Lieutenant-Governor for the Discharge of the same or any of them ; and the Commissioner of Agriculture and Public Works shall perform the Duties and Functions of the Office of Minister of Agriculture at the passing of this Act imposed by the Law of the Province of Canada, as well as those of the Commissioner of Public Works.

Great Seals.

136. Until altered by the Lieutenant-Governor in Council, the Great Seals of Ontario and Quebec respectively shall be the same, or of the same Design, as those used in the Provinces of Upper Canada and Lower Canada respectively before their Union as the Province of Canada.

Construction of temporary Acts.

137. The Words " and from thence to the End of the " then next ensuing Session of the Legislature," or Words to the same Effect, used in any temporary Act of the Province of Canada not expired before the Union, shall be construed to extend and apply to the next Session of the Parliament of Canada, if the subject Matter of the Act is within the Powers of the same, as defined

by this Act, or to the next Sessions of the Legislatures
of Ontario and Quebec respectively, if the Subject Matter of the Act is within the Powers of the same as defined by this Act.

138. From and after the Union the Use of the
Words " Upper Canada " instead of " Ontario," or " Lower Canada " instead of " Quebec," in any Deed, Writ,
Process, Pleading, Document, Matter, or Thing, shall not
invalidate the same.

As to errors in names.

139. Any Proclamation under the Great Seal of the
Province of Canada issued before the Union to take
effect at a Time which is subsequent to the Union,
whether relating to that Province, or to Upper Canada,
or to Lower Canada, and the several Matters and Things
therein proclaimed shall be and continue of like Force
and Effect as if the Union had not been made.

As to issue of Proclamations before Union to commence after Union.

140. Any Proclamation which is authorized by any
Act of the Legislature of the Province of Canada to be
issued under the Great Seal of the Province of Canada,
whether relating to that Province, or to Upper Canada,
or to Lower Canada, and which is not issued before the
Union, may be issued by the Lieutenant-Governor of Ontario or of Quebec, as its Subject Matter requires, under
the Great Seal thereof ; and from and after the Issue of
such Proclamation the same and the several Matters and
Things therein proclaimed shall be and continue of the
like Force and Effect in Ontario or Quebec as if the
Union had not been made.

As to issue of Proclamations after Union.

141. The Penitentiary of the Province of Canada
shall, until the Parliament of Canada otherwise provides,
be and continue the Penitentiary of Ontario and of Quebec.

Penitentiary.

142. The Division and Adjustment of the Debts,
Credits, Liabilities, Properties, and Assets of Upper Canada and Lower Canada shall be referred to the Arbitrament of Three Arbitrators, One chosen by the Government of Ontario, One by the Government of Quebec,
and One by the Government of Canada ; and the Selection of the Arbitrators shall not be made until the Par-

Arbitration respecting debts, &c.

liament of Canada and the Legislatures of Ontario and
Quebec have met; and the Arbitrator chosen by the
Government of Canada shall not be a Resident either in
Ontario or in Quebec.

Division
of records.

143. The Governor-General in Council may from
Time to Time order that such and so many of the Records, Books, and Documents of the Province of Canada
as he thinks fit shall be appropriated and delivered
either to Ontario or to Quebec, and the same shall thenceforth be the Property of that Province: and any Copy
thereof or Extract therefrom, duly certified by the Officer
having charge of the Original thereof, shall be admitted
as Evidence.

Constitu-
tion of
townships
in Quebec.

144. The Lieutenant-Governor of Quebec may from
Time to Time, by Proclamation under the Great Seal of
the Province, to take effect from a day to be appointed
therein, constitute Townships in those Parts of the Province of Quebec in which Townships are not then already
constituted, and fix the Metes and Bounds thereof.

X.—INTERCOLONIAL RAILWAY.

Duty of
Govern-
ment and
Parlia-
ment of
Canada to
make Rail-
way herein
described.

145. Inasmuch as the Provinces of Canada, Nova
Scotia, and New Brunswick have joined in a Declaration that the Construction of the Intercolonial Railway
is essential to the Consolidation of the Union of British
North America, and to the Assent thereto of Nova Scotia
and New Brunswick, and have consequently agreed that
Provision should be made for its immediate Construction by the Government of Canada: Therefore, in order
to give effect to that Agreement, it shall be the Duty of
the Government and Parliament of Canada to provide for
the Commencement within Six Months after the Union,
of a Railway connecting the River St. Lawrence with
City of Halifax in Nova Scotia, and for the Construction
thereof without Intermission, and the Completion thereof
with all practicable Speed.

XI.—ADMISSION OF OTHER COLONIES.

Power to
admit
Newfound-
land, &c.
into the
Union.

146. It shall be lawful for the Queen, by and with
the Advice of Her Majesty's Most Honourable Privy Council, on Addresses from the Houses of the Parliament of
Canada, and from the Houses of the respective Legisla-

tures of the Colonies or Provinces of Newfoundland,
Prince Edward Island, and British Columbia, to admit
those Colonies or Provinces, or any of them, into the
Union, and on Address from the Houses of the Parliament of Canada to admit Rupert's Land and the North-
western Territory, or either of them, into the Union, on
such Terms and Conditions in each Case as are in the
Addresses expressed and as the Queen thinks fit to approve, subject to the Provisions of this Act; and the
Provisions of any Order in Council in that Behalf shall
have effect as if they had been enacted by the Parliament
of the United Kingdom of Great Britain and Ireland.

147. In case of the Admission of Newfoundland and
Prince Edward Island, or either of them, each shall be
entitled to a Representation in the Senate of Canada of
Four Members, and (notwithstanding anything in this
Act) in case of the Admission of Newfoundland the Normal Number of Senators shall be Seventy-Six and their
Maximum Number shall be Eighty-two; but Prince
Edward Island when admitted shall be deemed to be
comprised in the third of the Three Divisions into which
Canada is, in relation to the Constitution of the Senate,
divided by this Act, and accordingly, after the Admission
of Prince Edward Island, whether Newfoundland is admitted or not, the Representation of Nova Scotia and
New Brunswick in the Senate shall, as Vacancies occur,
be reduced from Twelve to Ten Members respectively,
and the Representation of each of those Provinces shall
not be increased at any Time beyond Ten, except under
the Provisions of this Act for the Appointment of Three
or Six additional Senators under the Direction of the
Queen.

As to re-
presenta-
tion of
New-
foundland
and Prince
Edward
Island in
Senate.

SCHEDULES.

THE FIRST SCHEDULE.

Electoral Districts of Ontario.

A.

Existing Electoral Divisions.

Counties.

1. Prescott.
2. Glengarry.
3. Stormont.
4. Dundas.
5. Russell.
6. Carleton.
7. Prince Edward.
8. Halton.
9. Essex.

Ridings of Counties.

10. North Riding of Lanark.
11. South Riding of Lanark.
12. North Riding of Leeds and North Riding of Grenville.
13. South Riding of Leeds.
14. South Riding of Grenville.
15. East Riding of Northumberland.
16. West Riding of Northumberland (excepting therefrom the Township of South Monaghan.)
17. East Riding of Durham.
18. West Riding of Durham.
19. North Riding of Ontario.
20. South Riding of Ontario.
21. East Riding of York.
22. West Riding of York.
23. North Riding of York.
24. North Riding of Wentworth.
25. South Riding of Wentworth.
26. East Riding of Elgin.
27. West Riding of Elgin.
28. North Riding of Waterloo.

29. South Riding of Waterloo.
30. North Riding of Brant.
31. South Riding of Brant.
32. North Riding of Oxford.
33. South Riding of Oxford.
34. East Riding of Middlesex.

CITIES, PARTS OF CITIES, AND TOWNS.

35. West Toronto.
36. East Toronto.
37. Hamilton.
38. Ottawa.
39. Kingston.
40. London.
41. Town of Brockville, with the Township of Eliza-
    bethtown thereto attached.
42. Town of Niagara, with the Township of Niagara
    thereto attached.
43. Town of Cornwall, with the Township of Corn-
    wall thereto attached.

B.

NEW ELECTORAL DIVISIONS.

44. The Provisional Judicial District of Algoma.

The County of Bruce, divided into Two Ridings, to
be called respectively the North and South Ridings:—

45. The North Riding of Bruce to consist of the
    Townships of Bury, Lindsay, Eastnor, Albe-
    marle, Amable, Arran, Bruce, Elderslie, and
    Saugeen, and the Village of Southampton.

46. The South Riding of Bruce to consist of the
    Townships of Kincardine (including the Vil-
    lage of Kincardine), Greenock, Brant, Huron,
    Kinloss, Culross, and Carrick.

The County of Huron, divided into Two Ridings, to
be called respectively the North and South Ridings :—

47. The North Riding to consist of the Townships of Ashfield, Wawanosh, Turnberry, Howick, Morris, Grey, Colborne, Hullett, including the Village of Clinton, and McKillop.

48. The South Riding to consist of the Town of Goderich and the Townships of Goderich, Tuckersmith, Stanley, Hay, Usborne, and Stephen.

The County of Middlesex, divided into Three Ridings, to be called respectively the North, West, and East Ridings :—

49. The North Riding to consist of the Townships of McGillivray and Biddulph (taken from the County of Huron), and Williams East, Williams West, Adelaide, and Lobo.

50. The West Riding to consist of the Townships of Delaware, Carradoc, Metcalfe, Mosa and Ekfrid, and the Village of Strathroy.

[The East Riding to consist of the Townships now embraced therein, and be bounded as it is at present.]

51. The County of Lambton to consist of the Townships of Bosanquet, Warwick, Plympton, Sarnia, Moore, Enniskillen, and Brooke, and the Town of Sarnia.

52. The County of Kent to consist of the Townships of Chatham, Dover, East Tilbury, Romney, Raleigh, and Harwich, and the Town of Chatham.

53. The County of Bothwell to consist of the Townships of Sombra, Dawn, and Euphemia (taken from the County of Lambton), and the Townships of Zone, Camden with the Gore thereof, Orford, and Howard (taken from the County of Kent).

The County of Grey divided into Two Ridings, to be called respectively the South and North Ridings :—

54. The South Riding to consist of the Townships of Bentinck, Glenelg, Artemesia, Osprey, Normanby, Egremont, Proton, and Melancthon.

55. The North Riding to consist of the Townships of Collingwood, Euphrasia, Holland, Saint-Vincent, Sydenham, Sullivan, Derby, and Keppel, Sarawak and Brooke, and the Town of Owen Sound.

The County of Perth divided into Two Ridings, to be called respectively the South and North Ridings :—

56. The North Riding to consist of the Townships of Wallace, Elma, Logan, Ellice, Mornington, and North Easthope, and the Town of Stratford.

57. The South Riding to consist of the Townships of Blanchard, Downie, South Easthope, Fullarton, Hibbert, and the Villages of Mitchell and Ste. Marys.

The County of Wellington divided into Three Ridings, to be called respectively North, South and Centre Ridings :—

58. The North Riding to consist of the Townships of Amaranth, Arthur, Luther, Minto, Maryborough, Peel, and the Village of Mount Forest.

59. The Centre Riding to consist of the Townships of Garafraxa, Erin, Eramosa, Nichol, and Pilkington, and the Villages of Fergus and Elora.

60. The South Riding to consist of the Town of Guelph, and the Townships of Guelph and Puslinch.

The County of Norfolk, divided into Two Ridings, to be called respectively the South and North Ridings :—

61. The South Riding to consist of the Townships of Charlotteville, Houghton, Walsingham, and Woodhouse, and with the Gore thereof.

62. The North Riding to consist of the Townships of Middleton, Townsend, and Windham, and the Town of Simcoe.

63. The County of Haldimand to consist of the Townships of Oneida, Seneca, Cayuga North, Cayuga South, Rainham, Walpole, and Dunn.

64. The County of Monck to consist of the Townships of Canborough and Moulton, and Sherbrooke, and the Village of Dunnville (taken from the County of Haldimand), the Townships of Caistor and Gainsborough (taken from the County of Lincoln), and the Townships of Pelham and Wainfleet (taken from the County of Welland).

65. The County of Lincoln to consist of the Townships of Clinton, Grantham, Grimsby, and Louth, and the Town of St. Catherines.

66. The County of Welland to consist of the Townships of Bertie, Crowland, Humberstone, Stamford, Thorold, and Willoughby, and the Villages of Chippewa, Clifton, Fort Erie, Thorold, and Welland.

67. The County of Peel to consist of the Townships of Chinguacousy, Toronto, and the Gore of Toronto, and the Villages of Brampton and Streetsville.

68. The County of Cardwell to consist of the Townships of Albion and Caledon (taken from the County of Peel), and the Townships of Adjala and Mono (taken from the County of Simcoe).

The County of Simcoe, divided into Two Ridings, to be called respectively the South and the North Ridings :—

69. The South Riding to consist of the Townships of West Gwillimbury, Tecumseth, Innisfil, Essa, Tossorontio, Mulmur, and the Village of Bradford.

70. The North Riding to consist of the Townships of Nottawasaga, Sunnidale, Vespra, Flos, Oro, Medonte, Orillia and Matchedash, Tiny and Tay, Balaklava and Robinson, and the Towns of Barrie and Collingwood.

The County of Victoria, divided into Two Ridings, to be called respectively the South and North Ridings :—

71. The South Riding to consist of the Townships of Ops, Mariposa, Emily, Verulam, and the Town of Lindsay.

72. The North Riding to consist of the Townships of Anson, Bexley, Carden, Dalton, Digby, Eldon, Fenelon, Hindon, Laxton, Lutterworth, Macaulay and Draper, Sommerville, and Morrison, Muskoka, Monck and Watt (taken from the County of Simcoe), and any other surveyed Townships lying to the North of the said North Riding.

The County of Peterborough, divided into Two Ridings, to be called respectively the West and East Ridings :—

73. The West Riding to consist of the Townships of South Monaghan (taken from the County of Northumberland), North Monaghan, Smith, and Ennismore, and the Town of Peterborough.

74. The East Riding to consist of the Townships of Asphodel, Belmont and Methuen, Douro, Dummer, Galway, Harvey, Minden, Stanhope and Dysart, Otonabee, and Snowden, and the Village of Ashburnham, and any other surveyed Townships lying to the North of the said East Riding.

The County of Hastings, divided into Three Ridings, to be called respectively the West, East, and North Ridings :—

75. The West Riding to consist of the Town of Belleville, the Township of Sydney, and the Village of Trenton.

76. The East Riding to consist of the Townships of Thurlow, Tyendinaga, and Hungerford.

77. The North Riding to consist of the Townships of Rawdon, Huntingdon, Madoc, Elzevir, Tudor, Marmora, and Lake, and the Village of Stirling, and any other surveyed Townships lying to the North of the said North Riding.

78. The County of Lennox, to consist of the Townships of Richmond, Adolphustown, North Fredericksburgh, South Fredericksburgh, Ernest Town, and Amherst Island, and the Village of Napanee.

79. The County of Addington to consist of the Townships of Camden, Portland, Sheffield, Hinchinbrooke, Kaladar, Kennebec, Olden, Oso, Anglesea, Barrie, Clarendon, Palmerston, Effingham, Abinger, Miller, Canonto, Denbigh, Loughborough, and Bedford.

80. The County of Frontenac to consist of the Townships of Kingston, Wolfe Island, Pittsburgh and Howe Island, and Storrington.

The County of Renfrew, divided into Two Ridings, to be called respectively the South and North Ridings :—

81. The South Riding to consist of the Townships of McNab, Bagot, Blithfield, Brougham, Horton, Admaston, Grattan, Matawatchan, Griffith, Lyndoch, Raglan, Radcliffe, Brudenell, Sebastopol, and the Villages of Arnprior and Renfrew.

82. The North Riding to consist of the Townships of Ross, Bromley, Westmeath, Stafford, Pembroke, Wilberforce, Alice, Petawawa, Buchanan, South Algona, North Algona, Fraser, McKay, Wylie, Rolph, Head, Maria, Clara, Hagarty, Sherwood, Burns, and Richards, and any other surveyed Townships lying North-westerly of the said North Riding.

Every Town and incorporated Village existing at the Union, not specially mentioned in this Schedule, is to be taken as Part of the County or Riding within which it is locally situate.

THE SECOND SCHEDULE.

Electoral Districts of Quebec specially fixed.

COUNTIES OF

Pontiac.	Missisquoi.	Compton.
Ottawa.	Brome.	Wolfe and Richmond.
Argenteuil.	Shefford.	Megantic.
Huntingdon.	Stanstead.	

Town of Sherbrooke.

THE THIRD SCHEDULE.

Provincial Public Works and Property to be the Property of Canada.

1. Canals, with Lands and Water Power connected therewith.
2. Public Harbours.
3. Lighthouses and Piers, and Sable Island.
4. Steamboats, Dredges, and public Vessels.
5. Rivers and Lake Improvements.
6. Railways and Railway Stocks, Mortgages, and other Debts due by Railway Companies.
7. Military Roads.
8. Custom Houses, Post Offices, and all other Public Buildings, except such as the Government of Canada appropriate for the Use of the Provincial Legislatures and Governments.
9. Property transferred by the Imperial Government, and known as Ordnance Property.
10. Armouries, Drill Sheds, Military Clothing, and Munitions of War, and Lands set apart for general Public Purposes.

THE FOURTH SCHEDULE.

Assets to be the Property of Ontario and Quebec Conjointly.

Upper Canada Building Fund.

Lunatic Asylums.

Normal School.

Court Houses. ⎫
    in   ⎪
Aylmer.   ⎬ Lower Canada.
Montreal.   ⎪
Kamouraska. ⎭

Law Society, Upper Canada.

Montreal Turnpike Trust.

University Permanent Fund.

Royal Institution.

Consolidated Municipal Loan Fund, Upper Canada.

Consolidated Municipal Loan Fund, Lower Canada.

Agricultural Society, Upper Canada.

Lower Canada Legislative Grant.

Quebec Fire Loan.

Temiscouata Advance Account.

Quebec Turnpike Trust.

Education—East.

Building and Jury Fund, Lower Canada.

Municipalities Fund.

Lower Canada Superior Education Income Fund.

.

THE FIFTH SCHEDULE.

OATH OF ALLEGIANCE.

I, A. B., do swear, That I will be faithful and bear true Allegiance to Her Majesty Queen Victoria.

Note.—The Name of the King or Queen of the United Kingdom of Great Britain and Ireland for the Time being, is to be substituted from Time to Time, with proper Terms of Reference thereto.

DECLARATION OF QUALIFICATION.

I, A. B. do declare and testify, That I am by Law duly qualified to be appointed a Member of the Senate of Canada [or as the Case may be], and that I am legally or equitably seised as of Freehold for my own Use and Benefit of Lands or Tenements held in Free and Common Socage [or seised or possessed for my own Use and Benefit of Lands or Tenements held in Franc-alleu or in Roture (as the Case may be),] in the Province of Nova Scotia [or as the case may be] of the Value of Four Thousand Dollars over and above all Rents, Dues, Debts, Mortgages, Charges, and Incumbrances due or payable out of or charged on or affecting the same, and that I have not collusively or colourably obtained a Title to or become possessed of the said Lands and Tenements or any Part thereof for the Purpose of enabling me to become a Member of the Senate of Canada [or as the Case may be], and that my Real and Personal Property are together worth Four Thousand Dollars over and above my Debts and Liabilities.

APPENDIX I.

(See page ?).

GOVERNMENT HOUSE.

Halifax, Nova Scotia, 3rd October, 1864.

My Lord,

I have the honour to acknowledge the receipt of your Despatch of the 23rd ult.,* which reached me on the 30th ultimo, transmitting a Copy of an approved Minute of the Executive Council of Canada, dated the 23rd of September, 1864, and inviting me to name a deputation to represent Nova Scotia in the approaching Conference at Quebec on the 10th inst.

In reply I have the honour to state for your Lordship's information that I have laid your despatch and its enclosure before my Ministry, and I have appointed the Hon. Provincial Secretary, The Hon. Attorney General, The Hon. R. B. Dickey, the Hon. Jonathan McCully and Adams G. Archibald, Esqr., to form a deputation to meet the Delegates from the other British North American Provinces in Conference at Quebec on the 10th. inst., as proposed in Your Lordship's despatch.

I have the honour to be My Lord,
Your most obedient servant,
RICHARD GRAVES MACDONNELL.
Lieut. Governor.

His Excellency,
Viscount Monck,
Governor-General, &c., &c., &c.

Province of Nova Scotia.

R. G. MACDONNELL, Lt.-Governor.

By His Excellency, Sir Richard Graves MacDonnell, Knight Companion of the Most Honourable Order of the Bath, Lieutenant-Governor and Commander-in-Chief in and over Her Majesty's Province of Nova Scotia and its Dependencies, &c., &c., &c.

* See Appendix No. IV.

To Hon. Charles Tupper, Provincial Secretary; Hon. William A. Henry, Attorney General ; Hon. Jonathan McCully, M. L. Council ; Hon. Robert B. Dickey, M. L. Council ; Adams G. Archibald, M.P.P.

GREETING :

By virtue of the power and authority in me vested, I have thought fit to constitute and appoint, and do, by the advice of the Executive Council of the said Province, hereby, during pleasure, constitute and appoint you, the said Charles Tupper, William A. Henry, Jonathan McCully, Robert B. Dickey, and Adams G. Archibald, to be Delegates to confer upon the question of a Union of the British North American Colonies at a Conference to be held at Quebec on or about the tenth of October, A.D., 1864.

Hereby granting unto you all the rights, powers, and advantages which to the said office do or may lawfully appertain, and requiring you diligently to perform the duties thereof.

Given under my Hand and Seal at Arms, at Halifax, this Third Day of October, in the Twenty-eighth year of Her Majesty's Reign, A.D., 1864.

By His Excellency's Command,

JAMES H. THORNE, Deputy Secretary.

APPENDIX II.

(See page 5.)

Government House,

Prince Edward Island, 6th October, 1864.

My Lord,

I have the honour to acknowledge the receipt this day of your despatch dated 23rd September,* transmitting to me a copy of an Approved Minute of the Executive Council of Canada, respecting a proposal to hold at Quebec, on the 10th October, a Conference of Delegates from the Maritime Provinces with the Ministers of Canada to consider the question of a Union of these Provinces.

Your Lordship invites me to name a Deputation to represent P. E. I. at this approaching Conference.

I have accordingly with the advice of my Ministers named the following gentlemen, who will, I understand, proceed to-day, to Quebec in order to be present there on the 10th inst :

> The Hon. J. H. Gray, P. Ex. C.
>
> The Hon. Edward Palmer, Att'y Gen'l.
>
> The Hon. W. H. Pope, Col. Sec'y.
>
> The Hon. D. Davies, M.P.P.
>
> The Hon. A. A. Macdonald, M.L.C.
>
> The Hon George Coles, M.P.P.
>
> The Hon. T. H. Haviland, M.P.P.
>
> The Hon. Edward Whelan, M.P.P.

I have the honour to be, &c., &c., &c.,

GEORGE DUNDAS, Lieutenant-Governor.

The Right Hon'ble. Viscount Monck, &c., &c., &c.

---

* See Appendix IV

APPENDIX III.

(*See page 38. Note*)

Fredericton, April, 1865.

My Lord,

Upon the 12th November last your Lordship did me the honour to address to me a Despatch enclosing a Copy of the Resolutions agreed to by the Delegates appointed to consider the question of a Federation of the British North American Provinces.

To the copy so transmitted the following certificate was attached :—" I certify that the above is a true copy of the original report of the Resolutions adopted in Conference."

E. P. TACHÉ, Chairman."

In this copy the 24th Resolution stands as follows :—

"24.—The Local Legislature of each Province may from time to time alter the Electoral Districts for the purpose of Representation in the House of Commons, and distribute the Representatives to which the Province is entitled in any manner such Legislature may think fit."

In the copy of the Resolution presented to me on their return by the Delegates from this Province the same words are found.

In the papers laid before both Houses of Parliament by command of Her Majesty on the subject of the proposed Federal Union, a Despatch addressed by your Lordship to the Secretary of State for the Colonies on the 7th November, will be found (at page 4) transmitting to Mr. Cardwell a copy of the Resolutions, in which also the 24th Resolution is couched in the same words, and the accuracy of which copy is also certified by Sir E. P. Taché.

My attention has, however, been called to the fact that in the papers laid before the Canadian Parliament and transmitted to me by Your Lordship on the 30th January last, although the same Despatch from Your Lordship to the Secretary of State is printed at Page 3, the enclosure reads somewhat differently—the 24th Resolution standing as follows :—

"24.—The Local Legislature of each Province may from time to time alter the Electoral Districts for the purpose of Representation in such Local Legislature and distribute the Representatives to which the Province is entitled in such Local Legislature in any manner such Legislature may see fit."

This alteration is not altogether unimportant. In the one copy, the Resolution refers to the House of Commons of the Federal Legislature, in the other, to the Local Legislature alone.

I am requested by my advisers to ask Your Lordship to have the goodness to explain the cause of this discrepancy and to inform me, after directing a reference to the original document, which is, I presume, preserved at Quebec, which version was in fact that signed by the Delegates.

From the circumstance that in the papers laid before the English Parliament the same words occur as in the copy forwarded to me by Your Lordship on the 12th of November, it would appear that the Copy certified by Sir E. Taché, is correct and that the inaccuracy has arisen in copying the documents to be laid before the Canadian Parliament.

I am further requested to state that the Delegates from this Province have never authorized any alteration in the Resolution as signed by them, and that indeed their assent to any such alteration has never yet been sought.

I have, etc.,

ARTHUR GORDON.

The Right Hon'ble Viscount Monck, &c., &c., &c.

Provincial Secretary's Office, 4th May, 1865.

The undersigned has had the honour to receive a letter from Your Excellency's Secretary covering a copy of a Despatch from the Lieutenant Governor of New Brunswick, asking for certain information in reference to the proceedings of the Quebec Conference, and he now begs to submit for Your Excellency's information the following report :—

The 24th Resolution of the Quebec Conference as it stands in the original report by certain Members of the Conference (and which report is now in the possession of the undersigned) is in the words and figures following :—

" The Local Legislature of each Province may from time to " time alter the Electoral Districts for the purpose of Represen- " tation in the House of Commons, and distribute the Represen- " tatives to which the Province is entitled in any manner such " Legislature may think fit.'

In the papers submitted to the Canadian Parliament the 24th Resolution was made to read as follows :—

" The Local Legislature of each Province may, from time to time, alter the Electoral Districts for the purposes of Represen- tation in such Local Legislature, and distribute the Representa- tives to which the Province is entitled in such Local Legislature, in any manner such Legislature may see fit."

The above change was made because it was found that the Resolution as expressed in the original report, did not convey the true meaning of the Conference.   As Your Excellency is aware, the proceedings of the Conference towards the close of its de- liberations were very much hurried, and it was subsequently dis- covered that several errors had occurred in revising and re-arrang- ing its numerous resolutions which were adopted in the first in- stance without that exactness of expression and logical sequence so necessary in an instrument intended to present a complete scheme. Some of these errors were discovered and corrected at Montreal, by the unanimous consent of the Delegates present at a meeting held in that City for the purpose. There was no doubt in the minds of the Canadian Delegates (when their attention was called to the point) that the gentlemen who undertook the duty of reducing into form the Minutes and Resolutions of the Con- ference, had misapprehended the meaning of the Conference in reference to the subject embraced in the 24th Resolution.   It could never have been intended to destroy the independence of every Member of the General Parliament by giving power to the Local Legislature of his Province to " alter " and thus practically to abolish his Constituency whenever by speech or vote he might happen to displease a majority of that Legislature. The power to divide each Province into the proper number of Electoral Dis- tricts in the first instance (as provided by the 23rd Resolution) was given to the Local Legislatures *ex necessitate*, but the power to alter or re-adjust the Constituencies after Parliament is constituted belongs naturally, logically, and according to every constitutional precedent, to that Parliament, and not to an inferior Body. The undersigned is informed that on discovering the error in the 24th Resolution and also important errors in the 29th and 43rd Resolutions, in reference to Export duties on Timber and Coals, communication was had with the leading Members of the Governments of the several Maritime Provinces.

The undersigned is also informed that answers were received from those gentlemen expressing their concurrence in the suggestions of the Canadian delegates as to the fact of error in both cases and as to the mode by which it was proposed to correct them.

The undersigned regrets that he is unable to give to your Excellency fuller and more precise information in consequence of the absence from the country of those Members of the Government who conducted the correspondence referred to.

Respectfully submitted :

W. McDOUGALL, Secretary.

His Excellency The Governor-General.

APPENDIX IV.

(See pages 294, 296).

Quebec, 23rd September, 1864.

Sir,—I have the honour to transmit a copy of an approved Minute of the Executive Council of Canada respecting the proposal to hold a Conference of Delegates from the Colonies of Nova Scotia, New Brunswick, Prince Edward Island and Newfoundland with the Ministers of Canada to consider the question of a Union of these Colonies and to digest a scheme for the practical realization of the idea which may be submitted as embodying the joint opinions of the Governments of the several Provinces to the Secretary of State for the Colonies with a view to obtaining his sanction for legislation on the subject.

In conformity with the request contained in this Minute I have the honour to invite you to name a deputation to represent your Province in the approaching Conference which will meet at Quebec on the 10th October.

I have, etc.,

MONCK.

The Lieutenant Governors of Nova Scotia, New Brunswick, Prince Edward Island, and the Governor of Newfoundland.

Copy of a Report of a Committee of the Honourable the Executive Council, approved by His Excellency the Governor-General in Council on the 23rd September, 1864.

The Committee of Council has the honour to inform Your Excellency that the Deputation from the Executive Council who met the Delegates from the Maritime Provinces, at Charlottetown, on the 1st instant, in accordance with the Order in Council of the 29th ultimo, have reported that such Conference duly met, and that the question of a Confederation of the British North American Colonies was discussed at length, and such progress made, that it was thought desirable by the Conference that the subject should be resumed in a formal and official manner under the authority of the Government of the several Provinces.

The Committee have therefore the honour to advise and submit for Your Excellency's approval, that the several Governments of Nova Scotia, New Brunswick, Prince Edward Island and Newfoundland, be invited to appoint delegates, under the authority of the despatch of the Secretary for the Colonies to the Lieutenant Governor of Nova Scotia,, dated 6th July, 1862, and communicated by the Colonial Office to Your Excellency by a despatch of the same date, to confer with the Canadian Government on the subject of a Union or Federation of the British North American Provinces.

The Committee beg leave further to recommend that Quebec be selected as the place, and the 10th October next the time for the meeting, as they have ascertained that such time and place will meet the views and convenience of the several Governments.

Certified :

W. H. LEE, C. E. C.

APPENDIX V.

(*See page 59.*)

The Duke of Newcastle to the Earl of Mulgrave.

Nova Scotia.

No. 182.

Downing Street, 6th July, 1862.

My Lord,

I have duly received Your Lordship's despatch, No. 47, of the 21st of May, accompanied by a copy of a Resolution which was passed in the House of Assembly on the 15th of April, 1861, relative to an amalgamation of part of all the British Provinces in North America. The Resolution points out that the question might be considered either of a distinct union of the Maritime Provinces or of a general union of them with Canada and suggests that it might be desirable upon so important a subject to ascertain the policy of Her Majesty's Government, and to promote a consultation between the leading men of the Colonies.

Your Lordship explains that for various reasons your Government were of opinion that it would be inexpedient to act on this Resolution last year, but that they now wish it to be brought under consideration.

No one can be insensible to the importance of the two measures which are alluded to, and I am far from considering that they do not form a very proper subject for calm deliberation. They are, however, of a nature which renders it especially fit that if either of them be proposed for adoption it should emanate in the first instance from the Provinces, and should be concurred in by all of them which it would affect.

I should see no objection to any consultation on the subject amongst the leading members of the Governments concerned, but whatever the result of such consultation might be, the most satisfactory mode of testing the opinion of the people of British North

America would probably be by means of Resolution or Address, proposed in the Legislature of each Province by its own Government.

Beyond this expression of the views of Her Majesty's Government as to the preliminary steps which might be taken towards the decision of this great question, I am not prepared to announce any course of policy upon an invitation proceeding from one only of the British North American Provinces, and contained in a Resolution of so general and vague a character as that which you have transmitted to me. But if a Union, either partial or complete, should hereafter be proposed with the concurrence of all the Provinces to be united, I am sure that the matter would be weighed in this country both by the public, by Parliament, and by Her Majesty's Government, with no other feelings than an anxiety to discern, and to promote any course which might be the most conducive to the prosperity, the strength and the harmony of all the British Communities in North America.

I have, etc.,

NEWCASTLE.

The Right Honourable The Earl of Mulgrave, etc., etc., etc.

APPENDIX VI.

Westminster Palace Hotel,
London, S.W., Dec. 4th, 1866.

My Lord,

I have the honour to inform you that the Delegates from the Provinces of Canada, Nova Scotia, and New Brunswick, met this morning, and formed themselves into a Conference for the purpose of arranging the terms of Union of those Provinces.

The Gentlemen forming the Conference are as follows :—

CANADA.

The Hon. John A. Macdonald, Attorney General U. C., and Minister of Militia of Canada.

The Hon. G. E. Cartier, Attorney General of Lower Canada.

The Hon. A. T. Galt.

The Hon. W. McDougall, Provincial Secretary.

The Hon. W. P. Howland, Minister of Finance.

The Hon. H. L. Langevin, Postmaster General.

NOVA SCOTIA.

The Hon. Charles Tupper, Provincial Secretary.

The Hon. W. A. Henry, Attorney General.

The Hon. J. W. Ritchie, Solicitor General.

The Hon. J. McCully.

The Hon. A. G. Archibald.

NEW BRUNSWICK.

The Hon. P. Mitchell, President of Council.

The Hon. R. D. Wilmot.

The Hon. S. L. Tilley, Provincial Secretary.

The Hon. Charles Fisher, Attorney General.

The Hon. J. M. Johnson.

I have the honour further to inform Your Lordship that I was then appointed Chairman, and Lieut.-Col. H. Bernard, Secretary of the Conference.

I have the honour to be, My Lord,

Your Lordship's most obedient servant,

JOHN A. MACDONALD.

The Rt. Honourable
The Earl of Carnarvon.
Secretary of State for the Colonies.

Westminster Palace Hotel,
London, 25th December, 1866.

Dear Lord Carnarvon,

I am happy to inform you that the Delegates who have sat steadily from the 4th to the 24th inst., have arrived at a satisfactory conclusion, and have adopted by the unanimous vote of the Provinces, a series of resolutions which I shall transmit to-morrow morning to Your Lordship at the Colonial Office.

The Delegates desire me to convey to you their opinion that it is expedient to avoid any publicity being given to the resolutions until the Bill is finally settled and ready to be laid before Parliament.   They think that their early publication would answer no good purpose, and might tend to premature discussion on imperfect information of the subject both in this country and America.   Believe me,

Dear Lord Carnarvon,

Very sincerely yours,

The Rt. Honourable   JOHN A. MACDONALD.

The Earl of Carnarvon,

Secretary of State for the Colonies.

Westminster Palace Hotel,
London, December 26, 1866.

My Lord,

I have the honour to transmit to you by desire of the Conference of Delegates from Canada, Nova Scotia and New Brunswick, a series of resolutions.   They submit these resolutions for the favourable consideration of Her Majesty's Government with a view to the early introduction of a Bill into the Imperial Parliament based upon them.

The Delegates purpose to re-assemble here on Friday, the 28th inst., and shall be glad to wait on Your Lordship at your convenience for the purpose of arranging the course of action.

I have the honour to be, My Lord,

Your Lordship's very obedient servant,

JOHN A. MACDONALD.

The Right Honourable The Earl of Carnarvon.

Downing Street,

28th December, 1866.

Sir,—I am directed by the Earl of Carnarvon to acknowledge the receipt of your letter of the 26th instant, forwarding resolutions in which the Delegates from Canada, Nova Scotia and New Brunswick have embodied the principles on which they desire that a Bill may be introduced into Parliament for the Union of those Provinces.

Lord Carnarvon will at once give his careful attention to these resolutions, and as soon as His Lordship shall have had time to give them the consideration which they require, he will not delay to fix a day and hour when he may have the pleasure of conferring with you and the other gentlemen who are acting with you on the subject.

I am, sir, your obedient servant,

FREDERIC ROGERS.

The Honourable John A. Macdonald.

————

Private.

Highclere Castle,

Newbury, 28th December, 1866.

My Dear Sir,

I received this morning your official letter and the resolutions of the Delegates.

I found it difficult to consider them in their present form and have sent them to London to-day to be put into type ; but I will on their return to me lose no time in giving them my best attention. I will communicate with you, as soon as I have sufficiently mastered the changes introduced, to fix a meeting with yourself and the Delegates.

I quite agree in the expediency of considering the resolutions private for the present.

Believe me, my dear Sir,

Yours very faithfully,

CARNARVON.

The Hon. J. A. Macdonald.

Westminster Palace Hotel,
London, Feb. 28, 1867.

My Lord,

I have the honour to forward you a Resolution adopted by the Delegates from Canada, Nova Scotia, and New Brunswick, relating to Prince Edward Island, and to request that it may be communicated, should Your Lordship see no objection, to the Government of that Colony.

I have the honour to be, My Lord,

Your Lordship's very obedient servant,

JOHN A. MACDONALD,
Chairman of Conference.

The Rt. Hon.
        The Earl of Carnarvon,
                Secretary of State for the Colonies.

Resolved—

That in case the colony of Prince Edward Island should hereafter desire to join the Confederation of Canada, this Conference recommend that the Government of the Confederation should deal with the question of compensation for the proprietary rights in the Island, in the most liberal spirit.

That this preceding Resolution be communicated to the Rt. Hon. the Secretary of State for the Colonies.

Quebec, 29th November, 1866.

My Lord,—I have the honour to transmit herewith to Your Lordship an address to Her Majesty the Queen from the Provincial Association of Protestant Teachers of Lower Canada, and to request that it may be laid at the foot of the Throne.

I have, etc.,

MONCK.

The Right Honourable the Earl of Carnarvon, etc., etc.

Downing Street, 17th December, 1866,

My Lord,—I have the honour to acknowledge the receipt of Your Lordship's despatch, No. 203, dated the 29th November last enclosing an address to Her Majesty from the Provincial Association of Protestant Teachers of Lower Canada, complaining of certain alleged grievances in the educational system at present in force in Lower Canada, and praying that provisions may be introduced into the proposed Imperial Act of Confederation calculated to protect the educational interests of the Protestant inhabitants of Lower Canada.

The question of education is one of the important subjects which may be expected to be discussed by the North American Delegates when in conference in this country, and the present memorial, which has been duly laid at the foot of the Throne, shall then receive full consideration.

I have to request you to communicate to the Memorialists the substance of this despatch.

I have, etc.,

CARNARVON.

The Right Honourable Viscount Monck, etc., etc.

———

TO THE QUEEN'S MOST EXCELLENT MAJESTY,—The Petition of the Provincial Association of Protestant Teachers of Lower Canada,

Humbly sheweth :—

That, notwithstanding the legislative union of Upper and Lower Canada, there exists in each portion of the united provinces a distinct educational system.

That, under the educational law of Lower Canada, and in consequence of the denominational character of the schools of the Roman Catholic majority, your Majesty's subjects professing the Protestant faith are subjected to serious disadvantages : first, in being deprived of the benefits of a general system of education similar to that enjoyed by their fellow subjects in Upper Canada ; secondly, in their liability to be taxed for the support of Roman

Catholic schools: and thirdly, in the difficulties which they experience in establishing non-denominational or separate schools and seminaries of higher education for themselves.

That, though the injury thus inflicted on education has been the subject of frequent complaints on the part of the Protestant population, and, as your petitioners believe, has tended to discourage the settlement of Protestants in this Province, and has caused many families to leave this country for others in which they might avoid such inconveniences, no remedy has hitherto been granted by the Legislature.

That, in prospect of the Confederation of the Provinces, under the constitution adopted at the Quebec Conference, by which it was proposed that education should be under the control of the local legislatures, the Protestants of Lower Canada became alarmed lest they should continue to labour under these disadvantages: and, to allay the feeling thus generally existing, solemn pledges were made by members of the Government, that the grievances complained of should be redressed by Parliamentary action before Confederation.

That, though a bill for this purpose was introduced by Government in the last session of the legislature, it was almost immediately withdrawn; and unless provisions to this end can be introduced into the Imperial Act of Confederation, your memorialists fear that their educational rights will be left to the control of the majority in the local legislatures without any guarantee whatever.

That, while your petitioners would prefer a general and non-denominational system of education, they believe that so long as the present system of separate schools shall continue in Lower Canada, they may justly claim the following privileges as constitutional rights which should in no way depend on the vote of the local legislature.

1. That all direct taxes for the support of schools, paid by Protestants, unless otherwise designated by themselves, should be applied to Protestant, or non-denominational education; and that all public money given for the same purpose should be divided between Protestants and Roman Catholics in proportion to population.

2. That suitable and adequate provision should be made for the protection of the educational interests of Protestants, in the management of educational funds, the establishment and proper classification of schools and institutions of superior education, and generally in the administration of educational affairs.

Wherefore, your memorialists humbly pray your Most Gracious Majesty to take their case as above stated into your favourable consideration, with a view to the introduction of proper and just safeguards into the Imperial Act of Confederation, should such Act be passed.

And your petitioners will ever pray.

(Signed by the President of the Association and others.)

Montreal, Nov. 23rd, 1866.

To the Honourable G. E. Cartier,

Attorney-General, &c., &c.:

Sir,—I am directed by the Executive Committee of the Provincial Association of Protestant Teachers of Lower Canada to transmit to you a copy of the enclosed memorial.

The Committee, believing that the objects sought by the petition will commend themselves to your approval, and being assured that they are regarded as of the most vital importance by the Protestant population of Lower Canada, beg leave, respectfully, to solicit your support and countenance to the prayer of the petitioners.

I have the honour to be,

Your most obedient servant,

P. J. DAREY, M.A.,
Secretary of the Provincial Teachers' Association.

INDEX OF NAMES.

INDEX OF SUBJECTS.

G.

H.

I.

J.

N.

O.

P.

POPE CON.—21

Q.

R.

U.

W.